Barcelonawalks

BARCELONAWALKS

George Semler

Photographs by
Robin Townsend

An Owl Book

Henry Holt and Company · New York

Copyright © 1992 by George Semler
All photographs copyright Robin Townsend
All rights reserved, including the right to reproduce
this book or portions thereof in any form.
Published by Henry Holt and Company, Inc.,
115 West 18th Street, New York, New York 10011.
Published in Canada by Fitzhenry & Whiteside Limited,
91 Granton Drive, Richmond Hill, Ontario L4B 2N5.

Library of Congress Cataloging-in-Publication Data
Semler, George.
Barcelonawalks / George Semler; photographs by
Robin Townsend—1st ed.
p.   cm.—(Henry Holt walks series)
"An Owl book."
Includes bibliographical references and index.
1. Barcelona (Spain)—Description—Tours.   2. Walking—Spain—
Barcelona—Guide-books.   I. Title.   II. Title: Barcelonawalks.
III. Series.
DP402.B24S46   1992
914.6'720483—dc20   91-31841
CIP
ISBN 0-8050-1585-X (alk. paper)

Henry Holt books are available at special discounts
for bulk purchases for sales promotions, premiums,
fund-raising, or educational use. Special editions
or book excerpts can also be created to specification.
For details contact:
Special Sales Director, Henry Holt and Company, Inc.,
115 West 18th Street, New York, NY 10011

First Edition—1992

Designed by Claire Naylon Vaccaro
Maps by Jeffrey L. Ward
Printed in the United States of America
Recognizing the importance of preserving the
written word, Henry Holt and Company, Inc. by
policy, prints all of its first editions on
acid-free paper. ∞

1 3 5 7 9 10 8 6 4 2

For Lucie

Contents

Acknowledgments

This book would not have been possible without Barcelona's many amateur and professional historians. Every street seems to have its resident expert, as in, "I have no idea, but you should talk to so and so."

Many friends, neighbors, and complete strangers have shared stories, information, and documents of all possible descriptions. The Town Hall of Gràcia was especially helpful in the preparation of the section of the book on that part of town.

James and Suzanne Knowles were the catalysts for this book, Fifi Oscard and Nancy Murray put the players together, Theresa Burns gave expert and abundant editorial advice, Jennifer Lapidus contributed much-needed assistance, and Rebecca Holland did outstanding production/editorial work. I am deeply indebted to all of them.

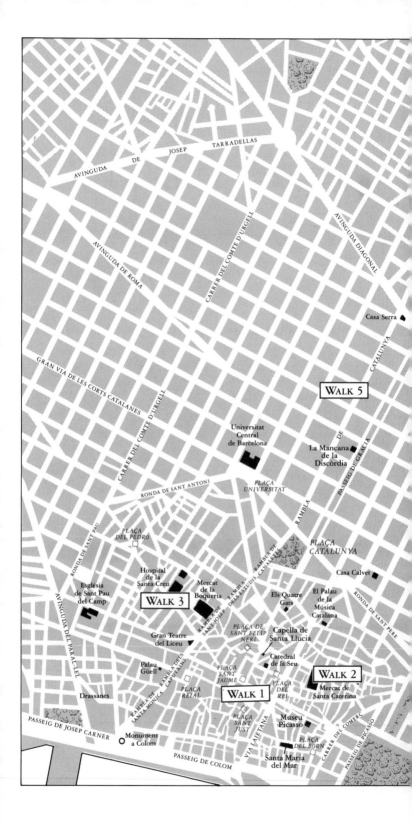

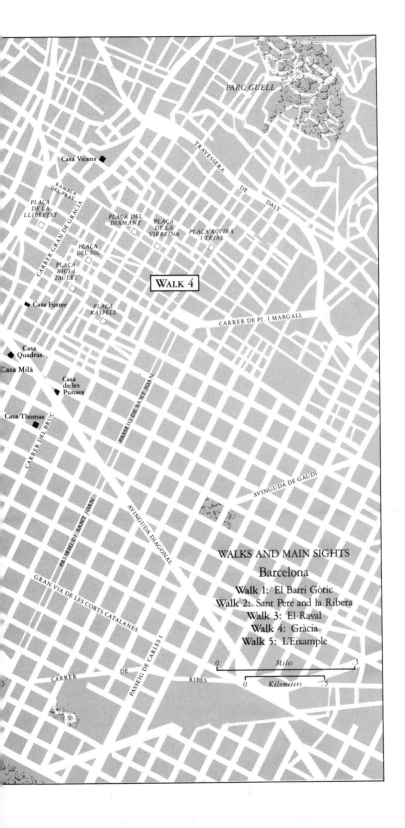

PARC GUELL

Casa Vicens ◆

RAMBLA
DEL PRAT

PLAÇA
DE LA
LLIBERTAT

PLAÇA DEL
DIAMANT

PLAÇA
DE LA
VIRREINA

PLAÇA ROVIRA
I TRIAS

CARRER GRAN DE GRÀCIA

PLAÇA
DEL SOL

PLAÇA
RIUS I
TAULET

WALK 4

◆ Casa Fuster

PLAÇA
RASPELL

CARRER DE PI. I MARGALL

TRAVESSERA

DE

DALT

Casa
Quadras ◆

Casa Milà

Casa
de les
Punxes ▼

Casa Thomas ◆

CARRER DEL BRUC

PASSEIG DE SANT JOAN

AVINGUDA DE GAUDÍ

PASSEIG DE SANT JOAN

AVINGUDA DIAGONAL

WALKS AND MAIN SIGHTS

Barcelona

Walk 1: El Barri Gòtic
Walk 2: Sant Pere and la Ribera
Walk 3: El Raval
Walk 4: Gràcia
Walk 5: L'Eixample

GRAN VIA DE LES CORTS CATALANES

CARRER

DE

PASSEIG DE CARLES I

RIBES

0   Miles   .5

0   Kilometers   .5

Introduction

Barcelona, the largest city on the Mediterranean Sea, is a rich blend of art and industry, color and passion, history and invention. In five intimate walking tours, this book will take you through Barcelona's most characteristic neighborhoods, in-depth explorations through streets and buildings, and the human dramas played out in and around them over the city's two-thousand-year history.

Described by poet Joan Maragall as *la gran encisera*, "the great enchantress," Barcelona has always celebrated her own romantic readiness, a flirtatious and restless drive to absorb new people and ideas while stubbornly clinging to local identity.

Above all, Barcelona is the capital of Catalonia, a country within a country, with its own Romance language—Catalan—linguistically closer to Provençal French than to Castilian Spanish, as well as its own literature, folklore, customs, and national personality.

Barcelona at the end of the twentieth century is experiencing its greatest cultural and political renaissance since the House of Aragón ruled the Mediterranean dur-

Gràcia street lamps

ing the Middle Ages. Spain's return to democratic government and the subsequent revival of Catalonia's autonomous rights, privileges, and institutions have sparked an
artistic, linguistic, and economic recovery comparable
only to the nineteenth-century *Renaixença* that produced
the ornate and ebullient *Moderniste* architecture you will
see splashed throughout the city. The Olympic Games of
1992 and the nationalistic pride and urban renewal triggered by the promise of this event have caused a powerful and passionate rediscovery and reinvention of
Barcelona's past, present, and future: another important
rendezvous for *la gran encisera*.

The five walks in this book are presented in historical
sequence. Thus, the Barri Gòtic, or Gothic Quarter, settled by the Romans in 133 B.C. comes first and the Eixample (or "widening"), constructed after the city's third
ring of walls was demolished in 1854, comes last.

The Barri Gòtic, Walk 1, is the oldest part of the city,
seat of government for Roman, Visigothic, and Carolingian rulers and later for the sovereign counts of Catalonia
and the kings of the House of Aragón. Barcelona's earliest
history unfolded within the original walls surrounding
this small piece of high ground.

In Walk 2, the Barri de Sant Pere is the early textile
district, while the Barri de la Ribera (the shore) was the old
waterfront neighborhood, both enclosed by Barcelona's second ring of walls.

El Raval, Walk 3, is the rough-and-tumble Barcelona
suburb that grew up outside the second set of city walls,
running down what is now the Rambla, and inside the
third ramparts that stretched along Carrer Pelai, the Ron-
das of Sant Antoni and Sant Pau, and the Avinguda del
Paral.lel leading down to the Drassanes shipyards.

Gràcia, Walk 4, was once a separate town, the most
independent and architecturally the most interesting of
Barcelona's *vilas agregats*, or incorporated townships.
These include Sants, Sarrià, and Sant Gervasi, outlying
villages that were gradually swallowed up as the city

moved out and away from the sea onto the slopes of the Collserola hills.

The Eixample, Walk 5, is the "widening," the part of the urban sprawl that looks like a waffle iron on the map and, perhaps surprisingly, contains some of the city's most singular structures. *Modernisme*, Barcelona's late nineteenth- and early twentieth-century explosion of art nouveau, found its home in the Eixample, virtually a living museum of art and architecture.

You might find it helpful to break up the walks in this book into before- and after-lunch sessions in order to rest and to allow time for reading up on the places you are about to explore. The longest walks are four hours and cover distances of up to nearly 3 miles. In order to see many of the sights mentioned, you really do have to look up, something I discovered while researching the book, and between mapping, reading, and spotting, there is an excellent chance of falling over curbs or being run down. Be especially careful of motorcycles. In the general din you don't hear them, and as you thread your way through stopped traffic, you run a serious risk of an ugly encounter with a speeding cyclist charging up the side lane behind a bus.

You will almost certainly see things along the way that incite your curiosity but are not included in the text. Every single walk through these streets uncovered fresh secrets and raised new questions—so much so, in fact, that finishing the book turned out to be something like trying to extinguish one of those trick birthday candles that refuse to go out.

Pablo Picasso, Salvador Dalí, Joan Miró, Pablo Casals, Antoni Gaudí, and a long list of less famous but equally productive artists, writers, and musicians have all tapped into Barcelona's primary natural resource, a heavy lode of energy and emotion. Public figures routinely weep in the course of both solemn and joyous events, and passions are never far from the surface in this busy crossroads between Europe, Iberia, and the Mediterranean.

Information
and Advice

BEFORE YOU GO

No visa is necessary to enter Spain as a tourist. After
1992, when Spain will become a full-fledged member of
the EEC and a united Europe, regulations could change,
but a valid passport will probably still suffice to cross the
Spanish border.

The Spanish Tourist Office and Barcelona's Patronat
de Turisme are producing ever better guides and studies
of all aspects of the city's art, history, and attractions. For
more information about publications, contact:

Tourist Office of Spain
665 Fifth Avenue
New York, NY 10022
Tel: (212) 759-8822

The Rambla

Patronat de Turisme
Paseo de Grácia, 35
08007 Barcelona
Tel: (011-34-3) 215-4477
Fax: (011-34-3) 215-4276

A map is fundamental in Barcelona, even for residents. Whether lost in the tiny and eccentric streets of the old city or adrift on the Eixample's unnumbered grid, you'll need to track yourself with a good map, the bigger the better. The small, two-volume *Guia Urbana* is a good investment. As in the Paris *par arrondissement* guide, streets are listed alphabetically and keyed on the city map.

The best months to visit Barcelona are October and May. July and August are hot, while the winter months can be cold and rainy but much more comfortable and culturally active than the summer. June and the second half of April are also good times, as are November and the second half of September.

The main festivals to keep in mind when choosing dates are the celebrations in honor of Barcelona's patron saint La Mercè (Our Lady of Mercy), which take place on and for a week after September 24; the Christmas season, including the traditional Three Kings celebration on January 6; Carnestoltes (Carnival), in late February; Saint George's day, on April 23; the Sant Ponce natural products fair, on May 11; and the Sant Joan celebration of the summer solstice held on the eve of June 24. These celebrations generally include open-air concerts, dances, processions, and a general intensification of Barcelona's already lively street life. Gràcia's town festival takes place in mid-August, while Sarrià's *festa major* is held during the first half of October. Both offer interesting glimpses into local folklore, customs, and traditions.

GETTING THERE

Getting to Barcelona from the United States is best accomplished via direct flights from New York on TWA and Iberia. Avoid "direct" flights via Madrid. These often involve delays in Madrid during which you disembark, go through customs, and either get back on the same plane or get on the first available shuttle.

KLM and Sabena offer connections via Amsterdam or Brussels that may seem out of the way but in fact turn out to be quieter and more comfortable, especially compared to the Madrid ordeal. The other advantage is arriving in Barcelona in time to freshen up, do a few things, possibly nap *briefly*, and get a great night's sleep, after which you will have no more jet lag problems. But by all means avoid serious sleep on arrival, or you'll be waking up and passing out at all hours for days.

The overnight train from Madrid to Barcelona has several advantages: You can carouse all over Madrid and be placed on the train at 11:00 in prime condition for sleeping. You awaken when the first sunlight reflects through your window off the Mediterranean on the coastline between Tarragona and Barcelona at about 7:00 in the morning. You have miraculously descended 2,000 feet from the high Castilian steppe to the sea, gotten a (sometimes rare) seven- or eight-hour night's sleep, saved one night of hotel expenses, and arrived in Barcelona at 8:00 in the morning with the entire day ahead of you. The Madrid-Barcelona plane is twice as expensive as tourist accommodations on the train, not always much faster, and costs you half a day. Driving is not especially beautiful (unless you take the twelve-hour route through Alcañiz and Tarragona), is very expensive in gasoline and tolls, and is dangerous. Good overnight connections from Paris, Seville, Rome, and most other European points are also available, although they may not get you in at the crack of dawn.

From the airport, only 7 kilometers away, trains run

every thirty minutes. These trains cost about $1.50 and, depending on what you have to carry, are the best way to go. The train will take you to Sants, Barcelona's central train terminal, or to Plaça Catalunya, the center of the city's system of communications. Taxis to Barcelona cost around $20.00, depending on where you have to go.

TRANSPORTATION

Once in town you have four choices of transportation: taxis, subways, buses, or walking. Although you will probably end up using all four eventually, walking is the secret. Even after almost twenty years here, old Barcelona hands still discover that routes they have covered (out of habit) by driving, bus, or subway are well within walking range and are reached faster, more beautifully, more healthily, and with less frustration on foot. Jaywalking is, of course, fundamental to rapid pedestrian transit. Never stop. And the *xaflanes*—the beveled-off city blocks you will read more about in Walk 5—really work in cutting down distances. For example, the walk from the Monastery of Pedralbes to Plaça Catalunya—an unthinkable trek for any decent Barcelona resident—can be achieved in under ninety minutes of vigorous marching.

Taxis presently start at about $2.50, and you get the first couple of kilometers for that flat rate. After that, the meter starts to ascend at 5 pesetas a click. Taxi drivers will almost never cheat or take you around the long way, so just relax and pay whatever he asks unless it seems truly outrageous. Often what you see on the meter is amplified by some extra charge the driver will have on a printed piece of paper, either last-minute adjustments in rates or special airport, train station, or luggage fees. The longest ride you can take within the city limits will never cost more than $8.00 or $9.00, and the normal taxi from the center of town to the periphery is about $5.00 or $6.00. Many times a combination of the $2.50 minimum and some walking at either end can solve your transportation problem nicely. But in any case, taxis are primarily a nighttime necessity for when the metro (subway) is shut down. During the day, depending somewhat on where you are going, walking is usually faster, and the metro, much faster.

A T-1 card will work on both the bus and the metro, whereas a T-2 is only for the metro. Either can be bought at Caixa (savings bank) offices or in metro stations for about 425 to 450 pesetas. The normal subway fare is 65 pesetas, so the ten-trip card lowers it to 45. The T-1 card can also be used for the Tramvia Blau, the trolley up to the Tibidabo funicular. Danger is not a factor on Barcelona subways. Everyone uses the metro at all hours, which are from 5:00 A.M. to 11:00 P.M. on weekdays and until 1:00 A.M. on Fridays, Saturdays, and on nights prior to holidays. The Sarrià train (FFCC: Ferrocarrils Catalans) is certainly the best and serves the upper part of town and also communities and cities outside of Barcelona such as Sant Cugat, Sabadell, and Terrassa. However, an additional fare is required to change to another line.

Buses have the advantage of remaining above the earth's surface, but the subway is faster, cooler, and more comfortable. Certain buses are especially useful. Number 64, for example, goes from Pedralbes in upper Barcelona all the way to the end of Passeig Nacional, to Barceloneta's newly restored beach.

Nighttime buses are available to certain axial points around the city and can be useful if you can figure out how to use them. They appear after 10:30 P.M., marked NB, ND, NF, NG, NH, NL, NN, NS, and NT. Many originate in Plaça Catalunya. If you are out late, out of money, and sore afoot from walking around Barcelona all day, have a careful look at the bus stop sign or check your city map to see if one of these nocturnals can get you somewhere near your destination. Most of them roughly parallel the sea, covering Barcelona's long axis out into the neighborhoods flanking the city. NB runs from Plaça Catalunya up to Avinguda Tibidabo at the top of Balmes until 3:00 A.M.

EMERGENCIES

The best thing to do in case of an emergency is to dial 010, the *Ajuntament*'s or town hall's, general information number, and ask for advice. This is a twenty-four-hour service armed with information in Spanish, Catalan, French, and English on anything from where to fix a flat tire to how to solve a dental crisis. Barcelona is world-famous for kidney and optical surgery, has an internationally respected obstetrical center, and can provide medical care as good as any in the world today, so there is no need to be wary of health care. Here are some useful numbers for emergencies:

Police assistance for tourists: 317-7020

For medical emergencies:
Hospital Sant Pau: 347-3133
Hospital Clinic: 323-1414
Hospital Cruz Roja: 235-9300

For dental emergencies:
Clinica Janos: 200-2333 (open weekends and holidays)
Clinica Dexeus: 418-0000 (open weekends and holidays)

For lost credit cards:
American Express: (91) 572-0303
MasterCard: (91) 435-4905
Visa: (91) 435-2445
Diners Club: (91) 247-4000

Consulates:
United States Consulate: 319-9550

United Kingdom Consulate: 322-2151
Irish Consulate: 330-9652
Japanese Consulate: 204-7224
German Consulate: 217-6162

GENERAL HEALTH CONSIDERATIONS

Barcelona water varies from one neighborhood to another as far as taste is concerned but is completely safe and sanitary. Most people drink bottled water in Barcelona simply because it tastes better.

Clams and mussels that have failed to open and mayonnaise-based *tapas* (hors d'oeuvres) that have been sitting out for a while are the only items that require special caution. In general, avoid weary-looking items included in counter displays.

Although there are a few public toilets around town, walking into any bar and proceeding directly to the *servicios* is a perfectly sound and sensible practice.

MONEY

The Spanish peseta is the local currency. The exchange rate is and has been in the general vicinity of 100 to the dollar. Traveler's checks are good to have when an establishment does not accept credit cards and you're either out of or prefer not to carry cash. Credit cards, especially MasterCard and Visa, are increasingly common all over Catalonia. American Express is somewhat less frequently advertised. Banking hours end at 2:00 P.M. (1:00 P.M. on Saturdays and during the months of July and August in many establishments). Automatic teller machines are available at the Banco Exterior de España office just to the left of international arrivals at El Prat Airport and at

the center of Sants train station. If your secret number doesn't work in the machine, then you will need to have the teller do your cash advance manually. Banks generally give better exchange rates than hotels.

TIPPING

Normally, in restaurants and nearly everywhere, the tip is included in the *cuenta*. Tipping is really not an issue here. Far from demanding tips, Barcelona taxi drivers have been known to ferry people beyond the end of their stated means: "I guess I'll get out here. I have exactly 300 pesetas . . ." The taxi driver clicks off the meter and says, "Where are you headed? I'm probably going by there anyway."

Why tipping is so live-and-let-live in Barcelona and all over Spain, and so cutthroat in neighboring France, is a mystery. Evidence suggests that a certain sense of chivalry below the Pyrenees dictates that one should have—or should appear to have—better things to do than hustle for loose change. In twenty-one years in Spain I have never heard a complaint or even a conversation between a waiter and a customer on this subject.

In any case, if it's a place you like and you want to make everyone understand how much you enjoyed it, a tip of 10 percent is an easy mathematical solution that will leave everyone more than pleased.

For porters, hotel maids, and people who perform special services around hotels, a 50- or 100-peseta tip is appreciated. Anything much less than that in present-day Spain may not produce much more than a chuckle. Better to tip well or not at all.

CLIMATE

Despite the pictures of palm trees you will see in advertisements, Barcelona can be cold, so don't underestimate the temperature changes and variations you might encounter here. Generally speaking, summer is hot and humid, and clothing cannot be too light. Winter is cold but seldom freezing, although the wet Mediterranean air can produce mornings chilly enough to require ski parkas and overcoats. Umbrellas are handy between November and March; on rainy mornings every hand seems to hold one. October and November and, in the spring, May and June provide Barcelona's most comfortable weather—warm enough for the beach but cool enough to enjoy the city.

CLOTHING

People dress casually but stylishly in Barcelona. Practically no one walks around the city in baseball hats and shorts except tourists. Although occasionally a dinner or an opera might call for suits and ties or even black tie or tails (rentals available at La Pimpinel.la de Sarrià, Carrer Major de Sarrià. Tel: 205-2576), Barcelona is not very rigid about dress codes. Church, for example, usually seems to call for no more than a shirt and sweater unless the occasion is a wedding or a funeral, and dinner and a night on the town only rarely require anything more formal than sweaters and casual jackets. A sports coat is a handy item for men to bring along.

Women in Barcelona—even in blue jeans—never seem to lose a certain sense of style and elegance. Many American women feel that their Barcelona counterparts far outdress them, so don't hesitate to bring some stylish suits and dresses if you want to avoid feeling underdressed.

Wearing hiking boots around Barcelona is an idea to consider. Ankle support and shock-resistant soles are important for getting around the city comfortably.

FOOD AND DRINK

Dining in Barcelona faithfully reflects Catalonia's privileged geographical disposition. The Mediterranean, the Pyrenees, and the "fruited plain" of the Penedes (and, of course, Valencia) supply the staples while local epicureanism and ingenuity provide the techniques for some of Europe's most robust and refined fare. (For an excellent introduction to Catalan cooking, *Catalan Cuisine* by Colman Andrews is delightful reading and manages to bring the subject to life.)

Catalan cooking differs from French and Spanish cuisine in several specific ways. Most dishes are based on the *sofregit* and the *picada*, the bookends, so to speak, of Catalan cooking: the preparation of a typical dish starts with one and finishes with the other. Sofregit, a combination of onions, garlic, and, perhaps, tomato, cooked for hours on low heat, provides the basic stock, while the picada is mixed with a mortar and pestle and consists of garlic, parsley, fried bread, and some kind of nuts (pine nuts, almonds, hazelnuts, or a combination). Sometimes chocolate or a mix of herbs is added to the picada, and this flavoring goes into the dish five or ten minutes before it's ready to be served.

Catalan cuisine's other two distinctive sauces are *al-lioli*—literally garlic (*all*) and oil (*oli*) gently beaten to a mayonnaiselike consistency—and *samfaina*, a combination of squash and peppers, almost a *ratatouille*.

Catalan cooking has a unique medieval quality. Anything with *naps* (turnips), for example, is by definition a recipe predating the discovery of America. The potato was discovered in the New World, and prior to that, *naps* were commonly used for stews and ragouts and civets of anything from duck to partridge to wild boar. Thus, anything with *naps* is probably a dish first concocted over five hundred years ago.

Game, seafood, wild mushrooms, and a wide selection of vegetables produce surprising combinations ranging from the classic *mar i muntanya* (coastal and upland products in the same dish—for example, chicken with shrimp) to *anec amb peras* (duck stewed in pears). Lamb, rabbit, duck, goat, wild boar, mountain goat, many species of fish, shrimp, prawns, shellfish, and pork in many guises and disguises are only part of a menu that includes a truly staggering variety of natural products.

Although many restaurants now have translated menus, a few fundamental Catalan dishes and their translations might be useful. First courses are usually vegetables, soups, or salads, but may also include shellfish or sausage. *Escudella* is a strong soup, excellent for winters in the Pyrenees, and typically includes onions, potatoes, carrots, cabbage, turnips, leeks, chicken, pork, ham, and sausage as well as various herbs, garlic, parsley, and a bay leaf. *Sopa de bolets* is a soup made from wild mushrooms, onions, herbs, carrots, bread crusts, and oil with a *picada* of saffron, toasted almond, and garlic. *Faves a la catalana* are lima beans with bacon, sausage, or ham, and might include garlic, onion, tomato, carrots, or mint. *Botifarra amb mongetes seques* are white sausages with white beans dressed in oil, garlic, and parsley—perhaps the most typical and least expensive choice you will find on any menu. *Espinacs à la catalana* is one of the most delicious inventions of Catalan cuisine: spinach prepared in garlic, olive oil, pine nuts, bits of cured ham, and raisins. *Truita* may be trout *or* omelette. Normally trout will be called *truita de riu*, river trout, to indicate that this is not a trout-shaped concoction of egg and, possibly, potato. *Escalivada* is another Catalan staple: cooked red peppers and strips of eggplant served cold in vinegar. *Trinxat de la Cerdanya* is a delicious Pyrenean specialty consisting of potato, cauliflower, lettuce, and garlic mixed to a paste and served with bacon. *Esqueixada* is a refreshing salad of raw salt cod mixed with onions, peppers, and olives, and dressed with oil and vinegar.

Main course specialties might include *bacallà a la llauna*, salted cod served with garlic, parsley, and tomato sauce; *suquet de peix*, a fish stew in a thick marinara sauce; *arros negre*, black rice cooked in squid's ink; *conill rostit amb allioli*, roast rabbit with *allioli* sauce; *ànec amb naps*, duck stewed in turnips; *xai rostit*, roast lamb; *costelletes de xai à la brasa*, lamb chops grilled over coals; *civet d'isard*, a stew of mountain goat; *civet de llebre*, stewed (presumably wild) rabbit; *civet de jabalí*, stewed boar; *fricandó*, veal stewed in *moixernóns*, a delicate mountain meadow strain of wild mushroom; *cabrit al forn*, roast young goat; *perdiu a la vinagreta*, partridge in vinegar; *guatlles farcidas amb fetge d'oca i raïm*, quail with foie gras and grapes.

There are two desserts that anyone discovering Catalan cuisine should try: *crema catalana*, a custardlike pudding with a hint of cinnamon and a burnt-caramel crust, and *mel i mató*, a curd cheese, either goat or cow, served with honey. Fresh fruit is another good choice, especially *maduixes*, strawberries (stick with the *maduixots*, or tame ones; the wild strawberries are usually disappointingly tasteless), served with cream or ice cream.

Tapas, small servings of hors d'oeuvres, are always available at bars and restaurants, and while Barcelona may not be the tapa capital of Spain, there are plenty of excellent places for small doses of wine and delicacies on the run. Casa Tejada at Carrer Tenor Viñas 3 (near Plaça Francesc Macià) is one of the best tapa emporiums of upper Barcelona. Even farther up is the Bar Tomàs at Major de Sarrià 51, famous for potatoes and *allioli*. Next to the Sagrada Família Cathedral on Carrer Provença, across from Plaça de la Sagrada Família, is an excellent display of tapas, especially *calamares fritos* (fried squid). Off Plaça d'Antoni Lopez, from the corner of the post office nearest the port, Carrer de La Mercè runs down three blocks to the Capitanía General, an army headquarters. This street is lined with good tapas bars, especially the Bar Celta, which has dishes from the northwestern Spanish region of Galicia, where *pulpo* (octopus) is served on wooden plates, and Ribeiro, a fruity white wine, is served in typical Galician ceramic saucers. Galician places are always a good choice for tapas.

Barceloneta is another good place for tapas, vinos,

conversation, and walking. Restaurante Perú at Passeig Nacional 10, a friendly family business with excellent *calamares fritos*, is one of the first and best stops on your way out into Barceloneta. The bars and cafés on the Mediterranean side of Plaça Barceloneta—the square in front of the baroque Sant Miquel del Port Church—offer some fine spreads of tapas, while moving farther toward the sea, the bars at the corners of Carrer de Santa Clara, Carrer Sant Miquel, and Carrer Baluard all have displays of assorted tapas.

Some of the finest tapas around are at the Boquería market, especially during the fall when fresh *bolets* (wild mushrooms) are just in from the countryside. You can buy some you've never tasted and ask one of the little *chiringuitos* (stands) to prepare them for you.

Standard tapas include *calamares fritos* (fried squid), *sepia* (a squidlike cuttlefish), *anchoas* (anchovies), *boquerones* (herring in vinaigrette sauce), *almejas à la marinera* (clams in a marinara sauce), *mejillones* (mussels), *gambas al ajillo* (prawns fried in olive oil and garlic), *tortilla* (Spanish potato omelette), *champiñones* (mushrooms), *morcilla* (blood sausage), *chistorra* (piquant sausage), *patatas bravas* (potatoes with hot sauce), *aceitunas* (olives), *alcachofas* (artichokes), *riñones al jerez* (kidneys cooked in sherry), *pinchos morunos* (veal shish kebabs barbecued in hot sauce), or *jamón serrano* (cured ham) with *pa amb tomaquet* (slices of country bread dressed with tomato and olive oil). The most common wild mushroom (*bolet*) is the *rovellón* (we call them chanterelles in English), usually prepared with garlic, parsley, and olive oil.

DRINKING TIPS

If you order a *tinto* in Barcelona (which means a black coffee in Bogotá, Colombia), you will perhaps be surprised to get not a glass of red wine, as you would in Madrid, but a small bottle of beer. In Barcelona red wine is *vi negre* or, in Spanish, *vino negro*. *Tinto* is understood as *quinto*, which is what they call the small one-fifth-liter beers now going for 50 to 75 pesetas in normal, "unimproved" surroundings. Ordering a *mitjana* (*mediana* in Spanish) or "middle-sized" beer will get you a standard 30-centiliter bottle of beer. Not counting imported beers, which are somewhat more expensive, the most frequently consumed Barcelona beer is the light Estrella Dorada brand marketed by the Damm company in Barcelona. Damm also has a darker beer, the lethal Voll-Damm, with a higher alcohol percentage. San Miguel is the lightest of the three bottled specialties, while a *caña* gets you a draft beer, which usually turns out to be the coldest, cheapest, and for some reason the most thirst-quenching.

Beers in night spots such as Otto Zutz and Up and Down, by the way, presently cost anywhere from $8 to $15 each, so be forewarned. Otto Zutz has live entertainment, jazz and country groups, while Up and Down is standard big-beat disco, usually taped. You get in without paying a cover charge, if they decide you deserve admittance, but ordering a few beers can be a hundred-dollar operation.

Coffee is another important field to master. In Barcelona, ordering a *café* will get you one espresso, black coffee. If you order a *café solo*, as you might in parts of the Spanish-speaking world, you get a look as if to say, "Foreigner, eh?" and an espresso. A *tallat* is coffee with a little milk (*tallar* in Catalan means "to cut"). In Spanish, this is called a *cortado*. Coffee with milk, which usually means about 50 percent milk, is *café amb llet* or, in Spanish, *café con leche*. A *carajillo* is coffee laced with rum, brandy, or whiskey, a fine way to stay awake without becoming sober.

CATALAN OR SPANISH?

While it's difficult to advise a visitor to Barcelona to brush up on Catalan at the expense of Spanish, considering that the rest of the Iberian peninsula and much of the rest of the world can be communicated with better in Castilian Spanish, the fact remains that Catalan is a full-fledged Romance language spoken by some eight million people (spoken more than Danish, Finnish, or Swedish). Catalan will be included as one of the EEC official languages in 1992. Although Spanish works throughout Catalonia, it bothers Catalan nationalists that visitors to their country use the language of the "empire" rather than the local idiom. Whatever you do, don't make the mistake of referring to (or even thinking of) Catalan as a dialect. Look it up; it's not. A few expressions will help you get around and go a long way toward reassuring your hosts that you recognize and respect their culture.

ENGLISH	CATALAN	SPANISH
Good morning	Bon día	Buenos días
Good afternoon	Bona tarda	Buenas tardes
Good night	Bona nit	Buenas noches
How are you?	¿Com està vostè?	¿Qué tal?
Very well	Molt bé	Muy bien
Thanks	Mercè (or Gràcies)	Gracias
Good-bye	Adéu	Adiós
See you later	Fins després	Hasta luego
See you tomorrow	Fins demà	Hasta mañana
What's your name?	¿Com us dieu?	¿Cómo se llama usted?
My name is . . .	Em dic . . .	Me llamo . . .
Pleased to meet you	Molt de gust	Mucho gusto
How much is it?	¿Quant val?	¿Cuánto vale?
What time is it?	¿Quina hora és?	¿Que hora es?
How do I get to . . . ?	¿Com s'hi va . . . ?	¿Cómo se va . . . ?

Closed	Tancat	Cerrado
Open	Obert	Abierto
Sorry	Ho sento	Lo siento
Please	Si us plau	Por favor
Breakfast	Esmorzar	Desayuno
Lunch	Dinar	Comida
Dinner	Sopar	Cena
Street	Carrer	Calle
Promenade	Passeig	Paseo
Square	Plaça	Plaza
Bridge	Pont	Puente
Palace	Palau	Palacio

OTHER POINTS OF INTEREST

There are a number of important Barcelona landmarks that have not been included in these walks, either because they were remote and difficult to include without recommending taxi hops or because they were such obvious tourist attractions and well documented in standard city guides.

Antoni Gaudí's **Sagrada Família Cathedral** is probably the most obvious omission. Located in the Plaça de Gaudí on the right side of the Eixample, the Sagrada Família is a visit few travelers should miss. Lluís Domènech i Montaner's **Hospital de la Santa Creu i de Sant Pau**, at the upper end of Avinguda Gaudí, is another important Moderniste tour de force, while Josep Puig i Cadafalch's **Casa Macaia** at Passeig de Sant Joan 114 (and whatever exhibit might be on there at the time) is not far away.

The promontory of Montjuïc overlooking Barcelona offers a series of museums (especially the **Miró Foundation**, the **Romanesque Art Museum**, and the **Pueblo Español**), all fundamental and exciting visits.

Other areas of the city that were hard not to include were the **Port**; the fishing and maritime neighborhood of **Barceloneta**; **La Ciutadella Park**, including the Museo de Arte Contemporaneo and the zoo; **Sarrià and Pedralbes** in the upper part of the city; and **Tibidabo** and **Vallvidrera** overlooking Barcelona.

The Golondrina (which means swallow) can be taken through the port to the end of the breakwater, for the half-ticket bargain rate of about $1.00, after which you can walk along the stone breakwater to Barceloneta, have a lunch of paella, and walk back into the center of the city through Barcelona's picturesque waterfront area. An alternative is to take the funicular across the port, descending at the midway station near the Columbus monument and the Rambla, or continuing over to Montjuïc.

Trains run out to Sarrià and Pedralbes, and there are funicular lines to haul you up to the Tibidabo amusement park and Vallvidrera, a cluster of houses perched on a promontory in the Collserola hills.

SIDE TRIPS FROM BARCELONA

There are three especially convenient and spectacular attractions for day trips around Barcelona: the Montserrat religious retreat, visible from parts of Barcelona when the air is clear; the beach at Sitges, a freewheeling mélange of Mediterranean village and Euro-spa; and the San Sadurní d'Anoia wine tour of the Freixenet or Codorniu producers of *cava*, Catalonia's own sparkling wine. All of these excursions can be accomplished by trains originating in the Sants terminal. (Call RENFE. Tel: 490-0202.)

For trips to the beaches and rocky inlets of the Costa Brava or for skiing in the Cerdanya, Camprodón, or farther west at Baqueira, a car is necessary.

HISTORY

Originally an Iberian settlement called Laia, Barcelona became part of the Roman Empire in 133 B.C. as Colonia

Favencia Julia Augusta Paterna Barcino, part of the Roman Hispania Citerior. The original walls of the Roman city of Barcino were completed in the fourth century, just before the reign of the Visigoth Ataulf, husband of Galla Placidia, daughter of Roman Emperor Theodosius I. Ataulf was assassinated in Barcelona in 415, but the city flourished until the eighth-century Moorish invasion. In 801, Charlemagne conquered Barcelona, which in one century had been ruled by Visigoths, Moors, and Franks.

This was the key moment in the development of Catalonia's separate identity on the Iberian peninsula. Barcelona became a *Marca Hispánica,* the southernmost edge of the sprawling Carolingian Empire, while the Moorish al-Andalus ended just south of the Llobregat River and Barcelona. Thus, Catalonia, in a sense, managed to fall through the cracks between the overextended Franks to the north and the Moorish empire to the south.

The Franks divided the *Marca* into geographical entities ruled by counts, of whom Sunifred and later his son Guifré el Pelós emerged as the strongest. The authority of the Frankish kings gradually weakened, and when Guifré died in 897 he passed his title on to his son as a hereditary right rather than by designation of the Frankish king, another step in the development of Catalonian sovereignty.

When al-Mansúr, Moorish regent of Córdoba, sacked Barcelona in 985, Sovereign Count Borrell II requested help from the Franks; he received none, and thus ended any vestigial feudal allegiance. As of 988, Catalonia was on its own, an independent state, with Barcelona as its capital.

Over the next four generations of sovereign counts, Barcelona and Catalonia consolidated authority over the former *Marca* and expanded into southern France. In 1137, Ramón Berenguer IV, through his marriage to the daughter of Ramiro II of Aragón, united Catalonia with the peninsular and landlocked House of Aragón, a fateful alliance that aided the rise of Catalonia in the Mediter-

Carriage port, Fiveller House

ranean but eventually led to historical differences resulting from Aragón's union with the Spanish crowns of Castile and León.

Jaume I conquered Majorca in 1229, later adding Ibiza and Valencia to Catalonia's Mediterranean empire. During his reign (1214–76) Barcelona grew rapidly. New walls were erected—the second set—encircling the Sant Pere and Ribera areas.

The dynasty continued to grow. Pere III (1336–87) controlled Majorca, the region of Roussillon in southern France (still known as Northern Catalonia by Catalan nationalists), Sicily, and Sardinia. During this reign Barcelona's third set of walls ringed the Raval as city life became more complex.

The final years of the fourteenth century were times of pestilence and pogroms for the last of the sovereign counts of the House of Barcelona. The crown passed to a nephew of Pere III, Ferdinand I of the Trastamara family. From this point on, Catalonia's fate depended largely on dynastic successions and marriages.

Ferdinand II (1479–1516) and his wife Isabella of Castile, known as the Catholic kings, brought about through their marriage the unification of the crowns of Castile and León with those of the House of Aragón, which included Catalonia. The last monarchs to rule from Barcelona's royal palace, Ferdinand and Isabella managed to unify Spain in 1492 (by reconquering Granada from the Moors); expel all non-Christians from the Iberian peninsula; establish the Spanish Inquisition; and discover America. During his sixty-four-year reign, Ferdinand unified the Spanish crowns and converted Spain to an Atlantic sea power, shifting influence away from Catalonia.

Under Carles I (1516–56), Barcelona was no longer the capital of the monarchy, although the Generalitat, Catalonia's autonomous government, remained in place. Carles I thrust Spain into the thick of his global quest for empire, making Madrid his capital and leaving Barcelona off the center of the European stage. Carles I did, however, swear an oath of allegiance to honor and defend Catalonia's constitution, thus setting the stage for the tragic and decisive events of the War of the Spanish Succession.

When Carles II died without an heir in 1700, three pretenders to his throne emerged. Catalonia was bound to Archduke Carles of Austria through the pledge made by his ancestor Carles I, while Felipe V of Anjou, grandson of Louis XIV, became the opposition favorite. All of Europe took sides in the developing Habsburg-Bourbon struggle for continental power. The Austrian archduke was named to succeed to the throne in 1700, but on his deathbed Carles II left his realm to Felipe V of Anjou.

War broke out immediately. Archduke Carles, with the help of England, invaded Spain and in 1704 established himself as Carles III in Barcelona with the support of Catalonian nationalists. When his brother Joseph I died and Carles succeeded him as the Holy Roman emperor, England, fearing Habsburg hegemony in Europe, withdrew, leaving Barcelona kingless, defenseless, and committed to resisting Felipe V. From August 1713 to the final battle on September 11, 1714—the day now celebrated as Barcelona's national day—Felipe V laid siege to the city. Two-thirds of Barcelona's houses were destroyed or damaged, and many more were ordered torn down to make fields of fire for the Ciutadella fortress. Dominated by the Montjuïc stronghold on one side and the Ciutadella on the other, eighteenth-century Barcelona was governed by occupation Bourbon troops, while all vestiges of home rule disappeared.

After 1714, although Catalonia had lost its institutions, the city prospered and grew. Between 1808 and 1813 Napoleonic troops took Barcelona and converted the city into the Imperial Department of Montserrat—a brief return to the Carolingian *Marca*. But whether governed by Bourbon or Napoleonic imperialists, Barcelona flourished; the population of one hundred thousand in 1800 tripled by the end of the century.

During the nineteenth century, industrialization created a dynamic working class. Barcelona was the scene of social violence followed by periods of armed repression in 1835 and again in 1848 when the artillery battery at Montjuïc shelled the city.

In 1860, Barcelona finally burst out of its walls, another key moment in the city's struggle to become more than a provincial capital. The Eixample, or "widening," opposed and manipulated by Madrid, nevertheless took place. Barcelona was moving farther from the watchtowers of the Ciutadella and the guns of Montjuïc. In 1868, after nearly seventy-five years of protest, Barcelona citizens were allowed to tear down the walls of the much-hated Ciutadella fortress.

The second half of the nineteenth century saw a reassertion of Catalonia's belief in its local identity and at the same time in its projection abroad. The Exposició Universal of 1888 marked the beginning of the city's modern cosmopolitanism, while the *Renaixença*, a rebirth of Catalonian nationalism, bloomed in the colorful and formally lavish Moderniste architecture that filled fin de siècle Barcelona.

Autonomous Catalonian government returned with the representational parliament known as the Mancomunitat, which lasted from 1914 until 1924. Under the Spanish Republic of 1931–39 the Generalitat de Catalunya again governed in Barcelona.

The Spanish Civil War of 1936–39, essentially an overthrow of the legally elected liberal and progressive government led by the army, the church, and the Spanish oligarchy, left Spain in the hands of the traditionalist right. The Franco regime (1939–75) and its Madrid-centered policies stressing Spanish national unity placed Catalonian culture under more repressive pressure than ever before. Bans on political and linguistic expression combined with the constant ideological presence of the fascist Movimiento Nacional.

Resentment of this attempt to rewrite history, denying Catalonia's distinct cultural heritage on the Iberian peninsula, ran (and still runs) deep, and when Franco died on November 20, 1975, the noise from *cava* corks popping in Barcelona was nearly as deafening as Felipe V's shelling of the city during the siege of 1714.

Since 1975, thanks in large part to the courage and popularity of another Bourbon, King Juan Carlos I, whom many predicted would be dubbed "Juan the short" for the anticipated brevity of his reign, Catalonia has lived through a Golden Age of national reformation. The king was instrumental in quelling the military coup of February 23, 1981, and far from repressing the Catalan language, uses it in speeches delivered in Catalonia, as he uses Basque and Gallego in Spain's other autonomous communities. With the 1977 return of Josep Tarradellas, president (in exile) of the Generalitat after his predecessor Lluis Companys was executed in 1940, Catalonia's legitimate democratic succession was completed. Since 1980, Jordi Pujol, once jailed for singing a forbidden nationalist ballad during the Franco regime, has occupied the Catalonian presidency.

Barcelona is now rapidly becoming a modern megalopolis. The walls presently checking the city's expansion are the very Collserola hills that have helped make Barcelona one of the most densely populated cities in Europe. Like the 1888 Universal Exposition, the success of Barcelona's long-frustrated Olympic movement has provided impetus for improving communications, restoring churches and monuments, and overhauling much of the city.

A NOTE ABOUT THE TEXT

The spelling and usage in this book have attempted to adhere as much as possible to the grammatical authority of Pompeu Fabra's *Diccionari general de la llengua catalana*, although certain Castilian Spanish terms and place names are used when they seem more appropriate. The Ebro River, for example, is referred to in the Castilian, as the *Ebro* instead of the Catalan *Ebre*, as it flows east from its headwaters in the Cantabrian mountains, through the Basque Country, across Aragón, and only becomes Catalan for the last 100 kilometers of its nearly 1,000-kilometer trajectory. Even this, admittedly, is debatable for a book largely if not exclusively confined to the city limits of Barcelona.

Accent marks also differ from Catalan to Spanish. The final "ia" is unaccented in Catalan as the two letters do not form, as they do in Castilian, a diphthong. Thus *Boqueria*, *Maria*, or *Dagueria*, in Catalan, are pronounced exactly the same as *Boquería*, *María*, and *Daguería* are in Spanish.

Any unwarranted confusions and/or contradictions in the text are undoubtedly my own, and have slipped through despite the best efforts of the editors, copy editors, production editors, and typesetters who have struggled so valiantly to standardize the text.

Walk · 1

El Barri Gòtic

EARLY ROMAN AND
GOTHIC BARCELONA

Fountain at Porta de l'Angel

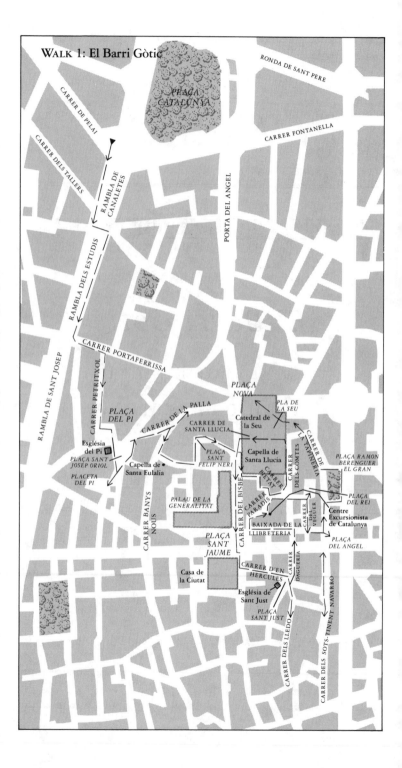

WALK 1: El Barri Gòtic

CARRER DE PELAI

RONDA DE SANT PERE

PLAÇA CATALUNYA

CARRER DELS TALLERS

CARRER FONTANELLA

RAMBLA DE CANALETES

RAMBLA DELS ESTUDIS

PORTA DEL ANGEL

CARRER PORTAFERRISSA

RAMBLA DE SANT JOSEP

CARRER PETRITXOL

PLAÇA NOVA

PLAÇA DEL PI

CARRER DE LA PALLA

PLA DE LA SEU

CARRER DE SANTA LLUCIA

Catedral de la Seu

Església del Pi

PLAÇA SANT FELIP NERI

Capella de Santa Llucia

CARRER DE LA TAPINERIA

PLAÇA SANT JOSEP ORIOL

Capella de Santa Eulalia

CARRER DELS COMTES

PLAÇA RAMON BERENGUER EL GRAN

PLAÇETA DEL PI

CARRER PIETAT

CARRER DEL VIGUER

PLAÇA DEL REI

CARRER BANYS NOUS

PALAU DE LA GENERALITAT

CARRER DEL BISBE

CARRER PARADIS

Centre Excursionista de Catalunya

BAIXADA DE LA LLIBRETERIA

PLAÇA DEL ANGEL

PLAÇA SANT JAUME

Casa de la Ciutat

CARRER D'EN HERCULES

CARRER DAGUERIA

Església de Sant Just

PLAÇA SANT JUST

CARRER DELS LLEDO

CARRER DELS SOTS-TINENT NAVARRO

Starting point: The top of the Rambla
Metro: Plaça Catalunya
Length: About three hours

This walk, like the other four, is best taken during the morning hours (between 9:00 and 2:00) of a typical weekday when you will find everything open and street life buzzing.

Hèrcules; Roman Consul Decius; the Visigoth Ataulf; the martyred virgins Eulàlia, Llucia, and Agata; the cries of the bandit Joan de Serrallonga tortured on the rack—the stones have tales to tell in these ancient streets, the oldest part of Barcelona.

Barcelona's Gothic Quarter, sometimes known as the *rovell d'ou*—the yolk of the egg—occupies the area around the high ground where the city was first settled. The prehistoric Iberian nucleus called Laia first overlooked the flats between the mouths of the Besòs and the Llobregat rivers from this gentle hill before the Romans founded Colonia Favencia Julia Augusta Paterna Barcino on the same site in 133 B.C.

Enclosed since the fourth century by the city's first set of walls, life at the center of Barcelona hasn't always been as peaceful as it is now. Today the reverberations of a music student's flute tracing the notes of some haunting medieval ballad in one of the old city's stone spaces all but reduce twenty centuries of humanity to a single moment, a hundred generations of ears and echoes.

The area around Barcelona's central cathedral, whether inhabited by the Laietans, Romans, Visigoths, Moors, Franks, or a long series of invaders, successors, regents, and viceroys, has always been Barcelona's nerve center. The nearby Plaça Sant Jaume is the site of the seat of Catalonian government, the Generalitat, as well as the Casa de la Ciutat, or Town Hall, while the cathedral—La Seu—continues to be the city's main ecclesiastical seat.

The streets and buildings on and around this ancient hill, called *Mons Taber* by the Romans, seem to run on different time than the rest of the city; hours and days are measured in grains of slowly falling sand rather than digital technology. As if protected from the city's rush and racket by Barcelona's original walls, El Barri Gòtic's mysterious hush is an acoustical oasis, a romantic retreat from the modern urban melee outside.

The **Rambla** is a good place to begin this walk, as much for contrast as convenience. Leaving the soccer and labor debates at the Canaletes fountain behind, the next part of the Rambla is the section where parrots, partridges, monkeys, hamsters, and all manner of little animals are sold on either side of the walk. This traditional market has come to be known as the *mercat dels ocells* (bird market), and that part of the Rambla, originally known as *Rambla dels Estudis* for the medieval university that once stood there, is now often called the **Rambla dels Ocells**.

Mimes and clowns frequently perform along this section of the Rambla; sometimes talented and amusing, they are often just more wildlife on the hustle. Barcelona, however, does have a strong tradition of mime and iconoclastic theater, so a Marcel Marceau in the making might be performing for nickels and dimes.

Student life was an essential ingredient in the medieval Rambla and is perhaps a contributing factor even today in the basically riotous and freewheeling sense of this unique stretch of bars, cafés, stores, restaurants, and hotels. Barcelona's first hotel, the Hostal de la Parra, faced the Rambla dels Estudis, as did many of the first public restaurants and cafés. Bars and bordellos seemed to stay close to the students of the Middle Ages, and these establishments flourished along the fourteenth- and fifteenth-century Rambla.

The Rambla dels Estudis was also the scene of George Orwell's bemused account of the Spanish Civil War in *Homage to Catalonia*: militia, anarchists, communists, and assault guards within the left and loyal ranks defending the legitimate Republican government of Barcelona in 1937, taking potshots at one another from the rooftops and doorways of the **Café Moka**, still present at no. 6, and the **Poliorama Theatre** across the way.

"Immediately opposite," wrote Orwell in chapter 10, "there was a cinematograph, called the Poliorama, with a museum above it, and at the top, high above the general level of the roofs, a small observatory with twin domes. The domes commanded the street. . . . As for the Civil Guards in the Café Moka, there would be no trouble with them; they did not want to fight and would only be too glad to live and let live." (Orwell later added that the troops he took as Civil Guards were not in fact Guardia Civil but Assault Guards, under the orders of the Republican government.)

In winter the two domed towers Orwell spent several nights manning are clearly visible above the Poliorama; from April on, you have to find an opening in the leafy canopy of plane trees to get a good look at them.

Felipe V, the perennial villain of Catalonian history,

who directed the siege of 1714 and the subsequent dismantling of all vestiges of home rule, suppressed the original university, or Estudi General, that overloooked this part of the Rambla in favor of army barracks. The student uprising of 1647 helped spark a general rebellion against centrist Madrid, and Felipe V thus disposed of a political threat and student hell-raising in a single stroke. Student life was temporarily banished to the university town of Cervera, a hundred kilometers west of Barcelona, and the Rambla was left for the moment in the hands of the army and the convents and monasteries nearby. Eventually the barracks were torn down (in 1843), and the Rambla gradually regained its raucous personality.

The Rambla, like many present-day streets in Barcelona, was originally a watercourse, generally dry, and known in Latin as *arenno*. The term changed during the Moorish occupation to *ramla*, derived from the Arabic for sand, *rmel*, and subsequently to Rambla (or Ramblas when referring to the various different sections that make up the Rambla). The Rambla was the principal riverbed, or *arroyo* (in Catalan *riera*), around the ancient city and during wet weather collected the runoff from the drainage system of the Collserola hills rising northwest of Barcelona. When the outer walls were constructed in the thirteenth century, it was logical to place them on the near side of the Rambla, or riverbed. Thus the Rambla lay just outside the second set of walls encircling the city of Barcelona. The Rambla was definitively fixed as a promenade or passageway after the appearance of the third and final walls, which ringed the area known as the Raval on the west side of the Rambla. Gradually the old walls were torn down, leaving an open space between the site of the second walls and the structures on the far side of the original watercourse.

The gates through Barcelona's second set of walls included the Santa Anna portal at the junction of what are now the streets of Canuda and Santa Anna, the Portaferrissa portal at Carrer de Portaferrissa and, farther down the Rambla, the portals at the Pla de la Boquería, Trentaclaus (opposite Carrer Escudellers), and Drassanes near the Christopher Columbus monument.

Leaving the Rambla at **Carrer de Portaferrissa**, opposite the baroque Betlem Church on the right, the **Portaferrissa fountain** occupies the corner on the right, with its ceramic tiles portraying the thirteenth-century walls and the gate at Portaferrissa itself. The inscription reads: "The 'Porta Férrica' was one of the portals of Barcelona's second walls, constructed in the thirteenth century. The steel bar, which was one of the city's standard measures of length, was set in the door and led to the portal's name as well as to that of the street that led to the 'Porta Férrica' from the center of the old city."

The **Palau Moja** at no. 9 Carrer de Portaferrissa was originally part of the city wall when it was built in 1702. Now the cultural headquarters for the Catalonian government, the building's *planta noble*, or main (second) floor, has an elegant salon overlooking the Rambla, with an adjoining chapel. The mural paintings inside were done by Françesc Pla, also known as El Vigatà. On the building's façade facing the Carrer de Portaferrissa are paintings al fresco, rediscovered during restoration work in the early part of the century and restored as much as possible. The scenes seem to portray, starting from the left, a pair of Roman soldiers, a soldier carrying a struggling woman away, another soldier with a tray, a Roman soldier greeting a woman and child, and on the far right, a soldier holding a baby by the foot, possibly a reference to the biblical slaughter of the innocents or the judgment of Solomon. Attempts to establish any clear connection among these scenes other than their possible suggestion of protest of foreign (Roman? European? Castilian?) domination have proved inconclusive and unconvincing.

Farther down Portaferrissa, just opposite the beginning of Carrer Petritxol, is another noble structure, at no. 7, with an excellent entryway and carriage patio.

Carrer Petritxol, one of Barcelona's most elegant little streets, leads down to the right toward **Plaça del Pi**. Lined with hot chocolate emporiums, art galleries, bookstores, and antique shops, Carrer Petritxol dates to the middle of the fifteenth century, when the narrow passageway was opened through the property of a family of the same name. At no. 5, **Sala Parés** is the oldest of Barcelona's art galleries, the setting for the expositions of many of the great Catalan painters, such as Ramón Casas, Isidre Nonell, Joaquim Mir, Pablo Picasso, and Santiago Russinol. The son of the Catalan poet Joan Maragall, great-grandfather of the present mayor of Barcelona, Pasqual Maragall, eventually owned the gallery. A haunting Maragall verse, perhaps the cry of the would-be believer in search of faith, appears just past the Sala Parés above a small fountain:

Per què ens mireu Verge Santa	Why do you look at us Holy Virgin
Amb aquests ulls tan oberts?	With those eyes so wide?
Doneu-nos l'esgarrifança	Give us the tremor, the thrill
dels vells miracles complerts!	The ancient miracles provide!

The famous nineteenth-century playwright Angel Guimerà, a public figure of great popularity known for his defense and renewal of Catalan language and letters, lived at **Carrer Petritxol no. 4**. A plaque with his bust in relief marks the house where the playwright died. The tile just across the street at no. 1 reads "From the balcony / you see trembling / the shadow of Angel Guimerà." Guimerà's bronze effigy presides over the café next to the Església del Pi, another congenial presence adding life and wit to the conversations around him.

The **Llibreria Quera** at Petritxol 2 is the best *excursionista* book and map store in Barcelona. The theme of "excursionism" is pursued very seriously in Catalonia as an expression of both patriotism and religion. During the

Franco regime and even today, youth groups fill the trains out into the country on weekends. The survival of the Catalan language and a special reverence for the land itself are fixed points on the agenda for these quiet outings. Routes for hiking or climbing and information on sanctuaries and remote Romanesque chapels to trek to in the Pyrenees are an important part of this peaceful, semi-mystical outdoor endeavor, and Llibreria Quera is one of the city's centers for orientation and information.

Carrer Petritxol leads down into the Plaça del Pi to the church of the same name: the **Església del Pi**. The famous *pi*—pine tree—a descendant of the original pine for which the fourth-century neighborhood was named, stands in the square under the church's immense rose window. The *barri del pi* was originally the western part of early Barcelona, tucked outside the first walls in a fold of land thought to be unhealthy because it lay close by a flat expanse of marshes and wetlands known as the Cagalell.

On Thursdays the intimate Mercat Gòtic fills Plaça del Pi and the adjoining Plaça Sant Josep Oriol. Antiques, rare books, pipes, silverware, and a wide range of quirky objects are on display and for sale in a quiet epicurean context. The dealers, unlike the usual flea market floggers, are usually students of their wares—herbs, goat cheese, woodcuts, and paintings—and the sense of the place is informed and uncommercial. On weekends there are art markets in the two squares.

Although the original church has been dated as far back as the tenth century, the present structure was begun in the early part of the thirteenth and consecrated in 1453. The church's symmetry is typical of fourteenth-century Catalan design, and in many ways the building seems a cousin to the more spacious Santa Maria del Mar (see Walk 2). The Església del Pi, one of Barcelona's most cherished minor churches, has struggled through the centuries—flooded, abandoned, burned, bombarded, restored, and still being restored. The huge rose window facing Plaça del Pi is said to be one of the largest in the world, and certainly within the confined space of its tiny square, it seems immense. The view from inside during the afternoon when the sun illuminates the rose window from the west, or from outside at night with subdued lighting coming from within the church, is one of the true gems of the Barri Gòtic.

Inside the church, the Sant Miquel altar and the altar of the Mare de Deu dels Desamparats are the most interesting. The latter includes a painting by the eighteenth-century painter Ramón Amadeu. The artist's wife and children were said to be the models for the image of the virgin and the children she is comforting.

Ask when the next wedding is taking place, and you might have a pleasant surprise. The creaky choir loft, one recent Saturday morning, seemed to barely suspend a chorus in which a young lady, later identified as the sister of the bride, sang a superb rendition of Mozart's Laudate Dominum, leaving the congregation gasping and leaky-eyed as the couple below finished out the responses as well as they were able. Later, in the bright morning sunlight in Plaça del Pi, the wedding party—identifiable mainly by their wide smiles—seemed a happy island in the tumultuous crush of Barcelona street life flowing by and around them.

The two open spaces around the church are good places to explore. On the corner of Carrer Petritxol, to the right as you face the church's rose window, is the building that was once the home of the Casa de la Congregació de la Puríssima Sang, often shortened to **Casa de la Sang** (House of Blood). This religious brotherhood, founded in 1342, was responsible for the last spiritual rites, comfort, preparation, and burial of prisoners condemned to death. It received sole authorization to accompany criminals and martyrs to the scaffold as late as the middle of the nineteenth century. In paintings and drawings such as Ramón Casas's famous *Garrote Vil* (1894), these specialists appear ghoulishly dressed in their long black cassocks and conical headgear, the high priests of capital punishment.

The engravings on the façade directly facing the rose window at no. 3 Plaça del Pi are the oldest in Barcelona, dating from the time of the building's construction in 1685.

The pharmacy on the corner of the square and Carrer del Pi, the **Farmacia del Pi**, bears a marble plaque explaining that playwright Angel Guimerà was born here into Catalan letters—a curious claim considering that on Carrer Petritxol we passed the house where Guimerà lived, worked, and died. The story is true inasmuch as Guimerà, who up to the early 1880s wrote in Castilian Spanish, was persuaded by members of his intellectual circle, or *tertulia*, who met regularly in the pharmacy, to compose his work in Catalan. Guimerà, known for his macabre sensuality, went on to great success as a poet and dramatist. *Mar i Cel* (1888) was his first successful play, and *Terra Baixa*, translated in 1914 under the title *Marta of the Lowlands*, has always been recognized as his masterpiece.

Hostal Jardí stands at the corner of **Plaça Sant Josep Oriol**. Oriol, a seventeenth-century Barcelona priest, was canonized for his good works and healing miracles. Hostal Jardí is one of the better situated and lower-priced lodgings in the city, while the café below, **Bar del Pi**, is perfectly located and is one of Barcelona's characteristic half-inside, half-outside cosmopolitan grazing spots. There's also a phone conveniently placed behind the coffee machine, so you can simultaneously pick up a bracer from the smell of the fresh-ground coffee beans, a breather with a relaxing glass of something, and a functioning telephone if you need it.

Take a moment to explore Plaça Sant Josep Oriol and the **Placeta del Pí** behind the church before continuing down Carrer de la Palla; there are several points of interest. Beginning at the far end of Plaça Sant Josep Oriol is the narrow street called Carrer Cecs de la Boqueria, or the

Angel Guimerà, Plaça Sant Josep Oriol

Blind of the Boqueria, originally built at the site of the cemetery for the blind. The cemetery was part of the Església del Pi, which was, through the offices of Saint Martin, the seat of the brotherhood of the blind.

The tiny Placeta del Pi allows a look at the church's bell tower as well as a view of the buildings on the sunny south-facing side of Plaça Sant Josep Oriol. These diminutive hideouts, with their flowery balconies and cozy attics and dormers, send a familiar Mediterranean signal of whatever the opposite of organized life is: independence, confusion, freedom, a sense of romance, simplicity, well-being.

Moving back into Plaça Sant Josep Oriol, you will see a marble plaque at the rear corner of the long and symmetrical church wall that reads: "On April 6, 1806, word of the approval of the miracles of God's servant, Dr. José Oriol, was received, for which reason the outside of this church was illuminated; as he passed over this bridge [high overhead to the left of the plaque], the director, José Mestres, fell flat to the ground without hurting himself in the least, in spite of his extraordinary obesity, as is duly recorded in the archives of the Royal Community, in memory of which this stone is placed here." That this mishap should be literally engraved in stone has always seemed extraordinary, and there are a wide range of explanations and interpretations available: Mestres was blinded by the light, tipsy from celebrating Oriol's canonization, too portly to watch his step, or just clumsy and lucky. In any case, the event was taken as another proof of Oriol's saintliness, a miracle, chiseled in marble for posterity *qua* Humpty Dumpty or even the Fall from Grace itself.

The elegant entryway and courtyard directly across from this piece of memorabilia, behind playwright Guimerà's bronze likeness, is the **Fiveller Palace**, at no. 4, now the seat of the Catalonian Agricultural Institute. Several rooms in the building, which dates from 1571, are decorated with ornate and colorful murals from the time of the Napoleonic Empire. It is from this house (as you will read in Walk 4) that the young Maria Francesca Fiveller is reported to have set off by carriage for the neighboring town of Gràcia, where she would confirm her brief but spectacular marriage to the powerful Viceroy Amat.

Continuing down **Carrer de la Palla**, named for its original proximity to the scales for weighing straw, there are several antique shops and doorways of interest. At the corner of Carrer Banys Nous (New Baths)—named for the baths erected in the medieval *Call*, or Jewish quarter, at the corner of Carrer de la Boqueria—the visible curvature of the street and wall traces the shape of the original city ramparts that encircled Roman Barcelona from the fourth century on.

Although our route will continue to the right down Carrer Banys Nous to the corner of the **Baixada de Santa Eulàlia**, a short stroll up Carrer de la Palla to the edge of

Plaça Nova is recommended, if only to get the feel of the walls that once stood there, parts of which are still visible through an open space left by the removal of a building. The antique shops, which specialize in documents and books, are some of the most interesting in Barcelona.

Moving back down Carrer Banys Nous from its intersection with Carrer de la Palla, a wooden door—usually wide open—reveals the notorious **Portalón**, one of Barcelona's most intriguing restaurants: cheap, exquisitely pungent, safe, friendly, and comfortable. Dominated by a

Portalón, a unique dining experience

mammoth 2,600-liter wine barrel standing by the bar, Portalón's signature event is the lady hanging out laundry or mopping the, for her, floor (for you, ceiling) on the translucent skylight over the dining room, the rope soles of her espadrilles sliding blackly overhead. Steer clear of the reserved table—the longest one, in the center of the room—where a group of local artists sets up for lunch around two o'clock. The best spots are the marble-topped tables just inside to the left. While some travelers will have no inclination to enter Portalón, much less dine

there, for others this former stable and carriage house has a primeval and ramshackle charm, an unpremeditated old-world allure. Available witnesses can attest to the spot's not-always-apparent hygiene, having survived many a meal there.

Continuing down Carrer Banys Nous, at the corner of the Baixada de Santa Eulàlia, leading up toward the cathedral, a plaque on the wall overhead to the right attests to the twelfth-century baths associated with Barcelona's Jewish quarter, or *Call*. Many of the streets around this area refer to the Call (from the Hebrew *qahal* for meeting): Arc de Sant Ramón del Call, Carrer Sant Domènec del Call, Carrer del Call. The Call occupied the zone just below and west of Roman Barcelona, established on the high ground around what was then the Temple of Augustus.

The city's Jewish community played an important part in Barcelona's medieval splendor, especially in the development of industry and commerce and in the sophistication of what emerged as the Iberian peninsula's first nonfeudal economic system. Leading poets, scientists, and astrologers were members of the Jewish community, which included two synagogues, hospitals, several baths, and a school. By royal decree the Call was closed to the Christian community between the thirteenth and early fifteenth centuries, opening only for special markets and produce fairs. Although protected by Barcelona's sovereign counts, who valued their wealth and needed their expertise, Jews were required to wear capes and hoods and distinctive red-and-yellow ribbons. In August 1391, Spain's generalized uprising against the Jews—as elsewhere a product of envy and poverty— reached Barcelona. Despite local government attempts to organize an army to protect the Call, hundreds of Jews were murdered, and the quarter was sacked. Although the government executed a handful of the leaders of the pogrom, the Call never recovered its medieval eminence. Stripped of their wealth, survivors were forced to convert, becoming so-called new Christians and changing their names to non-Hebrew ones such as Llobet, Pi, or Bosc (wolf cub, pine, forest). Over the next century the synagogues were converted to churches, Jewish cemeteries were destroyed, and the Jews were expelled from the Call. In 1492 the Spanish Inquisition officially expelled all non-Christians from Spain.

Since 1492 the diaspora of Sephardic Jews (from the Hebrew for Spain: *Sepharad*) has extended throughout the world, although many settled in North Africa and the Middle East. Efforts to permit the return of the Sephardim to Spain finally bore fruit: In 1925, after years of a campaign led by Senator don Angel Pulidó, Spanish dictator Miguel Primo de Rivera published a decree recognizing the citizenship of all Sephardim under the protectorate of Spanish consulates abroad. Since then, Barcelona's Jewish population has waxed and waned, growing to seven thousand in 1934–35. The Israeli Community of Barcelona at no. 24 Carrer Porvenir estimates the city's present Jewish community to be just over three thousand.

From Carrer Banys Nous, a left at the Baixada de Santa Eulàlia leads up a tiny and ancient passageway lined with antique shops, medieval entryways, and carpentry shops. This *baixada* (descent), like other streets so named, marks what was once the drop from the city walls. At the first corner coming up the street, a tiny chapel overhead on the right is built into the wall. It commemorates the martyrdom of Barcelona's patron saint, Santa Eulàlia, a beautiful but rebellious young Christian said to have been rolled naked in a barrel filled with broken glass down this same hill as part of a marathonian martyrdom to which she was subjected because of her beliefs. The figure in the alcove portrays Santa Eulàlia with the X-shaped cross upon which she was eventually crucified. The verse below by Catalan poet Mossèn Jacint Verdaguer describes the ordeal of the barrel:

Veyent acostar les flames   Seeing the flames die down
També recula Dacià   Decius also draws back

La tanca dins una tina	He closes her into a barrel
Que té sagetes per claus	That has spikes for nails
Tota encerclada de glavis	All encircled with glass
Y ganivets de dos talls	And double-edged blades
Baixada de Santa Eulàlia	Down the hill of Santa Eulàlia
Tu la veus rodolar	You see her rolling
D'un abisme a l'altre abisme	From one abyss to the other
Per aquells rostos avall	Down over this rough track
Dexant per rastre en les herbes	Leaving a trail in the grass
Un bell rosari de sanch.	A lovely rosary of blood.

According to legend, Santa Eulàlia was crucified in the Plaça del Pedró (Walk 3); her remains are in Barcelona's cathedral just up the hill.

Described as the exceptionally lovely daughter of wealthy Barcelona merchants, Santa Eulàlia became a fervent Christian to protest the corruption of the Roman Empire. When the Roman emperor Diocletian decreed in the latter part of the third century that Christians were to be persecuted, Eulàlia reported to Decius, the local authority. Decius demanded that she worship false gods, to which Eulàlia responded by throwing a handful of sand at the altar. For this she was imprisoned and subjected to thirteen progressively crueler martyrdoms: she was whipped; her flesh was torn with hooks; hot coals were applied to her feet and breasts; her wounds were treated with salt; she was scalded with boiling oil, sprinkled with molten lead, thrown into a vat of lye, rolled thirteen times down the hill now named for her in a cask of broken glass; she was thrown into a corral filled with ravenous fleas and then driven naked around town in a cart pulled by oxen. After each ordeal Santa Eulàlia is reported to have slowly shaken her head, faith intact. The twelfth ordeal was the attempt by the Roman consul's son to seduce Eulàlia and convince her to recant; she remained unpersuaded. Her final ordeal was crucifixion outside the city walls in the Plaça del Pedró. Today we can only hope that much of the story of Santa Eulàlia is fictitious. The monstrousness of the legend itself holds a certain morbid fascination for Eulàlia worshipers, however, as well as questions about the sadistic and misogynistic behavior of early Christian legend in general.

Farther up this same street, past the elegant house at **no. 5, Carrer de Sant Sever**, with its graceful patio and baroque façade, the Carrer de Sant Felip Neri leads left into one of Barcelona's most intimate enclosures, **Plaça Sant Felip Neri** and the church of the same name. The pockmarks on the walls of the church are said to be bulletholes left by executioners, although it is difficult to believe any firing squad could miss by that much unless they were trying to, a tactic favored by conscripts leery of having blood on their hands. More probable is the report that bombs fell into the *plaça* during the Spanish Civil War or that a hand grenade was detonated in the confines of the tiny square during one of Barcelona's many sieges, wars, uprisings, rebellions, or revolutions. Sounds of water echo hauntingly from the central fountain unless the children from the parish school are on recess, in which case the din is impenetrable. The baroque church of the order known popularly as the felipons stands at the left side of the square. The **Sala Newman**, an acoustical gem used for concerts and theater productions, is part of the church and certainly a good place to investigate whether something interesting is scheduled. The priests of this church, according to the *vox populi*, are famous for being the earliest rising confessors in the city. One of Barcelona's best-known pundits and chroniclers, Josep Maria Carandell, hypothesized that husbands and wives of Barcelona's progressive Catholic bourgeoisie stop at the church on their way home from late night cavortings "filled with remorse," later arriving home renewed and squeaky clean of conscience.

Barcelona's shoemakers' brotherhood, which developed into one of the world's first trade organizations, and the **Museum of Early Footwear** occupy the building on the right side of the square. The Brotherhood of Saint Mark, dominated by shoemakers, originally applied to the bishop of Barcelona in 1203 for permission to build an altar dedicated to the patron saint of cobblers. This brotherhood eventually became a guild that, in addition to regulating and organizing the shoemaking industry, was socially and politically active in the life of the city throughout the Middle Ages.

Apel.les Mestres, a famous late-nineteenth-century poet, composer, and artist, lived in Plaça Sant Felip Neri in what was originally his grandfather's house until he was forced to move, late in life, to the Passatge Permanyer in the Eixample (Walk 5). The son of Josep Oriol Mestres (the corpulent architect who fell from the footbridge back in the Plaça del Pi), Apel.les Mestres poignantly described the house in his book, *La Casa Vella*, brilliantly illustrated by himself. Grandfather Mestres was the gravedigger for the cemetery for prisoners that originally occupied the *plaça*. Many Barcelona heroes and not a few villains were buried there after being strangled, hung, or quartered at one of the standard spots outside the city walls. The famous antimonarchist bandit Joan de Serrallonga, the 1714 Resistance hero Josep Moragues, the so-called martyrs of the organ (whom you are about to meet), and a virtual Who's Who of Barcelona's executed elite found their final resting places under the cobblestones of Plaça Sant Felip Neri. Legend tells us that the executioner himself was also buried here, having been excluded from other parish cemeteries by the citizenry, who deemed it fitting that, in death, he join his victims.

Carrer de Montjuïc del Bisbe twists out and around to the Plaça de Garriga Bachs in front of the Santa Eulàlia door of Barcelona's main cathedral. **Plaça de Garriga Bachs** is a pleasant opening in winter or summer, after some of the moist and dark alleyways left behind. Musicians often perform in the acoustically favored squares

Plaça Sant Felip Neri

of the Barri Gòtic, and this forum is one of the most frequented and coveted.

The sculpture and murals in this *plaça* are in memory of the heroes of Barcelona's resistance to the early nineteenth-century Napoleonic occupation. After the 1808 uprising in Madrid (immortalized in Francisco Goya's *2 de Mayo* painting), Barcelona was next to declare its independence from Joseph Bonaparte I. France's response was to dispatch four thousand seasoned troops from Perpignan to punish Catalonia, where, despite the heroics of the legendary drummer boy of Bruc, Barcelona was soon under French military rule. The famous Bruc patriot, by drumming from different points around the rugged mountain pass of Bruc, 40 miles west of Barcelona near Montserrat, fooled the invading troops into thinking they were opposed by a large army, thus delaying their advance and allowing Catalonian forces from Manresa to deal the French column a stinging defeat. Nevertheless, the invaders were soon installed in Barcelona, and by June 1909 local Resistance leaders conspired to seize Montjuïc and throw off the yoke of the foreign regime.

The four scenes depicted in these murals record the story of five leaders of the struggle for independence as they are taken to their executions in the Ciutadella on June 3, 1809. The text describes their courage and composure as one by one they are garroted to death or hung (the garrote was reserved for the two clergymen because hanging was considered a lower and less humane form of execution). The other civilians present, described as traitors, are presumably collaborators who betrayed the five Resistance leaders.

In the fourth scene, on the far right, three other prisoners, visibly weak and exhausted, are seen in the presence of their military captors. As the text reads, they attempted to rally the city to revolt and save the first group by ringing the bells of the cathedral as the executions were taking place. French troops surrounded and ransacked the cathedral searching for them. After seventy-two hours of hiding in the organ, the three agitators are giving themselves up, having been promised amnesty, and are being revived by their captors. All three were executed on June 27, 1809.

The *garrote vil*—vile garrote—was an iron collar fixed to a high-backed chair; quickly screwed tight by the executioner, it simultaneously crushed the cervical vertebrae and cut off respiration. The *garrote vil* was last used in Spain on March 4, 1974, when Salvador Puig Antich, a leader of the revolutionary organization known as the Iberian Liberation Movement, was garroted to death in the courtyard of Barcelona's Carcel Modelo (Model Prison). It was to be General Franco's final *garrote vil*, carried out at the same time that Heinz Chez, a hapless northern European wanderer accused (as was Puig Antich) of killing a policeman, was executed in neighboring Tarragona. There was widespread protest over this double execution, the last gasp of an authoritarian regime; Franco himself died twenty months later. Albert Boadella's avant-garde theater troupe, *Els Joglars*, was court-martialed nearly three years later for performing *La Torna*, a satirical account of the trial and execution of Heinz Chez, portrayed as an attempt to distract attention from the political ramifications of Puig Antich's death. (In Catalonia, *la torna* was traditionally the extra scrap of bread placed on the scales to make up an even kilo when bread weight baked out short.)

Puig Antich's family publishes the announcement of his death in Barcelona newspapers every March 2, and many young Barcelonans named Salvador in memoriam will come of age about the time of the 1992 Olympics.

The door to the cathedral cloister that opens onto Plaça de Garriga Bachs is often closed, but if this entryway is open, cut through to the back door opening out to Carrer Pietat. If it's closed, continue up Carrer Bisbe Irurita to the corner of Carrer Pietat and make a left.

The cloister is particularly lush in summer and provides a cool break. From the cloister there are also doors to the Santa Llúcia Chapel and into the cathedral itself. White geese, said to symbolize Santa Eulàlia's virginal innocence, bob in the pond while the palm trees, orange trees, and magnolias seem doubly green in the penumbra. Children flock to the cloister during the celebration of Corpus Christi to watch the marvelous egg, known as *l'ou com balla*, dancing on the Gothic fountain, a tradition said to be an ancient symbol of fertility. The dance of the egg, which is hollow, dates from the 1700s and was first performed in Barcelona between 1800 and 1802, according to historian Ramón R. Comas. A dancing egg can also be seen at the Ateneu de Barcelona on Carrer Canuda (see Walk 2) during the celebration of Corpus Christi.

The interior doorway leading into the main apse is one of the mysteries of the cathedral. As Agustí Duran i

Sanpere notes in his *Barcelona i la Seva Història*, "Just looking at it one sees that this door is older than all the rest of the cathedral." The classical pillars and nearly semicircular arches suggest that the door, clearly Romanesque, may have been from the original eleventh-century cathedral, although the rich ornamentation is atypical of structures of that period. The tops of the columns, or capitals, some leafy and others with sculpted scenes, all elaborately finished in white marble, are especially anomalous—as if, concludes Duran i Sanpere, they had been borrowed from an original Roman monument, as suggested by some of the mason markings lettered on the stone blocks, apparently left from poorly erased inscriptions.

To the right of the Portal de la Pietat and out through

The Cathedral cloister

the door into the street are the **Cases dels Canonges**, originally part of the ecclesiastical community that almost completely ringed the cathedral. The *canonges*, or canons, were staff or clergymen who worked in liturgical and scholarly pursuits connected to the life and religious activity of the cathedral. The fact that the canons were collected together in one nuclear neighborhood was typical of medieval towns: Carpenters, shoemakers, potters, and other professionals tended to cluster together, as the street names of Barcelona often show.

One of the last residents of the block of houses across from the Portal de la Pietat was the canon Pere Font, a highly respected native of the Pyrenees who had worked his way into the religious community after a distinguished career in the provincial towns of Vic and Tárrega. Upon his death, the story goes, the rush of mourners paying their respects became so tumultuous that the doors had to be closed, only to magically reopen as a result of the strength of the grief his death had inspired.

The building, restored in 1931 to mixed reviews, is now used for the **Escola Professional de les Dones** (Women's Professional School). Lectures, workshops, and seminars (usually announced in the "Convocatorias" section of the daily newspapers) are held there regularly.

Continue around the back of the cathedral and down the Baixada de Santa Clara to the excellent restaurant **La Cuineta**. It overlooks this space from the second floor and, suspended in a mysterious, medieval setting of stone and lamplight, is a good place for dinner.

Follow the curve of the apse of the cathedral along the Carrer Comtes de Barcelona. The first great doorway on the right is the **Palau del Lloctinent** (or Lieutenant). This late-Gothic structure was completed in 1557 and inhabited by the viceroys and lieutenants representing the Spanish monarchy. The patio is especially interesting, with its carved wood ceiling over the stairway and a second-floor gallery overlooking the courtyard. There is a door on the stairway with a sculpted relief of scenes from the life of Sant Jordi (Saint George) by Josep Maria Subirachs, the artist charged with the controversial completion of Gaudí's Sagrada Família Church. The view of the Barri Gòtic from the watchtower is excellent. The Palau is now the archive for the House of Aragón and contains one of the world's best collections of documents from the Middle Ages. Christmas concerts are often held in the patio; different choral groups from around Barcelona and Catalonia perform from all four sides of the courtyard and from the stairs, converting the stone structure into a vibrant sound chamber.

Plaça Sant Iu is the next opening down the Carrer dels Comtes. It is another favorite spot for musicians, especially flutists and classical guitarists whose quiet tones echo wonderfully through the surrounding courtyards and arcades.

The **Museu Marés**, in Plaça Sant Iu, was created in 1948 with the private collection of Frederic Marés, noted sculptor and restorer of religious images and icons. Housing the best collection of medieval polychrome wood sculpture in Spain and one of the most important in the world, the Marés is considered by experts on a par with the Cloisters of New York City's Metropolitan Museum of Art. Some four hundred fifty medieval paintings and sculptures in the Marés have recently been recatalogued, many identified and attributed to their true authors for the first time. Fifteen hundred works of art and over thirty thousand collectors' items, from medieval kitchen utensils to ivory carvings, are included in the Marés trove and in the **Museu Sentimental**, which also has a collection of common artifacts and objects from the eighteenth and nineteenth centuries. The museum's special gems include Jaume Huguet's *Retablo de Sant Agustí*, the polychrome wood relief of Jesus' appearance to his disciples on the sea (by the master craftsman known simply as Maestre de Cabestany), and a *Virgin with child* attributed to Pere Moragues, the famous medieval wood sculptor.

The garden overlooks the modern city below—with the same ramparts used by the Romans to look down on the fourth-century settlements outside the city walls.

Continue on to the front corner of the cathedral. The building to the right is known as **Casa de la Canonja**, another staff residency for the medieval community of canons. The original house was torn down, and what is now visible was built around 1450, with the back wing added in the middle of the sixteenth century. The façade of the oldest section is decorated with reliefs of Santa Eulàlia, the passion of Christ, and the coat of arms of the cathedral.

The interior of the cathedral contains enough art and architecture to fill a book of its own. A moment of rest in the semidarkness, a tour of the side chapels, and another shortcut to the right through the cloister and out through the Capilla de Santa Llúcia will lead back to the Carrer de Santa Llúcia, directly across from the entrance to Casa de l'Ardiaca.

Stay outside and cut across Plaça de la Seu, the square in front of the cathedral steps, to arrive at **Casa del Degà**, or Deacon, the senior member of the cathedral staff. Originally built in the fourteenth century, the house forms part of the city walls; two towers are visible from the far side of the square. The next door down Carrer de Santa Llucia is **Casa de l'Ardiaca**, or Archdeacon, the chief jurisdictional authority appointed by the bishop. The twelfth-century structure is now the home of the city archives and the Historical Institute of Barcelona.

The marble sculpture to the right of the door portraying swallows and a tortoise was designed by Lluís Domènech i Montaner after the building was acquired by the Collegi d'Advocats (Lawyers Association) in 1870. Domènech i Montaner, one of the greatest of Barcelona's Moderniste architects (along with Antoni Gaudí and Josep Puig i Cadafalch), refused to mutilate the building's great wooden door when asked to install a letter drop. Instead he perforated the solid stone alongside, which he decorated with the marble relief. When the dean of the Lawyers Association asked the meaning of the sculpted figures, the architect is said to have replied that it symbolized the juridical process: The swallows have wings to fly to truth's highest realms, while the administrative procedures plod behind at a turtle's pace. The dean, less than thrilled with this unsolicited editorial in marble, asked if something else might be more appropriate. Domènech i Montaner is reported to have replied that there was an old saying from the Middle Ages that would have been perfect:

Advocats i procuradors	Lawyers and senators as well
a l'infern de dos en dos.	Two by two, straight to Hell.

The green cloister and the Gothic fountain are a welcome relief from the solid stone surroundings, while the building's interior contains a lifetime of drawings and photographs of a Barcelona that has largely disappeared. It also contains a collection of the city's publications, housed in one of the Roman towers, including Barcelona's oldest paper, *Diari de Barcelona*, founded in 1792 and still published today.

Capella de Santa Llúcia across the street, on the corner of Carrer del Bisbe, is another of Barcelona's most cherished spots. Santa Llúcia, patron saint of the blind and of the light of understanding, has always occupied a special corner in the city's collective heart. Barcelona's blind gathered there by the hundreds every December 13 through the nineteenth century, waiting in long lines to touch a Santa Llúcia religious artifact to their eyes, hoping for a miracle. Another popular tradition held that marriageable girls, especially those from outside Barcelona, would meet eligible young men to court them at the Fira de Santa Llúcia in December.

The story of Santa Llúcia is another cruel account of Christian faith and beauty martyred by the Roman authorities. According to legend, Santa Llúcia, the lovely daughter of a noble family, had blue eyes so overpowering that a young man fell in love with her and swore that if she would not give up her vows to the church and marry him, he would denounce her to the anti-Christian authorities. When she refused, the young man carried out his threat, and Llúcia was brought before the Roman consul, who also fell hopelessly in love with her. The consul begged her and finally threatened her, to no avail, for the girl remained faithful to her religious convictions. The consul stormed and raged and pleaded, vowing that Llúcia's blue eyes had seduced him so completely that he would do anything to have them. Llúcia, according to the legend, plucked out her eyes, put them on a plate, and had them delivered to the man who had thrown her in jail. The consul was so horrified that he ordered her to appear before him so that he could tell her that, in spite of her blindness, he would pardon her if she would marry him or her original suitor. Llúcia appeared, miraculously endowed with new, dark, and even more beautiful eyes. She again refused her two pretenders and was put to death. Typical images of Santa Llúcia, such as the Joan Llimona painting over the door of the chapel dedicated to her, show the saint bearing her two eyes, sunny-side up, on a plate.

The present-day Fira de Santa Llúcia is the beginning of the Christmas season; Christmas trees, arts and crafts, and especially crèche figures are sold in stands ringing the cathedral for two weeks prior to Christmas. If you happen to be here at Christmas, have a close look at the Nativity scenes and the figures. Barcelona has a strong tradition of *pessebristas*, or crèche-makers. Many of the figures are impressively wrought, intricate, and evocative. One mysterious Catalan personality, always present in the *pessebre*, is the *caganer*, which literally means "defecator." This unmistakable figure, usually placed behind the stable, graphically goes about his necessities, assuming the usual and unmistakable position, as the traditional personages gather to admire the newborn Christ. Explanations of the *caganer* tradition usually stress realism and getting on with everyday life as a foil to the religious event being played out inside the stable. Other opinions link this scatological cameo to anti-Christian, anticlerical, antiestablishment, and independentist sectors opposed to all forms of centralism, whether from Madrid, Rome, the geopolitical superpowers, or heaven above.

Uphill to the left, back through Plaça de Garriga Bachs and past Carrer de la Pietat, Carrer del Bisbe passes under the universally criticized pseudo-Gothic bridge built in 1928 to connect the Generalitat and the Cases dels Canonges. Considered excessively ornate and uncharacteristic of even the wildest excesses of Gothic vitality, the footbridge is perhaps the most vilified of all the restoration work to date.

Many of the buildings in Barcelona's Gothic Quarter have been restored, moved, or even invented long after the departure of the Romans and Visigoths, and there has been much hilarity and criticism of the neo-Gothic monumentalism practiced in the latter half of the nineteenth century. One Barcelona chronicler on this subject cites an amusing anecdote told by a Barcelona novelist: A foreigner, arriving in Barcelona at the beginning of the century, asks a young shopkeeper where this Gothic Quarter he has heard so much about might be found. When the boy doesn't seem to know, the owner pipes up, "Sure, you know—it's that neighborhood they're building around the cathedral."

Continuing under the offending footbridge, Carrer del Bisbe opens into **Plaça Sant Jaume**. The respective government seats of Catalonia and Barcelona have stood here for almost six hundred years, although they were never face-to-face until some intervening architecture was removed during the first half of the nineteenth century. The **Palau de la Generalitat de Catalunya** is immediately on the right, emerging from Carrer del Bisbe into the square, while the **Casa de la Ciutat** (the Town Hall) stands in opposition across the way.

The historical significance of the Generalitat as an institution goes back to the beginning of the thirteenth century when the Catalonian Parlament, also known as the Corts Catalans, first met. Later in the same century this body was formalized to represent three entities: church, military, and citizenry. In the early 1300s a council consisting of three deputies from each branch was created and entitled Generalitat de Catalunya. During the fifteenth, sixteenth, and seventeenth centuries the building itself was sumptuously improved and amplified until Felipe V abolished the Generalitat in 1714 and established the Real Audiencia, a kind of Bourbonic kangaroo court that lasted until 1908 when the provincial council, or Diputacion Provincial, was established. Between 1931 and 1939 the Generalitat was the government seat for an autonomous Catalonia, and since 1977 it has been once again the Generalitat de Catalunya, governing an autonomous Catalonian national entity within the Spanish state.

The Palau de la Generalitat can be visited on the first Sunday of each month, upon the pealing of the bells, which occurs "sometime during the morning," and on April 23, the Fira de Sant Jordi (Festival of Saint George), which coincides with the original Fira de les Roses. This tradition, also known as the Fira dels Enamorats (Lovers' Festival), when knights declare their amorous preferences by giving roses to their ladies, was originally established by the Catalonian parliament during the twelfth century. The rose festival was joined in 1436 by the Festa de Sant Jordi and then in 1926 by the book fair—Festa del Llibre—commemorating the date of Cervantes' (and, by coincidence, Shakespeare's) death. It is now traditional for the lucky ladies to receive roses from their suitors and to give books in return.

Sant Jordi has been Catalonia's patron saint since the eighth century when chapels, churches, and children were already being named in honor of the knight errant who converted a village to Christianity by slaying an oppressive dragon. Although there are different versions of the legend of Sant Jordi, the most universally accepted accounts include a dashing young knight, the beautiful daughter of a troubled feudal lord, and a fire-breathing dragon. Sant Jordi slays the dragon, symbol of evil, and wins the lovely maiden, whom he gallantly declines in favor of his vows of chastity and the carrying forward of his quest in defense of truth and justice. The blood of the dragon spouted forth and turned to roses, according to some versions, and Sant Jordi offered them to the young lady, hence the connection with the Fira de les Roses. The scene of Sant Jordi slaying the dragon appears everywhere around Barcelona, especially in the Modern-iste reliefs of sculptor Eusebi Arnau.

The Palau de la Generalitat is a lavish and impressive place and will dispel any lingering confusion about poverty and suffering below the Pyrenees. The Gothic stairway, the Sant Jordi chapel, the sixteenth-century patio with its orange trees, the Saló Daurat with its gilded ceiling, the Saló Torres Garcia with its murals al fresco, and the Sant Jordi hall all speak eloquently of Catalonia's rich past and expensive future.

The Casa de la Ciutat directly across the square is the seat of municipal government. Although the guards and doormen do not advertise this fact, there is a tourist information office just inside to the left. From there, after collecting free maps and pamphlets on different aspects of the city, you can request a meeting with the protocol officer to arrange a tour of the building. Between 9:00 and 2:00 and later, from 4:00 to 8:00, a trip to the protocol office should at least get you through the patio; and if protocol can arrange a visit or add you to a group tour later in the day, don't miss it. The Casa de la Ciutat, like the Generalitat, is astonishingly luxurious and rich in history, art, and architecture. The **Saló de Cent**, the main hall on the second floor, was built in the early 1400s and was the meeting place of the Consell de Cent (Council of

100), very probably Europe's first parliament. The origins
of this institution can be traced to the early *Assembleas*
held in Lyons in 1283 and, even earlier, in 1188, in Girona. Thomas N. Bisson, a Harvard medievalist awarded
an honorary degree by Barcelona's Autonomous University in May 1991, cited the 1188 meeting, which included representatives of the third estate, or bourgeoisie,
as a decisive event in the development of Western democracy, and lamented the "anomaly that Catalonia itself
does not sufficiently value its contribution to European
parliamentary history." The privileges of representative
and democratic government conceded to citizens of
Barcelona as early as the thirteenth century continued to
evolve when a listing of honored burghers was compiled
and made public; new names are added every year on
the first day of May. This body, originally known as the
comú, or "commons," became the Consell de Cent and
made Barcelona a virtual sovereign republic within the
monarchy, which lasted until it was dissolved (along with
everything else) by Felipe V in 1714.

Inside the building, the Saló de Cent, the Saló de les
Croniques with its murals by Josep Maria Sert, and the
Sala del Trentenari (a smaller council of thirty elected by
the larger body) are stunning and opulent chambers of
exceptional interest.

The outside of the Casa de la Ciutat is an object lesson in architectural history. The side of the building
around to the left, the old façade, is pure Gothic, ornate
and complicated, while the wall facing the Generalitat,
now the main entrance, is of a stark neoclassical austerity,
even and orderly. The Gothic façade was built between
1399 and 1402, while the neoclassical façade was constructed between 1831 and 1847. The archway on the
right side of the Gothic façade was obviously stuck onto
the nineteenth-century neoclassical addition. The sculpture on the left-hand corner of the Gothic side is an image
of Santa Eulàlia.

Carrer Hèrcules, named for the mythical founder of

Barcelona, leads to the left, down to the **Plaça Sant Just**, one of the hidden gems of the Barri Gòtic, a square almost completely unspoiled and untouched by the last millennium. On the way down Carrer Hèrcules, hug the left-hand wall for a lovely view of the bell tower of the **Església de Sant Just**—especially by night when the tower is exquisitely illuminated. Plaça Sant Just is said to have been where the first Christians were executed in Roman Barcelona. The church, dedicated to Sant Just and to Sant Pastor, is possibly Barcelona's oldest, placed as far back as the fourth century, although the present structure was erected in the fourteenth century over the early Christian burial ground. A section of the Roman sewer system, suspected to have been used as catacombs by the city's Christians, was once located below the Plaça de Sant Just. The statue of Catalonia's patron saint, La Moreneta, the black Virgin of Montserrat, was said to have resided first in Sant Just, before it was removed to the Montserrat monastery in anticipation of a Moorish invasion. The Latin inscription over the door—UNA ES CUM PUERIS JUSTO ET PASTORE BEATIS /VIRGO NIGRA ET PULCHRA NOSTRA PATRONA PIA—is a linguistic puzzle dedicating the church both to the child saints Just and Pastor, martyred at the age of seven, and to the black Virgin. Translated nearly backwards, it comes out as: *Our pious patron is the black and beautiful Virgin, together with the sainted children Justo and Pastore.*

According to popular legend, the Virgin of Montserrat was removed from its mountain hideaway and returned to the Església de Sant Just for safekeeping shortly before the 1714 siege in which Felipe V finally succeeded in conquering Barcelona and ending the War of the Spanish Succession. When, after the fall of Barcelona, Felipe V ordered all of Catalonia's institutional documents, constitutions, and charters burned, the city is said to have filled with a black smoke that stained the icon and turned the Virgin black from a combination of grief and soot, never to regain her original rosy complexion until Catalonia recovered its lost rights and liberties. (Scientists explain the pigmentation of the black Virgins of Montserrat and of Czestochowa, Poland—both symbols of countries that have been mistreated by history—as the result of the aging of the wood used to make them.)

The fountain in the Plaça Sant Just was constructed in 1367 by Joan Fiveller (the original Fiveller palace was on Carrer de Lledó before moving to the Plaça de Pi in 1571) after he discovered a spring while hunting in the Collserola hills and had it piped in as a water source to Barcelona. The image high on the fountain's façade is of Sant Just, while the falcons on the two sides refer to the hunt. The balustrade above encloses a lush hanging garden with ivy flowing down the walls of the fountain.

The **Academia de Buenas Letras** (Academy of Arts and Letters), at the end of Carrer del Bisbe Cassador, was an important link in the recovery of Catalan culture after 1714 and was the precursor of the Institute of Catalan Studies and the Real Academia Catalana. The patio, the exposed stairway, the Gothic loggia or open gallery, and the spacious halls inside are all fine examples of aristocratic seventeenth-century design. The outside of the structure overlooks the Carrer del Sots-Tinent Navarro and is built into sections of the original Roman walls that appear later in this walk.

Before moving down the narrow Carrer Dagueria (named for the ancient craftsmen who made daggers along this street), a short walk down Carrer de Lledó is a good chance to see some of the finest patios and carriage ports in Barcelona. The original Fiveller house is at no. 4, while no. 11, an eighteenth-century town house with a huge entryway and lovely exposed stairway, was the Lledó family palace. The female busts in relief over the first floor of the senior citizens center at no. 13, with Latin inscriptions, promote the virtues of strength and knowledge.

Carrer Dagueria begins with the rococo eighteenth-century Moixo palace with its playful floral engravings, crosses Carrer Jaume I, and leads into Carrer Llibreteria, a busy little thoroughfare originally known as the Baixada de la Presó when the medieval jail (*presó* means prison) was located in the tower over the Roman Porta Major, or main gate, through the walls of what is now Plaça del Angel. Later named for its bookstores, some of which are still there, Llibreteria leads back past the inviting **Mesón del Café**, a good place for a quick espresso, if it's not too crowded.

Returning to Plaça Sant Jaume, Carrer Paradís is a narrow crease leading back uphill to the right, just short of Carrer del Bisbe's opening into the square. **La Cuineta**, the restaurant on the first corner, is a cozy hideaway but not as spectacular as the upstairs dining room of its other location next to the cathedral. **No. 10 Carrer Paradís** marks the spot for a number of Barcelona essentials: the highest point of the Mons Taber—center of the original Roman Colònia Favencia Júlia Augusta Paterna Barcino, the remains of what is widely supposed to be a second-century Roman temple dedicated to Augustus—and the Centre Excursionista de Catalunya, one of the city's most important organizations. The entryway itself at no. 10 Carrer Paradís has a certain archaic truth and intimacy (remarkably, they've simply left it alone) that many of the spot's admirers find irresistible.

Inside to the right, the fluted Corinthian columns are visible, illuminated and behind glass. Alternately said to be the temple of Hèrcules, mythical founder of Barcelona, or the tomb of the Visigothic king Ataulf, assassinated in Barcelona in 415, the temple was in reality dedicated to the first Roman emperor, Augustus. Grandson of a sister of Julius Caesar, Augustus was known for wide-reaching reforms and especially for improving road conditions, which he recognized as the vital arteries of the Roman Empire. Barcelona's Via Augusta, the original Roman expressway across Barcelona, is named for Augustus.

The Hèrcules legend had the Greek hero, son of Zeus, creating the Pyrenees as a tomb for his beloved Pirene, drinking from the Mediterranean at Montjuïc, and after falling in love with Barcelona's rich plain, vowing to return to found a great city. Years later, returning from Greece, his expedition was blown off course by a storm. They landed at Marseille, losing a ship in the process. Working around the coast, Hèrcules and his fleet eventually found the missing ninth boat, *Barca-nona*, much to their surprise and joy, at the site of the city, and named the city after the lost and refound crew and ship.

The **Centre Excursionista** is up the stairway, where there is a better view of the Roman columns. This hiking and climbing club is a key part of city and Catalonian life. Founded in 1876, the Centre specializes not only in mountain climbing and exploring the Catalonian countryside but also in studying the history of the city itself. The Centre Excursionista blends a happy confusion of nationalistic and scientific activity with a thirty-thousand-volume library, film and photographic collections, as well as classes in skiing, mountaineering, speleology, geography, Catalan language, and history. Located at the historical center of the city, the Centre Excursionista has the feel of a microcosm, offering magical access to all of Catalonia.

The round millstone just outside the front doorstep of the Centre Excursionista marks the early settlement's highest point and was originally estimated to be 16 meters above sea level. Barcelona, however, according to more recent studies, seems to have grown taller, the result of successive building on its own ruins as well as the erosion caused by the *rieras* slicing through just outside the walls.

At the end of Carrer Paradís, the Baixada de Santa Clara continues to the right across Carrer dels Comtes and down into **Plaça del Rei**, often described as the city's most beautiful square. A modern bronze sculpture by Basque sculptor Eduardo Chillida occupies the space on the right at the entrance to the square. The spot at the top of the stairway, now the site of the **Palau Reial Major**, was the center of political power when Barcelona was a Roman colony and later under Ataulf during the early fifth century when the Visigothic king made Barcelona the capital of his empire after marrying Galla Placidia, daughter of Theodosius I and sister of the Western Roman emperor Flavius Honorius.

The present structure includes elements dating back to the tenth and eleventh centuries. Over the next few centuries the palace was the official residence of the counts of Barcelona, the dynasty of sovereign counts begun by Guifré el Pilos. These count-kings guided Barcelona to its apogee of power and influence in the Mediterranean. Barcelona is nicknamed *La Ciutat Comtal*, or City of the Counts, after this six-hundred-year line of sovereigns who presided over Catalonia and the House of Aragon until Martin I died without succession in 1410. The kings of the House of Aragón lived in the palace through the fifteenth century, near the end of which a wing was ceded to the tribunal of the Spanish Inquisition.

The **Santa Agata Chapel** stands to the right of the stairway, a single-naved structure with brilliantly painted wooden beams and tiny side chapels filled with coats of arms. The chapel is named after Santa Agata, another victim, like Santa Eulàlia and Santa Llucia, of the Roman consul Decius. According to legend, Santa Agata's breasts were cut off during the brutal torture preceding her execution and placed on a rock kept for centuries in the chapel's collection of holy relics. The legends of the martyrdom of Eulàlia, Llucia, and Agata are well known to most Barcelona natives and are routine elements in the city's early Christian history.

The **Saló del Tinell** is the main hall in the Plaça Reial Major, an architectural gem built between 1359 and 1362 during the reign of Pere III el Cerimoniós. This ample space is spanned by six wide arches and covered by wooden beams. Named for the vats (or *tines*) used for grain storage, the Saló del Tinell has been the venue for some of Barcelona's epic events, such as the funeral—including cavalcades and processions of entire villages of

Plaça del Rei

peasants—of King Joan II, the Catholic monarchs' reception of Christopher Columbus on his return from his most celebrated voyage in 1492, and the trials of the Spanish Inquisition. According to legend, Barcelona's rank and file were so terrified of the brutalities of the Inquisition that the stones in the walls of the Tinell were said to move if anyone attempted to tell a lie there.

The Spanish Inquisition, somewhat unfairly featured in the world's appreciation of things Iberian, was established by papal decree in 1478 and definitively suppressed only in 1834. Initially part of the program for religious and racial unity promoted by Ferdinand of Aragón and Isabella of Castile (the *Reyes Católicos*, or Catholic monarchs), the Inquisition's first victims were converted Jews and Muslims suspected of privately harboring heretical beliefs. Later, Spain's feudal aristocracy supported and prolonged the Inquisition as a weapon of class warfare in its pursuit of greater social and economic power. Although the inquisitors' early savagery led Pope Sixtus IV to protest, the Spanish Inquisition—organized and directed by the infamous Tomás de Torquemada—actually allowed the accused limited legal counsel, used torture only on special occasions, and was known to have the best prison accommodations that Spain could offer. Nobles, high-ranking royal officials, and even bishops were included in the long list of victims, notably Archbishop Bartolomé de Carranza, who was imprisoned for seventeen years. The *autos-da-fé*, or public burnings of condemned heretics, were important events in fifteenth- and sixteenth-century Spain, well attended and generally supported by the people. Once in place, the Inquisition became a means of enforcing militant conservatism, unity, conformity, and the notion of Spain as a closed society. To some degree the victim of bad press, especially in the early sixteenth-century anti-Catholic and anti-Spanish propaganda published by English, Dutch, and Italian protestant writers, the Spanish Inquisition, tragic as it was, executed fewer victims over nearly five centuries than Germany burned at the stake for witchcraft in the sixteenth and seventeenth centuries alone. And compared to the catastrophes perpetrated around the globe during this century, including the executions of the early Franco regime, the Spanish Inquisition, despite its place of honor in Spain's *Leyenda Negra*, or black legend, is difficult to rank as much more than a minor tragedy in the course of modern Western history.

To the left on the way out of the Plaça del Rei is the Clariana-Padellas house, now site of the **City History Museum**. This museum, much of it underground, planned around the actual Roman ruins, is a walk through the city's evolution, beginning with the neolithic settlement discovered on an upper Barcelona hilltop, and ending with a panoramic view from the building's highest point: to the east down into the Plaça de Ramón Berenguer III el Gran and to the west back into the Plaça del Rei.

Carrer Veguer leads out to the old Baixada de la Presó, now Carrer Llibreteria. The *veguer* was the royal representative charged with administering civil and criminal justice (*corregidor* in Castilian). Thus, the early jail, or *presó*, occupied a medieval tower nearby until the middle of the nineteenth century. It was precisely here that the

Catalan Robin Hood, Joan de Serrallonga, was imprisoned with his lover, Joana Macissa, on October 31, 1633. Serrallonga, a highwayman famous for fleecing travelers as they passed through the mountains between Barcelona and Ripoll, was known as a gentleman bandit who opposed the monarchy, nobility, and central power, and fought for the rights of peasants and the rural downtrodden in general. Jailed for robbery, the legendary folk hero was tortured in the *Sala dels Torments*, a dungeon said to have had massively thick walls so that the victims' screams would not echo through the streets. Stretched out on the rack in the presence of judges, scribes, and officials, Serrallonga soon broke down and revealed the names of all the friends, cohorts, colleagues, and collaborators he could remember. When sentenced in early January, Serrallonga was condemned to public whipping and a long series of abuses—including cutting off of ears and branding with a hot iron—to be performed "in the usual places" around the city, prior to his beheading and quartering. As a result of his supposed revolutionary ideals, the legend of Serrallonga as a romantic hero has been passed down in rhyme and song since the seventeeth century. The great Catalan poet Joan Maragall (among others) has immortalized the bandit and his lover Joana in his poem, "La fi d'En Serrallonga," and the avant-garde theater ensemble Els Joglars presented one of its finest productions, entitled "Alias Serrallonga," in 1971.

At the corner of Carrer Veguer and Carrer Llibreteria is the store annex of the City History Museum where a complete selection of Barcelona memorabilia and historical documentation is available. To the left, down Carrer Llibreteria, the **Subirà Cereria**—specializing in candles and wax items of all kinds—has lovely frescoes on the second floor and an interior restored to an almost exact replica of the store founded in 1761 and said to be Barcelona's oldest. Across the street, at the corner of Carrer Llibreteria and Plaça del Angel, is **La Colmena**, one of the city's oldest pastry shops, built in 1862. Note the beehive (*colmena*) on the corner and cut into the glass over the door opening into the square.

Plaça del Angel was the fourth-century Portal Major, then the most important entryway through the city walls. The square came to be known as Plaça del Mercadal for the major market located there, and later Plaça del Blat (wheat) for the market's specialty. The square was finally identified as Plaça del Angel after an angel appeared there during the late ninth century while Santa Eulàlia's remains were being transported from the Santa Maria del Mar church to the cathedral. According to the story, the procession came to a halt at Plaça del Angel when Santa Eulàlia's remains became too heavy to carry. Eventually, after prayers and supplications, an angel appeared and pointed to a cathedral official, who then confessed that he had broken off and pocketed one of Santa Eulàlia's toes. Once the toe was replaced, Eulàlia proceeded into the cathedral.

In 1616 an obelisk was erected in the center of the square, and the angel was placed on top. The revolutionary members of the city hall of 1823 tore down the monument; nothing prior to that date is left in present-day Plaça del Angel. The bronze angel still presides however with an outsized finger pointing accusingly over the square from her alcove on the façade at no. 2-3.

From Plaça del Angel, a short detour to the right down Carrer del Sots-Tinent Navarro provides an important look at the original Roman walls before moving back through the square and up Carrer Tapineria into the spectacular Plaça de Ramón Berenguer III el Gran. In fact, a complete circumnavigation of the walls, easily distinguishable on any street map, is an excellent way to get the feel of the original walled city. Just follow the only streets that curve: Correu Vell to Carrer Gignàs to Carrer d'Avinyó, which turns into Carrer Banys Nous, which becomes Carrer de la Palla before passing across in front of the cathedral into Carrer Tapineria.

Plaça de Ramón Berenguer III el Gran honors the

greatest of the sovereign counts under whose leadership Barcelona flourished in the Middle Ages. Some of the best sections of the Roman walls are visible from this garden square.

Carrer Tapineria is named for the medieval cork-soled shoes (*tapins*) made there when the street was the home of the cobblers' guild. The cork clogs, according to historian Agustí Duran i Sanpere, conferred the status of house mistress on women of the day and "to wear *tapins*" became a euphemism for marriage; thus a woman who would soon *calcar tapins* was about to be married.

Continuing along the Roman walls, the Baixada de la Canonja cuts back up to the steps of the cathedral. The square in front of the cathedral is the traditional spot for the *Sardana*, the Catalonian national folk dance, usually performed here on Sundays. This delicate and ancient rite of uncertain origins has been analyzed as an allegorical representation of the passing of time: The movement of the heavenly bodies revolve day and night in the long and short steps, and the morning rooster crows in the wailing of the high-pitched *flaviol*.

Plaça Nova, down the cathedral stairs to the left, was one of the gathering places just outside the original Roman walls. From this *plaça* two well-conserved cylindrical towers can be seen on either side of the entrance to Carrer del Bisbe. Like Plaça del Angel, this was a popular meeting spot as well as a place for executing criminals and a marketplace where all manner of goods, including slaves, were exchanged.

A minute's walk down Carrer de la Palla will take you back to Carrer Banys Nous. Portalón for lunch? Or La Cuineta? Casa Tinell? Or maybe out to Barceloneta for a paella on the beach.

Walk · 2

❀❀❀❀❀❀❀❀❀❀❀❀❀❀❀❀❀❀❀❀

Sant Pere and La Ribera

THE MEDIEVAL TEXTILE AND WATERFRONT DISTRICTS

Santa Maria del Mar

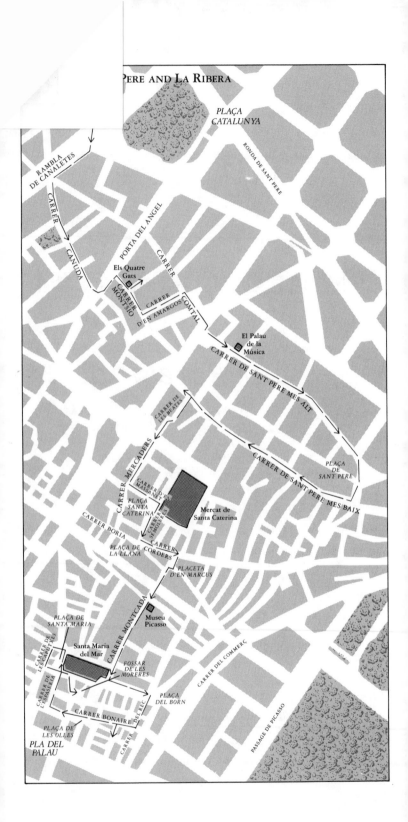

PLAÇA
CATALUNYA

RONDA DE SANT PERE

RAMBLA
DE CANALETES

CARRER

CANUDA

PORTA DEL ANGEL

CARRER

Els Quatre
Gats

CARRER MONTSIO

CARRER
D'EN AMARGOS

COMTAL

El Palau
de la
Música

CARRER DE SANT PERE MES ALT

CARRER DE
LES BEATES

CARRER MERCADERS

CARRER DE
MASSANET

PLAÇA
SANTA
CATERINA

CARRER BORIA

CARRER
SEMOLERES

Mercat de
Santa Caterina

CARRER DE
CORDERS

PLAÇA DE
LA LLANA

PLAÇA
DE
SANT PERE

CARRER DE SANT PERE MES BAIX

PLACETA
D'EN MARCUS

PLAÇA DE
SANTA MARIA

Museu
Picasso

CARRER MONTCADA

Santa Maria
del Mar

CARRER DE
LES CAPUTXES

CARRER DE
L'ESPARTERIA

FOSSAR
DE LES
MORERES

CARRER DEL COMERÇ

PLAÇA
DEL BORN

CARRER DEL REC

CARRER BONAIRE

PLAÇA DE
LES OLLES

CARRER

PASSAGE DE PICASSO

PLA DEL
PALAU

Starting Point: Café Zurich, on Plaça Catalunya at the head of the Rambla.
Metro: Plaça Catalunya
Length: About three hours

This walk takes us through Barcelona's early textile neighborhood, past the Sant Pere Church, and into the Barri de la Ribera, the early maritime neighborhood. Thick with some of the city's smallest and most medieval streets and alleys, the walk includes the Moderniste **Palau de la Música** concert hall and the Mediterranean Gothic Santa Maria del Mar Church, possibly the most disparate aesthetic extremes Barcelona has to offer.

Café Zurich, at the head of the Ramblas, is the place to start. A standard meeting point, Café Zurich is on the Plaça Catalunya side of the main entrance to the Barcelona metro. Originally the station house for the railroad train to Sarrià, the building is the oldest in Barcelona's Eixample, or "widening," and has remained nearly unchanged since its construction in 1862. Some sort of canteen or cold drink shop has occupied the corner on the Plaça Catalunya side since the very beginning, and since 1920, Café Zurich has been owned and run by the Valldeperas family. Neither nationalist bombing raids nor internecine warfare among rival Republican factions during the Spanish Civil War nor the Banco Central hijacking of 1981 has ever succeeded in closing down Café Zurich. It has traditionally been the setting for a wide range of artistic and professional clubs and intellectual gatherings of musicians, sculptors, poets, and journalists from *La Vanguardia*, generally considered Barcelona's best daily newspaper. This sidewalk café is nearly always sunny, a prime place to study people, run into old friends you didn't know were in town, read the paper, or write postcards. The wood-paneled interior has tables and booths that suggest a sense of intimacy, while the awning-shaded outside spots and the umbrella-covered tables on the new Rambla extension overlook festive old-world street theater.

Starting down the Rambla you will probably encounter a mob of orators in full harangue. Soccer and, to a lesser degree, politics and work are the usual topics of debate, with the criminal and congenital incompetence of coaches, club brass, politicians, and the managerial class in general the common thread running throughout. Don't be alarmed; in all probability no new global catastrophe has occurred. This has been going on for well over a thousand years. The spot used to be a piece of high ground just outside the city walls, a gathering place for beggars, thieves, gamblers, and hucksters of all kinds. Workers waited here outside the Santa Ana gateway into the medieval city, hoping to be hired. Perhaps for this reason, labor matters are still very much part of the agenda. These debates are intriguing: A speaker will hold the floor for as long as he is able to sustain the crowd's interest and assent. Any hesitation, confusion, repetition, or outright gaffe means immediate loss of forum, whereupon another speaker will take over and dominate for as long as he can—dialectics at its purest.

This section of the Rambla is known as **Rambla de Canaletes**, named for the iron fountain traditionally believed to be the source of Barcelona's coldest, best-tasting, and most fragrant water. According to legend, the water from Canaletes has magical powers: A foreigner drinking from this fountain will never be able to leave the city no matter how much he or she may desire or need to move on. It has been recorded that Barcelonans who wanted a visitor to remain in town would bring the foreigner to drink from Canaletes. Likewise, they would go to extraordinary lengths to avoid the fatal fountain with guests they wanted to get rid of. Probably named for the small canals or aqueducts that flowed through the second set of city walls here, the Canaletes fountain is one of the city's favorite symbols and becomes riotous after Barcelona soccer or basketball triumphs. Sports fanatics and Catalonian nationalists from all over the city converge to celebrate national or international championships . . . or victories over their historical nemesis, Madrid.

Carrer Canuda, named for the wife of a man named Canut, angles off to the left toward Plaça de la Vila de Madrid. "La Canuda," according to one story, was originally the beautiful domestic servant of a rich Barcelona resident who asked for her hand in marriage, only to be rebuffed by the girl's father, who believed that poor women who married rich men were doomed to lives of slavery and repression. The wealthy heir promptly called a notary and gave just over half of his fortune to the girl to even up the difference. They proceeded to be married, and La Canuda became well known in Barcelona for her kindness and generosity.

The **Ateneu Barcelonès**, or literary club, is at no. 6 Carrer Canuda, on the corner of the square. Founded in 1836, the Ateneu is a lush retreat with a graceful entryway and a second-floor "romantic garden" shaded and cooled by palm trees and fountains. An ancient and elegant oak-paneled bar overlooks Plaça de la Vila de Madrid below. There are solid wooden tables to work on, good natural light to read by, and armchairs which have presumably supported some of the best conversations ever held in Barcelona. The Ateneu was the city's cultural center until the end of the Spanish Civil War in 1939. The lovely and ancient library upstairs boasts one of the finest private collections of books in Spain as well as paintings by Françesc Pla, "El Vigatà." Special events and guest speakers include scholars, writers, and statesmen from all over the world. Profess an interest in joining, and you'll be allowed to look around, have a coffee, read the paper. Men can even get a haircut downstairs in what may be one of Barcelona's last real barbershops, surrounded by a spacious medieval entryway.

The plaque on the corner of Carrer Canuda over the square shows Madrid's Puerta de Alcalá flanked by Barcelona's Sagrada Família Cathedral, over the inscription, "The home of Madrid in Barcelona," a warm and unusual display of goodwill in an inter-city relationship that sometimes seems closer to a blood feud than a friendly rivalry. The sculpture presiding over the square is a *Maja de Madrid*, a Madrid beauty in typical folklorical dress, including fan and hair net, behind the municipal shields of Barcelona and Madrid.

The sunken garden in the Plaça de la Vila de Madrid contains the remains of a Roman road and tombs, including that of Roman Emperor Theodosius I, who died in 395.

At no. 24 Carrer Canuda is La Llibreria del sol i de la luna (Bookstore of the Sun and the Moon), which has been selling books at this location since 1766. The scrolled wooden plaque on the lower part of the door reads, EL LLIBRE FA LLIURE (Books make you free).

Continuing down Carrer Canuda to Porta de l'Angel, a quick left and right crosses to Carrer Montsió, named for a fourteenth-century order of nuns, followers of the Mare de Deu de Mont Sió (Our Lady of Mount Zion), whose convent was located there until it was moved stone by stone to Rambla de Catalunya in 1868. Casa Martí at no. 3 (bis) houses the famous café and beer hall known as **Els Quatre Gats**, a key landmark in Barcelona's turn-of-the-century art world. This pocket-sized neo-Gothic

Roman tombs, Plaça de la Vila de Madrid

gem, designed in 1895 by Moderniste architect Josep Puig i Cadafalch, was a favorite hangout for Moderniste artists and painters such as Ramón Casas and Santiago Russinol. Pablo Picasso first showed his work in Els Quatre Gats on February 1, 1900, to mixed reviews—begrudgingly praising his drawing while panning "Picazzo" as derivative and unoriginal. Although the expression "quatre gats" means "pretty much nobody," the place boiled with poets, musicians, and painters, including, among many others, Rubén Darío, Isaac Albéniz, and Isidre Nonell until Pere Romeu—owner and host—went broke in 1903, seven years after opening. Romeu, who died in 1908 at the age of forty-six, and Ramón Casas, his great friend, are the cyclists in the restored painting hanging in the café. Casas, short and wide, is in front while the tall, angular Romeu pedals behind. The conservative and Catholic Centre Artistic de Sant Lluc, of which Antoni Gaudí was a charter member, held meetings there from 1903 until 1936 when the space became a textile warehouse. Restored to a nearly exact replica of the original in 1983, Els Quatre Gats serves lunch and dinner and has different varieties of music and live entertainment, including a lady piano player who can roll out anything from ragtime to Rachmaninoff.

The sculpture at the corner of the building is a Eusebi Arnau rendering of Sant Jordi slaying the dragon. You will see at least two more Sant Jordi sculptures by Arnau (at the Casas Quadras and Amatller in the Eixample in Walk 5), but this is perhaps the largest and the most dramatic representation of this good-versus-evil theme, with Sant Jordi bearing the four-barred shield of Catalonia as he plunges his lance into the dragon's gaping maw. The other sculptures supporting and decorating the main-floor gallery are also intriguing. The somewhat sardonic monkey is a typical Arnau animal, while the men and women tucked into the vegetation under the window could represent any number of themes; architect Puig i Cadafalch puzzling over his plans, painter Ramón Casas lost in concentration, or Señora Martí napping in the grass.

The passageway next to the Quatre Gats leads down to an ancient doorway, all that remains of the Montsió convent. This alley, previously known as Passatge de Sant Josep, is now called Passatge del Patriarca. But from the doorway out to Carrer Comtal it is still known as Carrer Espolsa-sacs (literally, dust out sacks) named for the Augustinian monks known as the Frares del Sac for their baglike habits, which they shook out the windows over the street daily as required by the order's hygiene regulations. There was also a famous well on Carrer Espolsa-sacs, known to have healing powers; it specialized in home delivery of hot baths—salt or fresh water—during the mid-nineteenth century.

Continuing down Carrer Montsió, the doorway at **no. 8**, decorated with muscular cherubs and floral relief over the entry, is probably part of the original Mount Zion convent. At no. 9 is a barbershop for men, another of the remaining few. The next building on the right at no. 10 is the **Balmesiana Library**, a neo-medieval structure named for the early nineteenth-century philosopher Jaime Balmes, known for his defense of Catholicism and conservative ideology against liberals and protestant sympathizers. Born in Vic in 1810, Balmes died at the age of thirty-eight, leaving *Protestantism as Compared to Catholicism* as his fundamental opus. The entrance is on the far side of the building; some of the murals inside are of particular interest.

A sharp left away from the rock wall of the Balmesiana Library threads along tiny Carrer d'en Amargós. Amargós was, it seems, the landowner who permitted the original building along the street after the Valldaura Palace was torn down and the area was opened up for development. This narrow lane is lined with rustic entryways, wine shops, and restaurants. **Mercè Vins**, the first establishment on the left at no. 1-3, is a cozy bistro with a classic marble-topped bar and nooks, crannies, and balconies with tables for two (not very large) persons. The houses on the right side of the street stand, as the tiles just past no. 8 explain, at the edge of what used to be the gardens belonging to Catalonia's king or sovereign count, Guifré el Pilós, and are therefore of more recent construction than those on the left.

According to one popular story, a cobbler who once lived in Carrer d'en Amargós—possibly a forebear of Salvador, the "rapid" shoe repair specialist at no. 2—was well known for singing each day as he worked. His neighbor, the count, grew so tired of the shoemaker's endless performance, which echoed around the streets and throughout the stone spaces of his palace, that he sent down a bag of gold on the theory that if the man didn't have to work, he wouldn't need to sing. Initially overjoyed, the cobbler soon became more and more obsessed with losing his money, suspecting everyone of scheming to do him out of it until, unable to sleep and overcome with anxiety, he realized that the money was the source of all his unhappiness. He returned the bag of gold to the count and then went back to tacking shoes and serenading the neighborhood, while the count, headache and all, could only envy the man his peace of mind. Salvador, at no. 2, can barely speak in a hoarse croak and has never heard the story.

Carrer d'en Amargós runs into Carrer Comtal, named for Catalonia's sovereign counts. Guifré el Pilós, whose name is translated as either Wilfred the Hairy or Wilfred the Shaggy, was known to have favored this palace, originally thought to be a summer residence outside Barcelona's first walls. Guifré was at the Palau Valldaura when he received the call for help from his nephew Carles el Calb (Charles the Bald), a Frankish king who was battling the Norsemen, or Normans, in France. As legend has it, Guifré arrived just in time to turn the tide in favor of his ally but was mortally wounded in the process. Dying, the count bitterly lamented losing his life before winning a coat of arms for his realm, his shield still an empty golden field. Carles, placing his hand in Guifré's wound, said, "What better insignia than your own noble blood?" as he traced five red stripes against the golden background. This grant of arms became part of the basis for Catalonia's eventual independence from the Carolingian Empire. King Jaume I later suppressed one of the stripes, leaving four bars—*les quatre barres*—for Catalonia's four provinces: Barcelona, Girona, Lleida, and Tarragona, and the insignia has remained as the banner, or *senyera*, of Catalonia ever since.

The corner of Carrer Comtal and Carrer de les Magdalenes was once the site of the cage where the legendary Joan Garí was imprisoned by Guifré el Pilós. According to the legend, Garí, a Valencian nobleman, became a hermit living alone near the Catalonian religious retreat at Montserrat. Known for his miraculous healing abilities, Garí was asked to cure Guifré's ailing daughter, Riquilde, a young woman of unparalleled beauty. Unfortunately for Garí, he was unable to resist temptation and seduced the irresistible maiden; then, horrified by his sin, he killed the girl and buried her near his cave. Garí walked to Rome to confess to the Pope, who designed his penance: He was to return to Montserrat on his hands and knees and live on roots and herbs like an animal until he heard from the mouth of an infant that God had forgiven him.

Garí did as he was told. After years of living in the caves around Montserrat, his clothes rotted away. Covered with a long beard and curly hair that fell to his feet, he was discovered by Guifré's dogs during a hunt. Taken for some rare species of animal, Garí was brought back to Barcelona and locked in a cage until Guifré, during a feast celebrating the baptism of a son, remembered the strange beast and had it brought in to see if any of his guests could identify it. As the assembled company was being entertained by this strange creature, Guifré's three-month-old son rose up in his nurse's arms and announced in a clear voice: "Garí, stand up. God has forgiven you." At this point the hirsute figure was discovered to be a man. After telling his story, he took Guifré to Riquilde's grave where the girl was found alive and well, fresh and rested as if waking from a long sleep.

Directly across from the opening of Carrer d'en Amargós into Carrer Comtal, just to the left of the news-stand, there are two sets of tiles. The one on the left explains about the Palau Valldaura, Guifré el Pilós—founder of the nation and of Montserrat—and introduces the legend of Joan Garí, depicted in the four scenes painted by the famous Apel.les Mestres. Beginning at the upper left, we see Garí on all fours doing his penance. Scene number two is at the upper right, showing Guifré's dogs and Garí. In the third scene at the lower left, Guifré is showing Garí to his guests and his infant son instructs the monster to arise, and in scene number four, Garí shows Guifré Riquilde's resting place and the girl emerges alive, to the count's apparent joy and surprise. In Barcelona's History Museum (Walk 1) there are two wood carvings, one of Garí covered in thick hair falling like a cassock to his feet, and the other of the nurse with the babe in arms.

The building directly across from the Carrer Comtal on Vía Laietana is the house of the **Gremi de Velers** (Silkweavers Guild), at the corner at no. 1 Carrer de Sant Pere més alt. The structure is decorated on the south-

The Palau de la Música Catalana

eastern and southwestern façades with some of the best-preserved eighteenth-century engravings in Barcelona. In the engravings, Atlas and Caryatid figures, masculine and feminine, act as pillars for the building's main floor. The engravings on the far side are imitations added in 1930. The Silkweavers Guild, a craft respected on a par with silversmiths and engravers in early Barcelona, dates back to 1553, while the building itself was constructed in 1763.

Carrer de Sant Pere més alt soon broadens slightly into an opening dominated by a structure guaranteed to make you wonder if you've just stepped through the looking-glass. The **Palau de la Música** is a riotous formal and chromatic display as bright and unruly as a field of wild flowers. Designed by the fundamental architect of Modernisme, Lluís Domènech i Montaner, the Palau is Barcelona's most important music hall, home of the Orfeo Catalá, the city's best choral group, and setting for concerts by world-famous musicians ranging from Mstislav Rostropovich to Barcelona's own Montserrat Caballé to jazz combos and local choral ensembles.

The building itself was constructed between 1905 and

1908 by the prolific Moderniste, Domènech i Montaner, whose great-grandson and great-great-grandson, both named Lluís, carry on the family tradition in present-day Barcelona. Author of the lion's share of Barcelona's late-nineteenth-century architecture, Domènech i Montaner and his team of artists created their finest work in this elaborate and lyrical recital, which touches something essential in the Catalonian aesthetic sensibility.

Reactions to the Palau de la Música have not always been complimentary. Keeping in mind Flaubert's *"le mauvais goût c'est le goût de la génération antérieure,"* it is interesting to note that Spanish playwright Ramón del Valle-Inclán complained that "the mixture of brick, ceramics, glass, stone, and steel do not help me relax and listen to concerts in the least." Josep Pla, one of Catalonia's great chroniclers, a prose stylist of direct and classical taste, described the Palau in 1919 as "horrible, indescribably ugly" and objected to having to listen to music *"amb els ulls tancats"*—with his eyes closed. When Barcelona was preparing to host the Universal Exposition of 1929, journalist Carles Soldevila counseled in his brief guide to the city that anyone showing Barcelona to a visitor should explain about the Eixample and the "misfortune" of Modernisme. In February of the same year another critic of Modernisme, Manuel Brunet, published an article entitled "Is the Palau Salvageable?" He concluded, as the title suggests, that, alas, it probably was not.

But changes in style and taste aside, the Palau may be said to have withstood the test of time and is now universally acclaimed as one of Barcelona's most extraordinary buildings, possibly the flagship of Modernisme.

The façade's sculptures, by Catalan sculptor Miquel Blay, represent the Palau's commitment to popular choral music, an important Barcelona tradition. The busts, from left to right, are of Palestrina, Bach, Beethoven, and, around the corner, Wagner.

Inside the Palau, a catalogue of spectacular Moderniste devices—polychrome glass, ceramic mosaics, floral sculptures, and bas-relief statuary—clamors for attention. Flanking the stage are works originally attributed to the famous Catalan sculptor Pau Gargallo but later proven to have been sculpted by both Gargallo and his mentor, Modernisme's major sculptor Eusebi Arnau, a regular Domènech i Montaner colleague whose work will appear again later in Walk 5 in the Eixample. Gargallo's powerful equine figure on the right, inspired by the Wagnerian Valkyries, was conceived as a tribute to international music, while the Arnau sculpture of the young girls from the popular Catalan song *"Flors de Maig"* ("May Flowers") on the left is dedicated to traditional Catalonian music and Josep Anselm Clavé, creator of Barcelona's experimental workers' choral groups of the mid-nineteenth century. Antoni Rigalt i Blanch, the master glassworker of his time, designed the skylight, an eruption of heat and color over the main auditorium, while Lluís Bru did the ceramic mosaics, and Miquel Blay sculpted the exterior figures over the entrance, completing a juggernaut comprised of the greatest artists and craftsmen available in early twentieth-century Barcelona. The Palau, inside and out, is a feast.

Continuing on into the Barrio de Sant Pere on Carrer de Sant Pere més alt, there are a series of mansions built by the textile barons of early Barcelona. The Sant Pere district was the center of the textile industry, and even today many of the stores and workshops are involved in what has traditionally been the mainstay of Barcelona's economy.

At no. 18 is the building known as the **House of the Four Seasons**. The engravings on the second-floor façade represent the different seasons of the year: cherubim weaving garlands of flowers, harvesting wheat, cutting bunches of grapes, and roasting chestnuts. The **Palau Dou** at no. 27 was the home of one of the city's great textile families and is one of the most impressive buildings on the street, its neoclassical stone façade designed in the early nineteenth century. The other houses along Carrer de Sant Pere més alt include palaces constructed by prospering textile industrialists during the sixteenth, seventeenth, and eighteenth centuries. Josép Maria Sert, the painter of the epic murals of the Vic cathedral, the Barcelona city hall, and the murals in New York City's Waldorf-Astoria hotel, was born in 1874 at no. 49, around the corner from the family industry in what is now called Passatge Sert.

Plaça Sant Pere, at the end of Carrer de Sant Pere més alt, is the site of a hapless ninth-century church burned by the Moors in the tenth and eleventh centuries. Turned into a jail in the nineteenth century, it was later partially torn down by the state and twice burned during the twentieth century. Some experts on Barcelona art and architecture consider the attempts at restoration even more damaging to the Església de Sant Pere than the immolations and sackings.

The convent of **Sant Pere de les Puelles** (from the Latin for girl or maiden, *puella*) was a closed or cloistered retreat known for the beauty of its young ladies, all of whom were required to be of noble lineage. The abbess of Sant Pere de les Puelles was empowered to use several ecclesiastical symbols not usually conceded to women—such as the staff, the papal ring, and a fur stole over her left shoulder—and was authorized to preside over special religious events. Only the king and the Pope were allowed to enter the cloister. According to one legend, the king, on one of his visits, fell madly in love with one of the beautiful young maidens, returning to visit her again and again, to everyone's horror. The young *puella*, dedicated to the church, not to married life, rejected the king's proposal. The infuriated monarch announced that he was coming at the stroke of midnight to take her away, to which the lovely novice responded by dying of grief and confusion. When the king arrived, prepared to scale the wall, he found a great funeral ceremony in progress. The abbess threw open the doors and invited him into the main entrance to see what he had done. After kneeling at her feet, the king left in silence. According to Barcelona historian Joan Amades, the bells of Sant Pere ring the death knell at midnight on certain days of the year in memory of the innocent maiden who chose to die rather than compromise her faith by accepting the king's amorous advances.

Legend also has it that the Benedictine nuns, warned of the imminent arrival of al-Mansūr's forces near the end of the tenth century, decided to disfigure themselves, cutting off their noses and ears as a means of repelling or at least cooling the ardor of the invading Moors. The troops, expecting to find a trove of beauties, were so furious that instead of the routine round of violence and abuse, they decapitated the young ladies.

Moving away from the façade of Sant Pere de les Puelles past the entrance to the Carrer de Sant Pere mitjà to the intersection of Sant Pere més baix, Carrer Ocells, and Carrer Rec Comtal there is a glimpse of the massive Triumphal Arch looming out on the Passeig de Sant Joan. Any of these tiny streets can offer a tempting side trip with ancient and mysterious doorways and corners and a certain lived-in human pungence.

The various Sant Pere streets—*més baix, mitjà,* and *més alt* (lower, middle, and upper)—are the result of three different streets and their residents' original claim to Saint Peter's stewardship. Fourteenth-century municipal authorities finally settled the dispute in a Solomonic three-way division, thus equally satisfying and frustrating all parties.

Leaving Plaça de Sant Pere by Carrer de Sant Pere més baix there are several extraordinary houses sprinkled in among the small shops, bars, and cafés. The **Palau dels Marquesos d'Alòs** at no. 55, constructed by the textile-powerful Dou family—an important clan of leading statesmen, judges, professors, and scientists at the end of the eighteenth century—is one of the most impressive.

The **Farmacia Pedrell** (now Fonoll), the oldest pharmacy in Barcelona, founded in 1562, stands at no. 52. The entryway, beams, walls, and chandelier are Moderniste reforms added in 1890 by the architect Bernades. Isidre Nonell, Catalonia's famous Impressionist painter, whose work is every bit as evocative and appealing as the paintings of Monet or Boudin, was born, lived, and died in no. 50, the next house, as the plaque on the wall attests.

At no. 46 stands the **Casa de les Cortinatges** (House of the Curtains). The house itself dates from the fifteenth century although the engravings portraying cherubs drawing curtains (visible just above the second and third "A"s of the first-floor clothing store Alaska) were added in 1779.

The house at no. 42 offers a glimpse into the textile industry of the nineteenth century. Through an interior patio of this house, past a quick shoe-repair specialist and a hairdresser, a factory façade is still visible: large neo-Romanesque windows with dividing columns of reinforced concrete just behind a small palm tree. The city's rank and file were put to work in spaces such as this one during the latter half of the nineteenth century when Barcelona emerged as a European industrial power with all of the attendant social, intellectual, and artistic foment.

At no. 33 was the house of the Camille monks who, from the center's founding in 1662, specialized in providing care for the dying and were popularly known as the order of *agonitzants*.

A short walk to the end of Sant Pere més baix will take you to the old **Biblioteca Popular de la Dona** (Women's Public Library) at no. 7, which was not only the first public library in Spain, but, even more surprisingly, especially in a society that has never been described as matriarchal, was established exclusively for women. The reading room is presided over by philosopher Ramón Llull's inscription, *"Tota dona val mes quan letra apren"* ("Any woman is more valuable when she learns to read"), the truth and wisdom of which, currently beyond debate, was apparently not such an unrevolutionary idea in 1909 when the library was founded.

The library also offered the ladies another great nov-

elty: showers, along with rooms for meetings and a hairdressing salon, all part of the progressive thinking of
bourgeois antebellum Catalonia. After the 1936–39 Spanish Civil War succeeded in reestablishing law and order
as well as traditional notions about progress of all sorts,
the library fell into the hands of the feminine section of
the Falange, the official Spanish fascist political party, and
activities were reoriented toward homemaking and less
radical female pursuits. The building, formerly part of the
Santa Anna Church, is now occupied by the **Institut del
Teatre**.

Backtrack a few steps to Carrer de les Beates, named
for the convent once located on the street. This tiny thoroughfare leads down toward Plaça de les Beates and the
beginning of **Carrer de Mercaders** (merchants). This street
was named for the Catalan merchant seafarers who dominated the Mediterranean between the thirteenth and
eighteenth centuries, when it was popularly said that "not
even a fish dared to appear without the *quatre barres*,"
the four red bars of the flag of Catalonia and the House
of Aragón. Several entryways—at no. 42, for example, with
its carriage port and interior patio—provide a glimpse into
the elegant quarters of the city's merchants and moguls
of that era.

Farther down Mercaders, at no. 15, is the site of what
was once the Hostal de Girona, an inn frequented by the
Catalonian Robin Hood, Joan de Serrallonga, the re-
nowned highwayman. Serrallonga so frequently fleeced
rich and poor alike that a section of road between Vic
and Ripoll is still called *"el purgatori"* in reference to Serrallonga's "purges" of travelers' purses.

Carrer d'En Massanet is named for a legendary revolutionary known to have taken part in the burning of
the Santa Caterina Church during the anticlerical uprising
of 1835, sparked by a bad bullfight in the Barceloneta
bullring. Massanet was said to have been apprehended
and executed in the Ciutadella along with twelve other
convent burners, only to regain consciousness under a

pile of corpses on the way to the cemetery. He escaped and, disguised as a monk, survived. Alleged to have come back to participate in the murder of the notorious General Bassa, sent from Madrid to quell the uprising, Massanet continued his career as a revolutionary until he was killed in Rome in another rebellion against Pope Pius IX.

Carrer de l'Arc de Sant Silvestre leads to the **Santa Caterina Market**, another of the fresh and fragrant quasi-open-air markets scattered throughout Barcelona. These popular, bustling hangars filled with vegetables, fish, flowers, herbs, meat, and produce of all kinds have minuscule bar-café establishments and even, in some cases, excellent restaurants. The sensorial rush is much like the old early morning Les Halles of Paris, the colors, scents, and sounds obviously stimulating to anyone wandering into the cool cornucopia of these inner-city oases. Wild mushrooms (*múrqula, fredolics, camagrocs, rovellons*) or fish (*lluç, rap, gall, verat, sorell*), brightly illuminated and carefully laid out, seem to put a special, bright edge on everything. Check for the butcher's perfect teeth and the long lines of admiring *senyoras* waiting to have their filets and chops sliced just the way they like them by his expert, gleaming blade. Note the ladies and their daughters behind the counters, rouged and red-lipped, smiling, laughing. A certain hilarity reigns. Everything happens. Appetites balloon.

The market stands in the square once occupied by the Santa Caterina Church, one of the first Gothic basilicas constructed in Catalonia. In the opinion of some historians it was one of the most complete, including an immense rose window, an octagonal bell tower, and an intricately sculpted arcade and doorway. The Dominicans built the church in the early thirteenth century, but the structure was partly torn down, subsequently burned, and finally destroyed in 1837. Architect Josep Buixareu's simple neoclassical market, built in 1847, is a graceful space and one of the city's best markets, perhaps heir to some of the emotion and energy that went into the creation of the original Santa Caterina Church. The first bird market—now on the Rambla—was originally located in the Santa Caterina market, once an important center for buying and trading birds of all kinds.

Carrer Semoleres—named for processors of semolina, a wheat derivative—runs from Plaça Santa Caterina to **Plaça de la Llana** (wool), the old yarn and wool market, an uneven little square with all the dark and humid mystery of early Barcelona. Three streets open under archways into Plaça de la Llana: Carrer Semolers, Carrer Boquer, and Carrer Candeles. Carrer Boria leads down from Via Laietana and, farther uphill, the original Mons Taber, the Barcelona acropolis. Carrer Boria was once part of the old Roman Vía Augusta which led out to the north and entered the old city through the main entryway; thus, Plaça de la Llana has been traversed by virtually all of Barcelona's early history from Hannibal and his seven hundred elephants or Count Wilfred (Guifré el Pilós) on his way to fight the Normans in France to Saints Peter, Paul, and James going to and from Rome.

Carrer Boria was the scene of the public scourging and humiliation of criminals and miscreants of various kinds. Thieves and others judged guilty of antisocial activities were taken down what was then known as the Bajada de la Presó (today Carrer Llibreteria) lashed to a donkey, tied hand and foot, and naked to the waist. The donkey stopped at each street corner, the sentence was read aloud, and the executioner and his assistants proceeded to administer three lashes, the procession stopping at one hundred corners. The event was brought to a close by branding the victim's back with a red-hot iron bearing the municipal seal, at which point the procession returned through the streets to the jail where the prisoner's wounds were treated with salt and vinegar.

This tour was popularly dubbed *"pasar Boria avall"*— to go down Boria—as in "You'd better watch your step, or you'll end up going down Boria." According to Barcelona chronicler Isidre Torres i Oriol, the last public whipping took place on August 22, 1816. The victim, a fleshy matron known as Aunt Catherine, was sentenced to be whipped through the streets and to perform subsequent duty in the galleys for running an establishment specializing in the corruption of minors. Catalan painter Françes Galofré i Oller recorded a public whipping in his oil canvas entitled *Pena de Azotes*, first shown at the Galeria Parés on Carrer Petritxol in 1892. Long lines formed to see the painting, which caused a sensation possibly appealing to some half-remembered residual prurience. *Pena de Azotes* is now on display in the museum at Valls in the Penedès, west of Barcelona, the artist's birthplace.

From Plaça de la Llana, Carrer Corders—where rope or cord was manufactured in early Barcelona—leads to the Placeta de Marcús and on into Carrer Carders, named for the makers of the cards used in combing wool, another important part of the neighborhood's textile history.

The **Marcús chapel** at the corner of Placeta de Marcús was built by a wealthy twelfth-century banker and merchant who, according to popular history, had a dream in which he was told to go to the French town of Avignon. After waiting for several days on the bridge at Avignon, he met a young man who had had a dream of his own in which a chest of gold was buried in the Barcelona residence of a man named Marcús. Marcús returned, found the gold, and proceeded to build a hospital and a church dedicated to the Virgen de la Guía, the patron saint of travelers, presumably because of his various business trips throughout Europe. The diminutive Marcús chapel at the intersection of Montcada, Carders, and Corders was built in the twelfth century as part of the Marcús hospital and became the center for pony express mail between the Iberian peninsula and the rest of Europe.

Carrer Montcada begins in the Placeta de Marcús, crosses Carrer Princesa, and ends in the Placeta de Montcada next to Santa Maria del Mar Church at the western end of the Plaça del Born. One of Barcelona's most traditional and aristocratic streets, Carrer Montcada's history, unlike that of most city streets, can be traced directly to the year 1148 when Count Ramón Berenguer IV, during the battle with the Moors for Tortosa, ceded the land the street now crosses to Guillem Ramón de Montcada in return for organizing and financing the campaign. Montcada and nine other prosperous Barcelona merchants proceeded to build an unusually rectilinear trace through what had been known up to then as Vilanova de la Mar, one of the first neighborhoods to appear outside of the earliest Roman walls. Originally waterfront or beach (the sea originally reached almost as high as Vía Laietana), the sandy soil, though difficult to build on, permitted an orderly layout of streets unlike the curved and foreshortened alleys and byways inside the walls on Mons Taber.

Thus, Carrer Montcada became an enclave for Barcelona's most honored and wealthy families, and the *casas nobles* these eminent burghers built between the thirteenth and eighteenth centuries are some of the city's best examples of medieval and Renaissance architecture.

Casa Puigxuriguer is at no. 1, the first carriage port on the left starting down Carrer Montcada. Just inside to the left is a marble plaque attesting to the rainstorm that drove the Corpus Christi procession and the Host into the house of Joseph and Clarina Puigxuriguer for two hours on June 13, 1762. This event is still revered, and neighbors say that people still come looking for the *casa de la custodia*, or house of the monstrance, the chalice holding the consecrated Host.

Across Carrer Princesa, the third building on the right, at no. 12, is the **Palau dels Marquesos de Lló**, built in the thirteenth century. Once the home of the Royal Academy of Letters and later the site of the Workers' Atheneum, or cultural center, since 1969 it has housed the Rocamora collection of ancient clothing and the Museo

Textil, which is appropriate considering the Palau's proximity to the city's textile district. The collection of clothing includes inner and outer wear from as far back as the fourth century. The patio is one of Barcelona's best, with the loggia overhead, the sculptures around the windows inside, and especially the sixteenth-century ground-floor window to the left on the way out to the street. The mirror that was installed just inside the door during the palace's restoration creates a startling illusion of depth and space.

Across the street at no. 15 is the **Palau Aguilar**, originally built in the thirteenth century and owned by a

Palau dels Marquesos de Llío

series of families before it was bought by the Aguilars in 1463. Presently part of the Picasso Museum, the building itself is nearly as interesting as the artwork it houses—an elegant stone and glass space with abundant natural light, cool in summer, cozy in winter, and in general a pleasant place to spend time.

Marc Safont, the architect responsible for the sumptuous Generalitat, the Catalonian seat of government, is believed to have designed the Palau Aguilar as well. The patio, like the one in the executive mansion, features an open stairway leading to a main-floor balcony overlooking the staircase.

The Aguilar, Castellet, and Meca palaces are all part of the **Picasso Museum**, an important concentration of the artist's work. Included are nearly all of his graphic works, the main works from his Barcelona period, the forty-four studies of *Las Meninas*, as well as many childhood paintings and drawings.

Barcelona's claim to Picasso, it should probably be noted, is not airtight, as became evident in the late seventies when four different cities vied for the famous *Guernica* canvas. Pablo Ruiz y Picasso was born in 1881 in Málaga, where his father was an art teacher. After a brief period in the northwestern Spanish port town of La Coruña, the young Picasso, aged fourteen, moved to Barcelona when his father became a professor at the School of Fine Arts. Picasso, who chose to use his mother's more exotic and cosmopolitan-sounding last name, enrolled in art school in 1895 before attending the Royal Academy in Madrid two years later. He soon returned to Barcelona and the lively art scene at Els Quatre Gats where he showed his first work. After 1900, Picasso divided his time among Paris, Madrid, and Barcelona, although he did work in a series of studios in Barcelona until 1904. The famous Catalan Impressionist painter Isidre Nonell was an important friend and influence on the young Picasso, and many of the artist's strongest friendships were formed during the decisive nine years when he lived in Barcelona.

Thus, when the time came to return *Guernica* to Spain—in accordance with the artist's last will and testament—Málaga, Barcelona, Guernica, and Madrid all laid claim to what has undoubtedly become Picasso's most famous work. Each claim had its merits: Málaga, as his birthplace; Barcelona, as the scene of the artist's adolescence and key period of development; Guernica, the Basque village experimentally destroyed by German aviators supporting Franco's rebel forces in 1937, which is the theme of the work commissioned by the Spanish Republic; and Madrid, as the site of the Prado Museum specifically named in Picasso's will to be the painting's resting place upon Spain's return to a democracy.

The return of this antiwar masterpiece nearly caused a fresh outbreak of hostilities as Basques ("We supply the blood and Madrid gets the *Guernica*"), Catalans (Picasso once said he thought of himself as "a Catalan painter"), Andalusians (the painter's native soil), and Madrileños (under the explicit charter of the legacy) all battled for possession of the world's most controversial canvas. Madrid won, and *Guernica* is on display in a bombproof, armored building next to the Prado Museum.

Barcelona still counts Picasso—along with Salvador Dalí, Joan Miró, Antoni Gaudí, and Pablo Casals—as national patrimony, and Mayor Pasqual Maragall, in April 1991 (not coincidentally, soon after a Catalonian was appointed Spanish Minister of Culture), proposed bringing *Guernica* to the Olympic Games of 1992 so that "Spain can show off one of the nation's greatest works of art."

With or without *Guernica*, the Picasso Museum is a rich trove, holding nearly three thousand paintings, drawings, prints, ceramics, and other works created during Picasso's long career.

The Picasso Museum opened in 1963 after years of wrangling with Spanish authorities who were reluctant to approve public recognition of such a prominent anti-Franco figure and author of a work entitled *The Dream and the Lie of Franco* (1937). The museum was the idea of the artist's longtime friend Jaume Sabartés, who decided that the vast collection of works he had received as gifts over the years should be made public. Between Sabartés, Barcelona's Museum of Modern Art, and other donors, including Salvador Dalí, a monumental body of work was gathered together. Picasso himself gave his series of studies of *Las Meninas* in memory of Sabartés and later included some nine hundred works from his family collection. Beginning with the drawing Picasso did at the age of nine in La Coruña, through the oil paintings he achieved at the age of fifteen, the "blue period," his "rose period," cubism, and continuing through the studies based on the Velázquez original of *Las Meninas* he produced at the age of seventy-six, the museum requires several unhurried, untired hours of peace and quiet. This may be a place to return to after lunch, or maybe even another morning when the light in and around the museum will allow you to enjoy the building itself.

Although Picasso's greatest works are not in the Picasso museum, the artist's childhood doodling, his youthful studies and early works, and the prints, catalogs, and biographies available in the museum store provide an excellent opportunity to get to know the twentieth century's greatest artist, a creative giant who, when he died at the age of ninety-two in 1973, had managed to work through more than seven decades in an assortment of media.

Through Picasso's melancholy "blue period" between 1901 and 1904, when he was suffering from extreme poverty, including hunger and cold, during his first years in Paris, and into his less pessimistic "rose period" when his hues gave way to friendlier tones of brown and pink, the young artist struggled to establish himself in the art capital of the world. The list of artists who left Barcelona for Paris was long: Ramón Casas, Santiago Russinol, Miquel Utrillo, Juli González, Pau Gargallo, Joan Miró, Salvador Dalí, Isidre Nonell, and many others were forged and formed in the French capital only to return eventually to Catalonia.

Picasso stayed and took up residence in the Bateau Lavoir (a ramshackle barn named for the laundry barges on the Seine). He became friends with Georges Braque, with whom he would launch cubism, the poet Apollinaire, Gertrude Stein, and the writer Max Jacob. In a mere five years, by 1909, he was established as a young painter of exceptional talent, had left the Bateau Lavoir for the more comfortable Boulevard de Clichy, and took summer vacations in Spain and southern France.

Before World War I broke out in 1914, Picasso, at thirty-three, had achieved his most important work in the early masterpieces of his "rose period" and the creation of what art critics christened as *cubism*, a departure from Impressionism's emotion, color, and sensation in favor of a return to, in Picasso's words, "an architectonic basis in composition."

The war years brought a return to realism in Picasso's painting. After a number of liaisons and the death in 1915 of Eva, his second mistress, Picasso married Olga Koklova, a young Russian dancer, in 1918. Their son Paulo was born in 1921.

The 1920s were marked by surrealism. Although Picasso never formally joined the movement, he knew André Breton, Jean Cocteau, and Paul Éluard and shared in the influences of the period. The 1930s were a time of personal crisis for Picasso, whose liaison with the sensual blond model Marie Thérèse Walter, with whom he had a daughter, led to the failure of his marriage. The photographer Dora Maar succeeded Olga as Picasso's muse.

Guernica was painted in 1937 on commission from the Spanish republic. Two years later, World War II engulfed Europe. Picasso spent the war years at work in his studio in the Rue des Grands-Augustins in Paris, refusing to flee the Nazi occupation as many other artists chose to do, despite his precarious situation as a Spanish citizen enjoying persona-non-grata status with the Franco regime. Near the end of the war Picasso began his relationship with Françoise Gilot, a young painter forty years his junior with whom he eventually had a child. Picasso, now in his sixties, had become a public figure and received visits from André Malraux, Ernest Hemingway, Jean-Paul Sartre, and other famous personalities.

With Françoise, whose book *Life with Picasso* (McGraw-Hill, 1946) provides a fascinating personal view of this vital and complex creator, Picasso moved to Antibes in 1946 and then to the pottery town of Vallauris in 1948, after Françoise had borne Picasso's third child, Claude, in May 1947.

After the departure of Françoise Gilot in 1953, Jacqueline Roque, the cousin of a Vallauris potter, became Picasso's last woman companion and then his wife, after the death of Olga Koklova, in 1961. After living in Cannes and near Aix-en-Provence, Picasso and Jacqueline settled in Mougins in the mountains north of Cannes, where Picasso died on April 8, 1973.

Picasso, prolifically vital and restless throughout his life, appears to have been nearly as active erotically as artistically. Women found him irresistible, and he was voracious about the women who inspired him. His art was, in a sense, a synthetic dismantling of the modern human psyche, in his words "not a *trompe l'oeil* but a *trompe l'esprit*. I'm out to fool the mind rather than the eye."

No. 17 Carrer Montcada is **Palau Castellet**, also occupied by the Picasso Museum. Note the bust, in relief, high on the wall, representing the Supreme Being surrounded by angelic cherubim. Inside there is an elegant nineteenth-century neoclassical hall.

No. 19, the **Palau Meca**, is the third annex of the Picasso Museum and another excellent example of sixteenth- and seventeenth-century urban Barcelona architecture. The interior patio is especially spacious and includes a typical open stairway angling up to the baroque doorway of the main floor.

No. 14 is a Gothic and Renaissance building. The busts decorating the fourteenth-century window—an old man and a young woman—are of special interest, as is the doorway, which was added during the neoclassical nineteenth century.

The seventeenth-century **Palau Dalmases** at no. 20 is considered the best and most complete architectural unit on Carrer Montcada. The patio, the stairway, and the Gothic chapel on the main floor, with its angels bearing the key to the Epiphany, are all from the same period (fifteenth century) and have been preserved virtually intact. The sculptures decorating the stairway over the patio are especially intricate and portray the Rape of Europa and Neptune's Chariot, accompanied by bare-breasted maidens, young dancers, and musicians. The Palau Dalmases, still the home of the Marquis and Marchioness of Dalmases, is the site of the Omnium Cultural, forerunner of the Institut d'Estudis Catalans, devoted to the promotion and dissemination of Catalonian culture and history.

Across the street, the **Palau dels Cervelló**, at no. 25, a fifteenth-century building modified during the sixteenth, is the home of Barcelona's Maeght Gallery. The Maeght is always an interesting place to stop and browse through whatever exhibition of painting or sculpture is currently on display.

At no. 22 there is an important pause for *vino achampanado*, cider, or draft beer in the **Xampanyet**, a lively little establishment with small marble-topped tables, delicious anchovies, and brightly colored tile walls.

On the left as you come out into the Placeta de Montcada is the notorious Carrer de les Mosques, known as the smallest street in all of Barcelona—it is little more than a meter wide. Carrer de les Mosques was named for the clouds of flies (*mosques*) that used to collect in this narrow alley, attracted by the fruits and vegetables stored there by vendors from the Born market.

Emerging into the **Plaça del Born**, Santa Maria del Mar is to the right, and the Born's large black and red roofs are visible in the distance down to the left. The

Plaça del Born, the oblong space stretching between these two structures, is almost as important a piece of Barceloniana as the Ramblas. Originally used as jousting and tournament grounds and later as a popular gathering place for markets, celebrations, processions, carnivals and, during the Middle Ages, the burning of heretics, or autos-da-fé, this flat field was conveniently located behind the walls of the palaces where the aristocracy could watch the battles from their windows. The word *born* has several possible derivations: a unit of measure consisting of what fits into the palm of the hand, a handful, which may have been used in the early marketplace instead of scales, or the end or farthest point, as in the edge of town, perhaps marked by a stone. But the most commonly accepted definition is the point or business end of a jousting lance, which produced the verb *bornear*, meaning to joust. Whether named for the end of the lance or for the edge of town where the tournaments took place, the joust seems intimately related to the origin of the name of this square, the heart of the city from the thirteenth to the eighteenth centuries, when the demolition of the second set of walls converted the Rambla into the central promenade between the old city and the Raval to the west. *"Roda al mon i torna al Born"* ("Go around the world and return to the Born") is the popular dictum expressing the importance this piece of terrain has traditionally held for Barcelona natives.

A look around this elongated rectangle reveals several gems: From the glassed-in niche on the first balcony at no. 13 Plaça del Born, the figure of Saint Anthony, patron of herdsmen, overlooks the site of early livestock markets; no. 15 has lovely balconies and floor-to-ceiling windows; and the narrow wooden door and scrolled pillar at no. 18 support a heavy and ancient crossbeam and a façade embellished with Moderniste decorations.

The Plaça del Born is endowed with a number of

Café, Carrer Montçada

popular bars, saloons, and restaurants, such as the tiny upstairs and downstairs spot on the right at no. 26-28 called El Born, which opens at 7:00 P.M. The bar on the corner of Carrer del Rec, known as El Guinness, has a convenient glassed-in place for reading.

Past the far end of the jousting grounds, the old Mercat del Born, once the city's major outlet for food products from all over Catalonia, is an ornate iron hangar built by the Catalan architect Josep Fontseré in 1874. The marketplace is now used for public events, exhibitions, and musical and theatrical performances.

Carrer del Rec leads down to the right; its Gothic pillars and porches support low terraces, and it is one of the oldest streets in Barcelona's Barri de la Ribera, or waterfront neighborhood. The buildings and loggias seem to have been haphazardly stuck together, creating a lovely weathered and natural effect, as if conglomerated in layers century after century. The fruit and vegetable vendor at the corner of Carrer de la Esparteria—Almacen Santa Maria—is an operation that hasn't been altered for the better part of a millennium, since the porches were originally built for the protection and sale of merchandise.

The *rec*, or irrigation canal, was once a briskly flowing stream, an extension of Barcelona's main water supply. Mills stood along the *rec* as one of the street's early names, Molins de Mar, confirms.

The western side of the street is clearly medieval, built in the thirteenth and fourteenth centuries, while the other side dates from the end of the eighteenth. At the end of the siege of 1714, seven convents and nearly seven hundred houses were ordered removed by the victorious troops sent by Felipe V and led by the Duke of Berwick and Próspero de Verboom, in order to make space for the Ciutadella fortress. Over five thousand citizens were left homeless, having been commanded not only to evacuate but to tear down their own homes stone by stone.

El Born market

Barceloneta, the Cartesian fishing village, Europe's first artificially designed urban project, was constructed to compensate the citizens of the Barri de la Ribera who had lost their homes to the Ciutadella, but it was to take almost forty years to begin building; thus, the parties finally compensated were largely children and grandchildren of the original victims.

When construction was finally allowed on the east side of the Carrer del Rec, during the final years of the century, the first buildings were allowed to be only two stories high, like those of Barceloneta, to avoid masking the Ciutadella's fields of fire. These were principally oriented *toward* Barcelona, not against the foreign invader, as the fifty cannon bays and the esplanade, or glacis, between the fortress and the city made all too clear.

The Ciutadella would remain as a symbol and strategic stronghold of Barcelona's captive condition until, after many initiatives and attempts to demolish the unpopular fortrress, General Juan Prim ordered its demolition in October 1868.

From Carrer del Rec, turn right along Carrer Bonaire at the second corner down from the Plaça del Born. A short detour up Carrer Pescateria, the second left, will reveal an excellent spot for lunch. **El Raïm** at no. 6 is a semi-secret little restaurant specializing in truly authentic Catalan cuisine (they begged to be left out of this book).

Crossing Carrer Vidrieria, Plaça de les Olles is a quiet, sunny square with an iron fountain and a fishing equipment store on the corner. The building at no. 6 over the excellent Café de la Ribera has colorful mosaics decorating the second and top floors. The lower mosaic is difficult to see, but the upper one has been restored and sparkles brilliantly in the morning sun reflecting off the water of the nearby port.

The building at **no. 2** on the corner of Carrer de les Dames, built in 1910 by Enric Sagnier i Villavecchia, is a neo-Gothic marvel with a corner turret decorated with gargoyles and pinnacles and narrow floor-to-ceiling windows paned with old glass.

The next square, **El Pla del Palau**, is named for the royal palace that stood along its left or northern side until destroyed by fire in 1875. This palace was used by the House of Austria as a residence for the viceroy of Catalonia during the War of the Spanish Succession, and the Bourbons installed their military governor there after 1714. The fountain in the middle of the square was part of a project designed in 1825 by Francesc Daniel i Molina, the architect who built Plaça Reial. The marble fountain in the center is dedicated to the Geni Catalá, the *volkgeist* or national spirit of the Catalan people, with representations of the four rivers of Catalonia (Llobregat, Ter, Ebro, and Segre) and the four provinces (Barcelona, Girona, Lleida, and Tarragona).

The **Llotja**, at the far side of the square, was the medieval trading center and today houses the Barcelona stock exchange in its spectacular Saló Gòtic, or Gothic Hall. The Llotja was the most important civil structure in the cities of the Catalano-Aragonese confederation of the Middle Ages and can be found in Perpignan, Castelló d'Empuries, Tortosa, Valencia, Mallorca, and Zaragoza. Barcelona's original exchange was little more than a series of arcades erected between 1352 and 1357 by architect Pere Llobet to protect merchandise and traders from the elements. In 1380, however, King Pere el Cerimoniós ordered a great closed hall constructed, and it was completed in 1392. Although the main façade faces the Pla del Palau, the doors there are presently closed, and access to the building may be found along the sides.

The arcades visible across the main thoroughfare between the Pla del Palau and the port are Porxos d'En Xifré, the colonnaded passageways around the splendid Cases d'En Xifré. Josep Xifré, an early nineteenth-century Catalan businessman, was said to be one of the first to return from the new world with great wealth. As he set about building what was Barcelona's largest house in the 1830s, word began to circulate that he was out of money and was going to be unable to finish construction. When Xifré heard the gossip, he ordered a large granite stone removed and replaced it with a solid gold block as a demonstration of his solvency. The gold block overlooked the corner nearest the Pla del Palau and was replaced by a granite stone when the structure was finished. This stone is said to have been lighter in color, having been placed at a later date, and was distinguishable from the street until 1983 when restoration of the façade left all of the stones the same color. The corner space under the arcade houses the well-known Set Portes restaurant, open for business from one in the afternoon until one in the morning.

El Passadis del Pep, at the end of a carefully unmarked corridor at no. 2 Pla del Palau, is a good place to remember because it's probably the best restaurant near the end of this walk.

Up Carrer L'Espaseria from the Pla del Palau is a dramatic and dizzying view of Santa Maria del Mar's bell tower—much painted and photographed—framed by the walls on either side of the street. Carrer L'Espaseria is named for the twelfth-century sword makers who made Barcelona swords so famous throughout medieval Europe. Along with the secret of their special temper, they were thought to be charmed and able to inflict wounds straight from the scabbard by merely looking at them. Much of Catalonia's military and naval success in the medieval Mediterranean was attributed to the quality of Barcelona steel, while sword makers were regarded as demidemons and sorcerers.

Santa Maria del Mar, especially after a heavy dose of Catalonian Modernisme, is of almost breathtaking unity, purity, and simplicity of purpose. Known as the most harmonious example of Mediterranean Gothic architecture standing today, Santa Maria del Mar has been likened to the German *Hallenkirche*, or one-naved basilica, and is certainly one of the four or five stops I would advise a visitor to schedule during a three-hour layover,

Santa Maria del Mar

the others being Antoni Gaudí's Sagrada Família Cathedral, Paseo de Gràcia's Moderniste structures, and the Rambla.

Built in record time between 1329 and 1383, much of Santa Maria del Mar's classical harmony is a result of the speed and continuity of its construction in contrast to, say, the Barcelona cathedral, which was begun in 1299, interrupted in 1430, and finally completed between 1887 and 1913. Critics of Santa Maria del Mar's "coldness" have charged that it seems more the work of engineers than of architects. In fact, Berenguer de Montagut was neither; the designer of this profoundly moving edifice was a mere *magister operis*, or contractor, as well as a stonemason and sculptor. Berenguer's clean lines and clear draftmanship adhered closely to the geometrical laws in use in the Middle Ages, and with them he created a structure of almost mathematical balance and proportion. The completely unadorned octagonal columns are of an almost transparent slenderness accentuated by the sweep and mass of the fluted supports rising to the vaulted ceiling. The pillars open out at exactly 15.5 meters, just halfway to the keystones of the vaults 31 meters above the floor. This halfway point is reiterated in the cornice running around the side walls of the church. The result of all this balance and symmetry is a light, agile, airy sense of space in which, indeed, less is more.

At the sixth centennial of the completion of Santa Maria del Mar in December 1983, the trebles, countertenors, tenors, baritones, and basso profundos of Saint John's College Choir of Cambridge, England, performed a program of Christmas and liturgical music, much of which was written only shortly after the church was built and the choir itself was founded. Choirmaster George Guest was astonished and terrified by the six-second acoustic delay that took place as overtones echoed back from Santa Maria del Mar's almost completely unbroken space. He rehearsed his young choristers ferociously, holding closing chords until the eight- to twelve-part polyphony going out finally matched what was coming back. The concert, performed before a packed audience, was a moving event: The purity and simplicity of the boys' voices, especially the trebles, produced a particularly haunting effect in Santa Maria del Mar's pristine sandstone spaces, confirming Saint Augustine's credo that music and architecture are "twin arts."

Around Santa Maria del Mar are some of the most antique and beautiful alleys and byways in the city. On the way to lunch at Raïm or Set Portes or El Passadis del Pep, a walk around the fountain opposite Santa Maria del Mar's main door through Carrer de les Caputxes offers a look at some archaic and unreformed porches supported by octagonal Gothic columns. Little altered since the fifteenth century, this very short street seems glued together beam by stone, as much decay as endeavor. The balconies are particularly anarchical and quirky.

Just around the fountain to the left you can see someone's tiny terrace garden above the fountain itself, with laundry hanging and plants crowding over the edge. A

walk under the archway past the ancient pillar on the
right, under the wooden beams supporting a tiny room
above on the left, brings you to Carrer de L'Anisadeta—
named, according to one version, for a woman who sold
water laced with anise during the eighteenth century, and
according to another, after a former local tavern. A left
turn takes you back into Plaça de Santa Maria del Mar
and provides the best view available of the church's
façade.

Along the sea side of Santa Maria is the **Fossar de
les Moreres** (Cemetery of the Mulberry Trees) and the
monument at the burial site of the martyrs of the 1714
siege that ended the War of the Spanish Succession. The
Diada, or Catalonian National Day, September 11, is held
in observance of Catalonia's loss of sovereignty to the
professional armies of Felipe V and the Bourbons. It is
always celebrated in the Fossar de les Moreres by the
more radical and emotional groups of Catalan nationalists. The Frederic Soler "Pitarra" verse engraved along the
wall reads as follows:

En el Fossar de les Moreres	In the Fossar de les Moreres
no s'hi enterra cap traidor	No traitor lies
fins perdent nostres banderes	Even losing our banners
será l'urne d'honor.	It will be the urn of honor.

The wording of Pitarra's couplets refers to the me-
ticulous separation of Barcelona patriots and invading
soldiers that occurred as the dead—there were some thirty-
five hundred in all—were delivered to the Santa Maria del
Mar cemetery. As if these bitter enemies might continue
the battle in the next world, the gravekeeper carefully
separated the bodies, burying the invaders outside the
ring of mulberry trees and the fallen and defeated defenders of Barcelona inside. Pitarra's opening lines are

said to have been the words of the gravekeeper himself. Legend has it that this same aged gravekeeper, recognizing his own son who had fought with Felipe V among the dead, didn't hesitate to bury him where he belonged, outside the sacred sanctuary.

En el Fossar de les Moreres no s'hi enterra cap traidor . . .

Despite the gravekeeper's efforts, the Fossar de les Moreres has continued to be a battleground in one way or another ever since the events of 1714. The crumbling gap in the center of the eastern wall of the square and the lighter-colored stones where the passageway entered the church are all that remain of the notorious bridge built in 1700 by order of the viceroy of Carles II of Austria, the Prince of Darmstadt. This elevated corridor served as a private entryway for the viceroy or military governor assigned to maintain order in Barcelona, allowing him to come to mass at Santa Maria del Mar from his quarters in the Pla del Palau without risking assassination in the streets below (an indication of the popularity enjoyed by this public figure).

Massanet, the convent-burning revolutionary who survived his own execution in 1835, is said to have been one of the leaders of the group of rebels who used the passageway to reach General Bassa. The general was the unlucky emissary from Madrid who volunteered to re-establish order in tumultuous Barcelona with the promise "Either the people or me," news of which reached Barcelona ahead of him, driving revolutionary fervor even higher. Unaware of the bridge's existence, Bassa was seized in his office and thrown from the balcony to the multitude below; the mob lynched him with a rope from the nearest well. The general was then dragged through the streets to the Rambla where, after being displayed from the balcony of the Carmelite convent across from Plaça Reial, he was incinerated along with the library and documents of the Carmelites.

The marble plaque bearing Pitarra's verse was re- moved at the end of the Spanish Civil War in 1939 when all expressions of Catalonian national identity, including the language, literature, and folklore, were suppressed by Franco. The plaque was replaced, however, soon after the historic celebration of Catalonian nationalism, the *"Diada,"* of September 11, 1977, the first such celebration permitted in forty years. The passageway—like the Ciu- tadella, a hated symbol of centrist repression—was finally torn down in 1987, and the Fossar de les Moreres has become a symbol of fervent Catalonian patriotism.

Walk · 3

El Raval

WEST OF THE RAMBLA

Raval façade

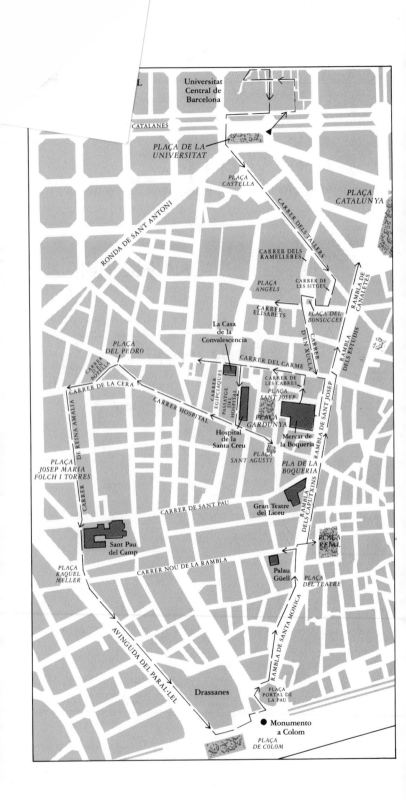

Starting point: Plaça de la Universitat (near Plaça Catalunya)
Metro: Universidad or Plaça Catalunya
Length: About four hours

The rough and bawdy Raval is one of Barcelona's least-known areas, off the tourist track, a cauldron filled with some of the city's most varied and colorful sites and sociology. Originally meaning "slum," the Raval is to the right descending the Rambla. First a no-man's-land outside Barcelona's second set of walls, the Raval became enclosed by the building of the third walls along what are now Carrer Pelai, the Ronda de Sant Antoni, Ronda de Sant Pau, and Avinguda del Paral.lel.

The Raval is traversed by all manner of human spectacle: a clown on his way home from work on the Rambla, his trunk of tricks rolling behind him on a dolly, paint, nose, and orange hair still in place, no longer comic; a family of Gypsies back from a Saturday morning's work begging for change in the Plaça Catalunya train station; a blind man feeling his way along the sidewalk; a pair of slightly-too-painted ladies getting a few daytime errands out of the way.

The construction of the third walls during the four-teenth century encouraged building in the Raval. During the nineteenth century industries sprang up and later the lower end became notorious for bars, brothels, and all the pungent excesses characteristic of a typical Mediter-ranean port city. Today, despite continuing efforts to gen-trify the Raval, the famous *Barrio Chino*, the corner of the Raval nearest the port, remains a good place to avoid at any time of day or night. So named for the preponder-ance of immigrants of all nationalities including Spanish (collectively dismissed as aliens or "chinos") who have lived in that part of the Raval, generally in misery, the Barrio Chino is no Chinatown. Even though the alcohol-ics, drug addicts, prostitutes, transvestites, and thieves here are nearly outnumbered by uniformed policemen, the area between Carrer Nou de la Rambla and the port is better seen from the relative safety of the Rambla Santa Mónica.

A look at the map will help. The Raval is almost evenly divided into three wedges by the Carrer Hospital and the Carrer Nou de la Rambla. From the top of the Raval at Carrer Pelai to Carrer Hospital, the streets are colorful but safe. Between Carrer Hospital and Carrer Nou de la Rambla life begins to feel risky, and from Carrer Nou de Rambla on down, it's no-man's land.

Almost all of this walk, which begins at the univer-sity, is confined to the area above Carrer Hospital, while the points of interest recommended below this zone— Sant Pau Church, the old shipyards and the Maritime Museum at Drassanes, Antoni Gaudí's Palau Güell, and the Liceu Opera House—are accessible from Ronda de Sant Pau, the Paral.lel, or the Rambla.

Barcelona's **Universitat Central**, just outside the upper edge of the Raval, is a good place to start. A few minutes' walk from Plaça Catalunya are the university buildings on the Gran Via de les Corts Catalanes at the intersection of Ronda de Sant Antoni and Ronda Universitat, between Carrer Aribau and Carrer Balmes.

The history of university studies in Barcelona reflects Catalonia's long struggle for, if not independence, at least an identity and perhaps a measure of national dignity. While Catalonia's first universities were founded in Lleida in 1300 and in Perpignan in 1350, it wasn't until 1401 that King Martí I founded Barcelona's Estudi d'Arts i Medicina, enlarged in 1450 to include theology, law, and philosophy. The building itself was begun on the Rambla dels Estudis in 1536. In 1714 Felipe V of the Bourbon dynasty took command of Barcelona "by military conquest," suppressed Catalonia's rights, privileges, and institutions, and in 1717 exiled the university to Cervera. Student demonstrations on the Rambla in favor of land reforms in 1647 had helped to provoke the uprising that led to the Guerra dels Segadors, a peasant revolt against landowners and the central government of Castile. Felipe V solved the problem of student subversion by placing it 100 kilometers west of Barcelona. The university didn't return to Barcelona until 1837, and the present building was erected between 1861 and 1889.

Entering by the door on the right, directly across from the Bar Estudiantil on the corner of Gran Via de les Corts Catalanes and Plaça Universitat, there are several lush interior courtyards to the right and straight ahead. The Paraninfo auditorium, with its historical paintings, and the stairway up to it are especially noteworthy, as is the library, which contains over 250,000 volumes collected from monastic archives and libraries all over Catalonia. The Pati de Lletres, to the left, is perhaps the best-known architectural gem in the university, with its two floors of arcades around an interior courtyard with orange and cypress trees. Through a side exit off this courtyard, a door opens out into the moist and leafy garden that leads around to the right behind the building, through an area of fountains and pools, and back into the space around the grand stairway and the main door back to the street.

The work of architect Elies Rogent, the university's Romanesque dignity is a welcome lull before entering the raucous Raval.

Crossing Carrer Aribau, Gran Via de les Corts Catalanes, and Ronda de Sant Antoni, you reach Carrer Tallers, which runs back across toward the top of the Rambla parallel to Carrer Pelai. *Tallers* means "cutters" in Catalan and was the name of the neighborhood known for butchers since the twelfth century. Originally the area behind the old fifteenth-century university, Tallers was once a zone of bordellos and beer halls, stuck in under the city walls running along what is now Carrer Pelai, until their removal in the nineteenth century opened the area to commerce, industry, and more presentable pursuits.

Entering Tallers from Ronda de Sant Antoni, Plaça Castella is the first opening, dominated by the baroque façade of the seventeenth-century **Església dels Mercenaris**, now the parish church of Sant Pere Nolasc. The order of Mercenaris, which was originally dedicated to saving the souls of slaves and captives, is now primarily occupied in fighting juvenile delinquency, which has become a growing problem in the Raval.

Continuing down Tallers past Carrer Gravina, the street is filled with stores, bars, cafés, bakeries, and a rush of pedestrian traffic. A right on Carrer de Les Sitges, a block short of the Rambla, leads down past the well-known **Ovella Negra**, a student beer hall built in a large cavelike space, all but intact from fifteenth-century university days, including brawling students and flying beer. **Bar Castells**, on the corner of Carrer de Les Sitges and Plaça del Bonsuccés, is a good place for a stop, another convenient, largely unimproved corner bar and café where in summer you can lean up against the marble bar from the sidewalk itself. Don't miss the enormous shelving against the mirror behind the bar, or the upstairs dining room, in case you're ready for lunch or want to come back for dinner.

Turning right through the Plaça del Bonsuccés and

into the interior patio and garden of what was formerly a seventeenth-century convent, a look left to the buildings at and around no. 9 Carrer dels Ramelleres offers a view of the kind of cozy eccentricity typical of old Barcelona. Just to the right of no. 17 Carrer dels Ramelleres, a ring of wood set in the wall just above waist level marks the ancient *torno*, or turntable, where, up until well into this century unwanted babies were spun into the safe and supportive arms of the nuns of the *Casa de la Misericordia*. Now cemented in, this wooden circle once contained a partitioned revolving shelf, a standard means of exchange with convents and nunneries but of special significance at this one. Answering the knock of a woman in distress, the nun on duty at the *torn* would answer, "Ave María," to which the new mother replied in kind as the turntable creaked her newborn out of one life and into another. The coin slot above to the left, fed by wealthy gentlemen, poor cleaning girls, and wayward matrons alike, was used for contributions to this community of foundlings.

At the corner of Carrer dels Ramelleres and Carrer Elisabets, turn right at the ancient DROGUERIA sign on the corner of Carrer d'En Xuclà. A short walk down Carrer Elisabets leads to the main entry of the ancient **Casa de la Misericordia**, the former chapel of which is now El Llar del Llibre, a bookstore, at no. 6. The gardens, filled with trees of bitter oranges used for marmalade, surround a home and school for girls from destitute families that was founded in 1581 by theologian and scholar Don Diego Pérez de Valdivia as a home for the poor. Originally known as La Casa dels Angels, the center began operations in 1583; faced with an overflow of homeless, from 1771 on it limited its work exclusively to girls from the city of Barcelona. The Casa de la Misericordia has specialized in the guidance and education of the daughters of the poor and almost-poor, transforming into "useful and productive women" many girls who "might otherwise have perished in poverty or stumbled into the pitfalls of immorality," as one historian put it.

After moving back up Carrer Elisabets, Carrer d'En Xuclà continues its narrow course past the **Herboristeria Guarro** herb store at no. 23, a delicious olfactory adventure that no one passing by should miss. A bouquet of rosemary (*romaní* in Catalan) or thyme (*farigola*), which doesn't cost much more than a coffee, will provide an instant Proustian rush of associations, all of them far removed from Barcelona's metropolitan clamor. The marble sculpture of the mid-nineteenth-century painter Marià Fortuny—with brushes clutched in his left hand—known for his brilliant portraits of North African life, dominates the corner of the street named for him.

The comfortable-looking restaurant and taurine club **Los de Gallito y Belmonte** at no. 5 Carrer d'En Xuclà offers excellent coffee and an even better selection of tapas. Continuing along the western façade of the Betlem Church, Carrer d'En Xuclà emerges on Carrer del Carme next to the dramatic sculptures on the corner of the church itself. Just across the Rambla is the Portaferrissa fountain, jumping-off point for Walk 1 through the Barri Gòtic. Out on the Rambla, the third building on the right on the Rambla de les Flors was the intown eighteenth-century palace of Viceroy Amat, named for his young widow, Maria Francesca Fiveller, after his death in 1782. This is the **Virreina** (viceroy's wife) known to most Barcelonans. The palace is the site of many of the city's best art exhibits as well as the home of the famous Cambó Collection of paintings, including works by Rubens, Tintoretto, Van Dyck, Goya, and others.

The Virreina Maria Francesca, widowed at the age of nineteen, enjoyed great popularity for over half a century following her brief but spectacular marriage to the viceroy, the story of which is recounted in Walk 4.

The **Rambla de les Flors** is undoubtedly the most fragrant and the most romantic stretch in this area. The flower vendors of early Barcelona were known for their

Casa de la Misericordia

beauty, and a certain erotic aura remains: People take their time squeezing through; eyes meet eyes. The famous turn-of-the-century Catalan painter Ramón Casas is known to have discovered the woman who became his model and later his wife selling flowers here. The flower stands make the Rambla seem narrower, pushing the human traffic closer together. Small groups often stop to talk, perhaps following the tradition of the *tertulias*, or intellectual conversations, that used to take place around the flower stalls during the last century.

The **Boqueria** market, officially known as the **Mercat de Sant Josep**, is the next opening on the right, and this is the real reason we have emerged from the Raval for a moment. Each of the Boqueria's entrances has its own personality: The side entrance through Carrer de les Cabres into the greengrocers' bright and open square possesses a natural rustic charm; the Passatge dels Coloms tunnels into the heart of the market in quiet penumbra; the back entrance—who can resist a back door to anything?—outflanks all the Rambla formality, offering a surprise approach to some unsuspecting squid, partridge, wild mushroom, or melon. But the main door to the Boqueria market, the wide entryway opening out onto the Rambla, is undeniably the most spectacular—colorful, massive, and light—a good place to start.

Originally occupied by a Carmelite convent built in 1593, the space now covered with a gigantic steel structure is really an arcaded plaza built by architect Francesc Daniel i Molina between 1836 and 1840. Molina's classical square, said to have been inspired by John Nash and his 1818 Regent Street Quadrant, is almost completely obscured by the iron frame covering some two hundred stands selling produce of every conceivable kind.

The name *Boqueria* probably derives from the early *boc*, or goat butcheries, favored by Barcelona's medieval Jewish community, which was originally located near the

Boqueria market

market in the *Call*, or Jewish Quarter. The largest and best-known of Barcelona's three dozen open markets, the Boqueria is a mighty display of provender, colorful and busy, fresh and aromatic. Although not known as a late-night spot, as Les Halles in Paris was up until the late 1970s, the Gardunya Restaurant at the back of the market serves dinner (including an excellent onion soup) until two or three o'clock after opera performances in the neighboring Liceu Theatre.

The life and personality of the Boqueria are endless, one of the city's most exciting and invigorating explosions of vitality. Aside from the animal, vegetable, and mineral attractions, there are over half a dozen *chiringuitos*, little bars and restaurants, serving irresistible specialties ranging from wild mushrooms to fried octopus and baby eels.

The wild mushroom and herb display offered by the popular Petrás at the Boqueria's back entry—PETRAS FRUITS DEL BOSC (forest), illustrated with a snail, next to the Gardunya Restaurant—is an essential visit. The genial Petrás holds court daily, producing the fall's first *camagrocs* or the spring's first *múrgulas*, both species of wild mushrooms essential to a wide range of Catalan dishes. Petrás is a powerful force throughout Catalan cuisine, a sort of high priest of dining, depended on by chefs and doted on by food lovers all over town. Colman Andrews, American author of *the* book on Catalan cuisine and all but a national hero in Barcelona, is a Petrás regular when he visits the city. He can usually be found there at the hub of a gang of eager gastronomes exchanging recipes and names of secret restaurants.

The ladies of the Boqueria stationed behind their counters of produce are master salespersons: intimate, direct, and persistent. It is almost impossible, once in their clutches, not to buy anything and everything they propose. Their eyes rove and grip; their dialectical skills are overwhelming. For contrast, try the truck farmers selling greens out in the Plaça de les Pagesos, tucked in between the Boqueria and the back of the Virreina at the end of the brief Carrer de les Cabres. Sunburned and

taciturn (as opposed to the painted and loquacious ve-
dettes inside), these field-workers bring daily produce to
the market from the farms and plantations around Barcelona: long-stemmed onions *(calçots)* in season, cauliflower, fruit, potatoes.

The Boqueria market is best exited through Carrer de
les Cabres. The greengrocers' market is usually sunny,
and one of the tiny cafés bordering it might be the perfect
place to take a little morning sun to warm up after the Boqueria, which can be cool in summer—chilled by the
shade and the ice under the fish—and cold in winter. The
street leading out into Carrer del Carme will place you
just down from the mouth of Carrer d'En Xuclà and the
Betlem Church.

The **Barri del Hospital**, the area around the city's
early hospital, is shaped like a triangle, with its base on
the Rambla and its point at the Plaça del Pedró. Originally
plantations between Roman Barcelona's Mons Taber and
the high ground at Montjuïc, the area was gradually populated with institutions that had a chance of surviving
safely outside the walls—convents, hospitals, and
churches—between the tenth and the fourteenth centuries. After the construction of the third walls brought
about more buildings, the Portal de Sant Antoni became
the main entryway through the walls for travel to and
from the rest of Spain. Multitudinous receptions were organized for entourages entering through the Portal de Sant
Antoni, either along Carrer Hospital to the Pla de la Boqueria and into Plaça Sant Jaume and the center of the
old city for government authorities, or through Carrer del
Carme and Portaferrissa to Plaça Nova and the cathedral
for bishops and church officials.

Moving down Carrer del Carme, the heavy wooden
portal at no. 9 is a good example of the kind of safe and
secure barrier it might be cozy to live behind surrounded
by downtown Barcelona's chaos.

At no. 23 is the Mas Grau pharmacy, decorated in
wood and glass, with a floral copper framework and coat

of arms featuring bare-breasted goddesses over the door. The balconies above, supported by arrows complete with feathered butts, are another manifestation of Barcelona's playful early twentieth-century architecture. The storefront of El Indio at no. 24 is a surprising structure with its elaborate engravings and columns. Dating from 1870, this textile store was redecorated in 1922 by designer Vilaró y Valls and is cataloged among the city's protected

Farmer's market, next to Boquería

Moderniste (in this case somewhat post-Moderniste) façades. The wooden tables inside, originally built and still used as counters for measuring bolts of fabric, are magnificent slabs of oak and mahogany. One table of lovely dark mahogany is valued in the tens of thousands of dollars. No. 31, over the Passatge 1800, is a tunnellike arcade lined with boutiques leading back into the Plaça de la Gardunya behind the Boqueria. The passage-

way was built during the eighteenth century and has engravings with mythological and pastoral themes dominated by landscapes and wildlife. No. 34 is a Moderniste façade, ornate and complex. An archaic PELUQUERIA DE SENORAS sign advertising a nineteenth-century hairdressing salon overlooks the street at no. 37. Passing the entrance to the hospital on the left, the intersection of Carrer del Carme with Carrer dels Angels on the right opens into a square occupied by a school building designed in 1916 by the architect Josep Goday.

At the corner of Carrer del Carme and Carrer Egipcíaques—named for a convent dedicated to Santa Maria Egipciaca that once stood opposite the hospital—a sculpture of Saint Paul (Sant Pau), patron saint of the Casa de la Convalescencia, leans pensively and wearily over the street from a large baroque corner alcove. The matching (and empty) alcove at the corner of the building across the street is an exact copy—down to the last rococo detail—of the one housing Sant Pau, and occupies the corner of the twentieth-century Center for Scientific Research, which is connected to the hospital by a footbridge.

Some fifty yards farther down Carrer del Carme at no. 63 is the **Bar Muy Buenas**, a recommended detour for a look at a unique Moderniste saloon and restaurant with some exquisitely cold draft beer on tap at its unfortunate new zinc bar. The original bar stands inside to the left, a lush marble and wood affair more than one hundred years old, but the true pièce de résistance is the photograph to the right just inside the front door showing the Bar Muy Buenas, circa 1931–36, with a handwritten menu and the special offer of a weekly meal ticket with no fewer than fourteen three-course meals with bread, wine, and dessert included for the overall total of twenty-three pesetas (1.6 cents per meal). This offer is embellished with notes promising excellent and à la carte service, and underscored with an emphatic "Tips will not be accepted!"

Moving back past the corner of Carrer Egipcíaques

and Carrer del Carme, the entrance to the hospital is the first opening on the right. The buildings of the **Hospital de la Santa Creu** (Hospital of the Holy Cross) were begun in 1401, although the hospital itself dates as far back as the end of the tenth century and is one of the oldest in the world. Gradually the Hospital de la Santa Creu absorbed the functions of the other medical centers of the city until it became the Hospital de Colom under the leadership of the canon Guillem Colom. At the end of the fourteenth century Barcelona's different hospitals united under the Hospital de la Santa Creu. The Casa de la Convalescencia was built in the seventeenth century; the Academia de Medicina was added in the eighteenth under the leadership of the famous surgeon Pere Virgili, whose bust presides over the Royal Academy of Surgery and Medicine. The latter part of the nineteenth and the first quarter of the present century marked a period of decline for the hospital, which was unable to meet the needs of a city that had grown too big. In the late 1920s the Hospital de la Santa Creu became part of the new Hospital de San Pablo, located at the far edge of the Eixample. World-famous Moderniste architect Antoni Gaudí, creator of the Sagrada Família Cathedral, one of the last patients, died at the Hospital de la Santa Creu in the Raval after being struck by a trolley on his way to mass at San Felip Neri Church on June 7, 1926, shortly before the hospital was closed.

Since 1929, when the College of Surgery was carefully restored in order to house the Academy of Medicine, Hospital de la Santa Creu has become an important venue in the city's cultural and academic life. Casa de la Convalescencia has been converted into the Institut d'Estudis Catalans, and the huge Gothic nave houses Barcelona's largest library, La Biblioteca de Catalunya. The Escola Massana School of Fine Arts occupies the *pati nou* at the far end of the courtyard on Carrer Hospital, and the chapel and the first floor have ben the site of important art exhibits. Other organizations, including the children's

and young persons' libraries, also have their centers in
the Hospital de la Santa Creu: the school of Bible studies,
the Academy of Pharmacy, and the center for the Amics
de Sardenya (Friends of Sardinia), which studies and
maintains Catalonia's ancient ties with this Catalan-
speaking Mediterranean island, now part of Italy.

Entering from Carrer del Carme, the Royal Academy
of Surgery and Medicine, an eighteenth-century stone
building, is on the left side of the narrow patio leading
straight ahead to the simple fifteenth-century Gothic
façade of the hospital.

The **Casa de la Convalescencia**, to the right, is an
irresistible conglomeration of patios, terraces, towers, and
stairways; each architectural facet is more surprising and
inviting than the last. The façade is unadorned dark marble, while the vestibule is a cross-vaulted square space
flanked by the spectacular polychromatic tile scenery created by Llorenç Passolas in 1680–81. The ceramic representations are chapters from the life of Saint Paul, the
saint of the building's benefactor, Pau Ferran. The first
scene to the left of the door opening into the patio portrays the saint's conversion, a treatment obviously based
on *The Conversion of Saint Paul* by Rubens, who was, in
turn, inspired by Leonardo da Vinci. The second scene
is of Saint Paul preaching to the Jews. The third shows
his flight from Damascus, with Saint Paul suspended over
the walls in a basket. The fourth scene portrays Saint Paul
and Barnabas curing the sick and doing good works in
Lystra. The fifth shows the saint embarking on a sea voyage, perhaps to Ephesus where he wrote his letters to the
Corinthians. The sixth scene, to the left of the door, shows
Saint Paul brought before the magistrates for having
treated the evil spirit of a soothsayer or seer, while in the
background we see Paul imprisoned with his disciple Si-
las. In the seventh scene, Saint Paul writes his epistles
under an olive tree. In the eighth, Peter and Paul meet in
Rome. The ninth scene represents Saint Paul's martyrdom. The tenth, just right of the door into the courtyard,
is the glorified image of the saint in heaven.

The patio of the Casa de la Convalescencia was built between 1655 and 1678 and served as a model for numerous Barcelona courtyards, with twice as many arches on the upper floor as on the lower level. The patio makes an immediate impression for its symmetry and proportions; at once balanced and light, ornate and tranquil. The elevated garden on the second floor, a favorite feature of early Mediterranean architecture, dedicated to Catalan novelist Mercè Rodoreda, is visible through the two sets of arches. The ceramic tiles encircling the walls of the patio are also the work of Llorenç Passolas. An image of Saint Paul sculpted between 1662 and 1677 occupies the center of the patio.

The stairway to the left of the vestibule entrance leads to the second floor and the chapel, the **Institut d'Estudis Catalans**, and **La Biblioteca de Catalunya**. The elevated garden at the rear of the building is a green and peaceful platform, and the diminutive stairway up to the third floor, an exercise in balance and economy, seems a wonderful place to set up a studio, lock yourself in, and throw away the key.

The third-floor offices include that of the famous Don Ramón Aramón, "secretary-general for life" of the Institut d'Estudis Catalans. Sr. Aramón was a moving force in the clandestine meetings of this organization after the fall of the Republic at the end of the Spanish Civil War. Recently asked whether it was true that meetings were held at his home during the Franco regime, Sr. Aramón chuckled and shrugged his shoulders: "Hombre, we met in a lot of places."

The fifteenth-century Gothic halls of La Biblioteca de Catalunya, open and powerful, are an interesting and striking contrast to the more ornate, baroque, seventeenth-century patio. The wide stone arches support polychrome wooden beams, while the simple, south-facing windows (like the arches, pointed) admit abundant light for a structure of this epoch. It would appear that architect Guillem Abiell, who also built the gloomy Església del Pi (Walk 1), had a clear idea of the practical problems a hospital faced when he took over the direction of the work in 1417.

The Institut d'Estudis Catalans, the Catalonian counterpart to the Real Academia de la Lengua Española in the world of Spanish culture, has suffered through many years of neglect and suppression since its founding in 1907. Presently composed of five sections—history and archeology, science and technology, philosophy and social sciences, biological sciences, and philology—the Institut was given the Casa de la Convalescencia in 1930 by the Generalitat de Catalunya. La Biblioteca de Catalunya, created at that time, was virtually kidnapped by the centrist Madrid government (placed under the control of the provincial authority or Diputación) after the Spanish Civil War ended in 1939. The Institut virtually ceased to exist until it began to hold meetings at, among other places, the home of Sr. Aramón and later in the Omnium Cultural at the Palau Dalmases (Walk 2) in Carrer Montcada. Finally, in 1977, after the death of Franco and the change of regime, the Institut was returned to its rightful home in the Casa de la Convalescencia. Today the Institut is enjoying what amounts to a golden age of Catalan culture and has become an important part of city life. The library will soon be completely renovated, computerized, and acclimatized for the safekeeping of books and documents.

Leaving the vestibule of the Casa de la Convalescencia and turning right, a lovely Gothic stone door, reinforced with massive wedges of granite over the lintel, opens into the Gothic cloister and the patio beyond: a tiny armored opening into a light, open space. The cloister at the head of the garden looks out through ogival (pointed) arches, while the stairways on either side—originally one for men and one for women—led to the two main hospital bays. The large stone cross separates the new part of the patio from the fifteenth-century Hospital de la Santa Creu. The building on the left at the end of the garden, however, was part of the fourteenth and fifteenth centuries' Hospital de Colom and later was the hospital archives, while the seventeenth-century structure on the right is the Massana School of Fine Arts, one of Barcelona's most respected centers for training in sculpture and painting. The balcony to the left of the Escola Massana entrance is a graceful medieval detail that looks as if it would fit perfectly into a production of *Romeo and Juliet.*

The hospital's Renaissance façade on Carrer Hospital is a rich cluster of sixteenth-century Catalan art and architecture, including gargoyles; fourteenth-century windows from the old Hospital de Colom, which predated the Hospital de la Santa Creu; and especially the door with its Italianate columns and the shell-shaped coat of arms flanked by Gothic candelabras.

The early hospital chapel just to the right of the doorway into Carrer Hospital, under the eighteenth-century *Caritat* or *Caritas* theme (a woman comforting two children) sculpted by Pere Costa, is a lovely stone space now used as the Sala d'Exposicions de la Capilla del Antic Hospital, an art exhibit funded by the city. The outside wall is older than the hospital façade to the left and is topped with ivy falling from overhanging wooden eaves. Inside this refreshing sound chamber, a wooden choir loft hangs over the entryway, and the largely bare stone expanse holds a stillness and a sense of mystery, something deep and dreamless and straight from the twelfth century.

On Carrer Hospital between the Hospital and the Rambla, shops and human traffic are thick. On May 11 this section of Carrer Hospital is the traditional site of the Fira de Sant Ponç, the festival of the patron saint of herbalists and beekeepers. Originally the day when farmers sold surplus winter produce in order to make space for new goods, Sant Ponç has become a forum for the promotion of natural medicinal herbs, ecology, and the environment, and a celebration of nature itself. Markets specializing in natural products materialize at dawn in certain streets and squares around Barcelona as artesans and country

Hospital de la Santa Creu

people from all over Catalonia bring natural goods of every kind to the city. Honey, jams, jellies, cakes, dried wild mushrooms, herbs, wooden spoons and forks, crepes, and *cava*, along with a delicious assortment of other products, fill Barcelona with a special fragrance matching spring's final collapse into summer on this always leafy, aromatic day, one of Barcelona's best. The time between Sant Ponç and Sant Joan's midsummer eve, marking the solstice on June 24, is about as sweet and promising as any six-week season on Barcelona's calendar.

Teatre Romea, now the Centre Dramatic de la Generalitat, at the corner of Carrer Junta de Comerç, is a key

138

landmark in the development of Catalan theater and a good place to check for a production to see. Many of Barcelona's avant-garde companies, such as Els Joglars, El Fura dels Baus, Els Comediants, and others, perform there regularly. Language is not necessarily an impediment to appreciating modern theater in Barcelona as many of these productions rely heavily on experimental, nonliterary, mime, and dance-oriented dramatic techniques. The Romea, named for Julián Romea, a famous nineteenth-century Spanish actor, was constructed in 1863 after succeeding the old Odeon as the heart of Barcelona's theater life. The Odeon, now Fonda de Sant Agustí, originally produced performances in the Sant Agustí convent until the convent and church were burned during the anticlerical rebellion of 1835.

Plaça de Sant Agustí and the area around it are cavernous, tree-shaded spaces, leafy and restful. The church itself, unfinished, was designed by architect Pere Bertrán in 1728. The façade, projected as a baroque design by stonemason and sculptor Pere Costa, was never completed because of funding problems. The San Agustí Church was the scene of several important moments during the last months of the Franco regime. One of these was the semiclandestine funeral of the executed Salvador Puig Antich (the Franco regime's last *garrote vil* victim, mentioned in Walk 1). Attended by many of Catalonia's leading intellectuals and nationalists, the casket was carried out on the pallbearers' shoulders under the watchful scrutiny of an ample detachment of *grises*, gray-uniformed riot police, who were sent to ensure that Puig Antich's last rites didn't turn into a celebration of Catalonian nationalism. The late Alexandre Cirici i Pellicer, in his *Barcelona Pam a Pam*, recounts the story of the important Catalonian Assembly that took place in the Sant Agustí Church during the Franco regime:

> On November 7, 1971, in the central nave of the Sant Agustí parish, the first plenary session of the *Assemblea de Catalunya* was held, destined to create a common platform against "franquismo" around the main points of "Liberty, Amnesty, and the Autonomy Statute." The meeting was not discovered by the police, but as a result of it, Josep Andreu i Abello, Josep Solé Barberà, María Vila Abadal, and this writer were all jailed.

"Illegal association" during the Franco dictatorship covered any unauthorized meeting of three persons or more; noisy parties were occasionally broken up as "illegal associations." Although the authorities did not find out about the meeting in time to break it up, Cirici and others were rounded up and incarcerated after the fact. This first plenary session was followed by an ever stronger popular movement in favor of the reestablishment of Catalonia's original rights and institutions, and the Statute of Autonomy—"Volem l'Estatut!" ("We want the Statute") was a rallying cry of the mid-seventies—was approved in 1975.

From this point we will walk back down Carrer Hospital through the Plaça del Pedró to the Sant Pau del Camp Church, Barcelona's medieval shipyard Drassanes, past the Columbus monument, and back up the Rambla, stopping at Gaudí's Güell Palace, Plaça Reial, and the Liceu Opera House on the way back to Plaça Catalunya. This might be the place to divide this ambitious hike in two if one is inclined to do so. Carrer Jerusalem, directly in front of the church, leads past the boisterous Egipte Restaurant at no. 12 Jerusalem, past the confusingly named but separate and quieter Egipto across the street at no. 3 Jerusalem, past Petrás's *fruits del bosc* stand, and into the back of the Boqueria market, where the Gardunya Restaurant is another good choice for lunch.

Carrer Hospital, the early road from Barcelona south and west across the Llobregat River into the rest of Spain, offers a rich catalogue of commerce and city life: a varied assortment of people in all conditions and from all continents, few of them tourists, many of them of advanced age, in sizes and configurations seemingly shaped by the tiny nooks and crannies of the Raval itself. On the corner of Carrer de la Junta de Comerç, just across from the front of the chapel, is a sidewalk bar that serves excellent espresso and provides a convenient perch for watching some Carrer Hospital street life. At no. 67 the effigy of a chef announces a store specializing in kitchen apparel. There are seven bakeries, pastry shops, or croissanteries between Carrer Hospital and Plaça del Pedró; the first two are on the left side of this block. No. 83 is trimmed with decorative floral relief; no. 99 has another chef hung outside over an ancient wooden storefront and sells work clothes, jumpsuits, and smocks.

Carrer Hospital is choked with tailors, haberdasheries, dry-goods stores, furniture bazaars, and snack bars. The Passatge Bernardí Martorell opens out under the floral-relief–decorated façade of no. 99 into an alley of tiny bars, barbershops, cobblers, and sundry shops and businesses. Back across Carrer Hospital, there are engravings over the deadly-looking Bar Kabaka (subtitled El Rincón del Pollo, or Chicken Corner), while over the Granell Pharmacy heads of cavaliers are engraved over the second- and third-floor balconies.

The Moderniste **Sastre y Marqués Pharmacy** on the corner of Carrer de la Cadena at Carrer Hospital no. 109 is said to have been redecorated by architect Josep Puig i Cadafalch, designer of Casa Martí on Carrer Montsió and of many important structures in the Eixample. On the floor of the pharmacy is an intricate wrought-iron lamppost felled in 1988 by a truck, but by the time you read this, it might be back in place over the corner. The wooden door's looping curves, the rich floral sculpture, and the trim around the edges of the upper floor are all Moderniste devices you will see frequently in Gràcia and the Eixample.

Other points of interest between the pharmacy and the Plaça del Pedró include the narrow six-story apartment building at no. 113; the signs painted on the second floor at no. 115 (above the F 1800 R over the door) that advertise special carriage covers, among other things; the scrolled Moderniste crest atop the building on the corner of Carrer de Sant Jeroni; the hams hanging in the doorway to no. 139; and the corner bar where Carrer de la Cera and Carrer Hospital come to a needle-sharp point, a fine observation site especially if the corner stool is empty. Looking up, you may notice that Carrer Hospital has its own live gargoyles, faces looking down over the turmoil in the street in expressionless amazement, as if seeing it all for the first or, more likely, the last time.

Plaça del Pedró is named for a stone pillar erected at the point where the road forked, leading to Portaferrissa or the Porta de la Boqueria entering Barcelona or to the Llobregat River via Carrer de Sant Antoni Abat, or Montjuïc via Carrer d'en Botella, on the way out. Even today there is a sense of *partage*, of significance and choice, about this point of space where Carrer del Carme and Carrer Hospital meet to form something like the fore-deck of a sailboat, the prow of a ship. Church and state separated here on the way into town; Santa Eulàlia was martyred here, and her presence is somehow still palpa-ble in the air. Sant Llàtzer Church battles to survive amid the "profane" edifices that have all but swallowed it. All of this contributes to a sense of crossroads as much meta-physical as geographical, both spiritual and secular, sa-cred and ribald.

This is the spot where legend tells us Santa Eulàlia, the stubborn victim of Roman Consul Decius, was cru-cified on an X-shaped cross, her naked body chastely covered by a fresh fall of virgin snow. A wooden mon-ument was first erected over the fountain during the late seventeenth century, only to be alternately destroyed and restored by history's oscillating tug of war between anti-clerical revolutionaries and faithful Eulàlia devotees. In 1820 neighborhood residents defended their statue from the rampaging mob, affection for Eulàlia and local loyal-ties overriding their disaffection with the Catholic church, but the 1835 uprising brought Eulàlia down. Subse-quently rebuilt, the monument was again destroyed by radical leftists at the outbreak of the Spanish Civil War in 1936. The present marble likeness of Eulàlia and her cross, sculpted by Frederic Marés, was erected in 1951.

The bell tower and empty alcove at the base of the triangular *plaça* are part of the twelfth-century Sant Llàtzer Church, now almost completely surrounded by neigh-boring buildings. Sant Llàtzer is in the process of being restored and separated from the walls that have been pushed up against its façades over the centuries. Used as a medieval hospital when originally constructed in open country between 1144 and 1171 for the treatment of leprosy, the chapel was initially dedicated to the Verge dels Malalts (Our Lady of the Infirm) and in the fifteenth century was named for Sant Llàtzer, the newly appointed patron saint of lepers.

Plaça del Pedró and the streets around it have a certain brisk and bawdy momentum, improvised, vital, at once temporary and definitive.

From the Santa Eulàlia monument, a look down Carrer de Sant Antoni Abat will reveal the 1913 Església del Carme on the right and Església de Sant Antoni Abat, with its three-arched Gothic porch. Across the Ronda de Sant Antoni, the large structure visible from Plaça del Pedró is the famous Mercat de Sant Antoni, built by Antoni Rovira i Trias, whose figure in bronze occupies a bench in the square named for him in Gràcia. Considered Barcelona's masterpiece of steel architecture, the Mercat de Sant Antoni is especially interesting on Sundays for collectors of books, antiques, and used clothing.

The other way out of Plaça del Pedró is the Carrer d'en Botella, leading into Carrer de la Cera and out to the Ronda de Sant Pau. Carrer d'en Botella slices down along the old Roman road to Montjuïc into a lively opening with an excellent and inexpensive restaurant, **Vila de Meira**, which specializes in food from Galicia, a seagoing region on the Atlantic Ocean in Spain's northwestern corner. This simple spot is a lunch place for workers and artists, and you can sometimes spot the well-known Catalan-American sculptor Tom Carr replenishing his abundant energy with a *braon* or a *pulpo*, two of the typical Galician dishes served in this busy and friendly place.

Along the way down Carrer d'en Botella, don't miss the house at **no. 16**, built during the 1700s when it was surrounded by fields and gardens. The engravings decorating the building depict scenes of country life: a little boy with scissors cutting flowers; a shepherd with a lamb on his back; a river personified; Neptune and the sea with Hermes.

The intersection of Carrer d'en Botella and Carrer de

la Cera ("wax," named for a former candle factory) is at the edge of one of Barcelona's two communities of bourgeois, well-dressed, Catalan-speaking, prosperous Gypsies. (The other is in Gràcia around the Plaça Raspall.) The Verbena de Sant Joan, the all-night festival of fire preceding the saint's day on June 24 when Barcelona's neighborhoods erupt in bonfires, is said to be celebrated with exceptional frenzy by the Gypsies at this little intersection. Young swains leap wildly over the flames, while the *paya* (non-Gypsy) bonfire burns politely up the street at Plaça del Pedró.

The tiny café at the point of the triangle formed by Carrer d'en Botella and Carrer de la Cera is another unique event, occupied by the celebrated "Quiosco Antonio," a wedge-shaped sandwich and beer spot owned and operated by—who else?—Antonio. He is a popular poet whose verse, generally dedicated to oddly spelled rhymes extolling the quality and especially the size of his sandwiches, covers the walls of his minuscule establishment. Antonio's is an excellent place for a sidewalk coffee or a *carajillo* (coffee cut with rum or brandy) or, better still, a *fino*: chilled dry sherry.

Between the fork with Carrer d'en Botella and the Ronda de Sant Pau, Carrer de la Cera is lined with lively bars and restaurants, notably the popular **Can Lluís**, a busy bistro at no. 49.

Carrer de Reina Amalia, the last street on the left before emerging into the Ronda, was named for the third wife of King Fernando VII. It is presently lined with undistinguished nineteenth-century buildings, but the street is known as the site of the prison that stood there until it was moved to the Travessera de les Corts and later to Carrer Entença where the so-called Carcel Modelo, or Model Prison, now stands. Carrer de Reina Amalia remained the women's prison until it too was moved; the building was torn down and the space converted into the Plaça de Folch i Torres. The area closest to the Ronda was formerly the infamous Pati dels Corders (ropemakers) where the *gar-*

rote vil brought the condemned to justice and large crowds came to boo and hiss the criminals as they were led out, only to sniffle in compassion after they had been dealt with. Children were brought here to witness the wages of mis-behavior, and it was here that the anarchist Santiago Salvador, author of the 1893 bombing of Barcelona's Liceu Theatre that killed twenty-two and wounded fifty, was garroted to death before a big crowd, the convicted murderer crying "Viva el anarquismo" and gamely singing a hymn until the steel collar snuffed it out.

Another block down is the oldest church in Barcelona, **Sant Pau del Camp**, survivor of Moorish invaders, anticlerical vandals, and hundreds of years of progressive urban planners. Although the earliest material evidence of the church is from the year 912—the date is engraved on the tombstone of Guifré II—historian Jeroni Pujades published evidence in 1829 showing that a Roman cemetery may have occupied the spot as early as the second century. In 1931 historian Agustí Duran i Sanpere took part in excavations that uncovered, among other things, part of a Visigothic bronze buckle, suggesting that the cemetery may have been used between the second and the seventh centuries. In addition, remains of an unidentified structure from the sixth or seventh century were also found, helping to explain the classical marble capitals atop the columns that form part of the church door. The death of Count Guifré-Borrell, known as Guifré II, in 911 suggests that the church must have been there for some time before that date, although it is also possible that he founded the monastery himself sometime during the last quarter-century of his life. It is accepted fact that al-Manṣūr, the Moor whose invading forces sacked the *Puelles* convent (in Walk 2), destroyed the monastery in 985 and that the Moors destroyed it again in 1114–15 after it had been restored. The gravestone inscriptions of viscounts Geribert and Rotlandis indicate that they founded the monastery again in 1117 and that most of the present church structure was built during the twelfth century.

Sant Pau del Camp

Sant Pau del Camp's three apses reflect the shape of a cross, with an octagonal tower rising over the junction of the nave and the apses. This tower is topped by a flat-sided bell tower that was added during the eighteenth century. The door, a continuing mystery, has two Visigothic marble columns under wedges supporting a rugged archway. Historians Agustí Duran i Sanpere and Alexandre Cirici i Pellicer agree that these capitals seem of another era, as do the five symbols of the Evangelists and the hand of God. In Cirici's words, they are "vestiges of an archaic epoch in which images were avoided." Saint Mark and Saint Luke are represented by the lion and the bull sculpted just above the capitals, while Saint Matthew is the winged man and Saint John is the eagle on either side of the hand of God.

The cloister, the main attraction of the church's interior, can be reached through the door on the right leading to the Sala Capitular, from which another right leads into the tiny and ancient arcaded garden, another of Barcelona's most exquisite hidden gems. The peace and calm of Sant Pau, called *del Camp* for its original location in the distant fields outside Barcelona's early walls, seems to have been preserved and concentrated in this retreat, with the fountain's quiet trickle echoing a millennium of human meditation in the heart of the Raval.

From Sant Pau del Camp, Avinguda del Paral.lel roars toward the port, running along the walls of **Les Drassanes**, the medieval shipyards that launched Catalonia's fleet throughout the Mediterranean during the Middle Ages. This long stretch of wall was built during the fourteenth and fifteenth centuries; its two entryways are located at Porta de Cagalell near Sant Pau del Camp and at the Porta de Santa Madrona. The shipyards, begun in 1378 at the height of Catalonia's maritime dominance in the Mediterranean, soon included eight parallel construction areas capable of building thirty ships at once. Three larger bays were constructed between 1612 and 1618, and eight more bays were added during the same century. The Spanish army moved into the shipyards, converted it to a barracks in 1663, and remained until well into the twentieth century, when this historic structure was completely restored to its original condition. Drassanes is now partly occupied by Barcelona's **Maritime Museum**, one of the world's finest collections of naval memorabilia. The interior is dominated by a series of gigantic semicircular arches supporting a wood-beamed ceiling.

The Maritime Museum has a variety of major attractions. The full-scale model of naval hero Joan d'Austria's flagship fills an entire bay, while the models for *Ictineo*, history's first submarine, designed by Narcís Monturiol and launched in the port of Barcelona in 1859, are carefully preserved along with its original plans and designs. The sailors' trunks or seagoing chests, decorated with paintings alluding to the dangers posed by women, provide a glimpse into the minds and worries of medieval seafarers. These allegories include representations of the falsely accused and imprisoned Joseph (Genesis: 39), betrayed by the wife of his master Potiphar, and (repeated in various paintings) the even more convincing example of Judith and the head of Holofernes, seduced and slain to save her city of Bethulia (Judith: 2–13).

The famous Spanish naval battle of Lepanto (in which Cervantes lost his left arm) is another important theme, including drawings and charts. Perhaps of maximum interest is the display featuring charts, maps, sextants, and paraphernalia from the voyage that discovered America. Now often used as the setting for convention banquets and professional gatherings, the Drassanes shipyard is an unforgettable place for cocktails and dinner surrounded by the cradle of Catalonia's medieval Mediterranean naval power.

Across from Drassanes, the sumptuous **Duana**, or customs building, stands at the spot where the old canal used to float vessels from the shipyards into the port. Crowned with gigantic winged sphinxes, the building was designed in 1895 by the least Moderniste of the Moderniste architects, Enric Sagnier i Villavecchia, in a style described by art historians as "colossalist," which surely would and have been dubbed either white elephant or wedding cake had it been built during this century.

At the center of the circular *plaça* where the Rambla meets the Mediterranean is one of Barcelona's most cherished and controversial symbols: the **Christopher Columbus monument**. Nearly everything about Columbus—birthplace, name, nationality, language, character, leadership, sanity, and burial site—has been and continues to be hotly debated.

Thought to have been born Cristoforo Colombo in 1451 in Liguria near Genoa, Italy, the great discoverer is known in Spanish as Cristóbal Colón. Colombo, which means "dove" in Italian, may have been translated to *colom*, Catalan for dove or pigeon, with some confusion (not uncommon) on the final consonant. New theories on the birth and nationality of Columbus come forth almost daily. The latest of these—the favorite of the Catalonian "Columbists" (who really must *have* him for 1992)—claims that the mystery surrounding Columbus begins with his birth as Joan Colom in the northern Catalonian city of Girona, son of a priest and a servant girl. While it is not inconceivable that historians could confuse Girona (Gerona in Spanish) with Genoa (Genova in Italian), especially with the help of Columbus himself, the weight of evidence supports his Italian origin, despite the fact that his surviving writings are in Castilian, Catalan, and Portuguese, not Italian.

Columbus was shipwrecked off Portugal in his early twenties, an event that was probably decisive in the course his life would take. Columbus married into an important Lisbon family and gained respect as a chart maker, sea captain, and navigator. During his years living on the island of Madeira with his young wife, Columbus caught the local enthusiasm about island discovery in the Atlantic and became familiar with the vagaries of the northeast trade wind. His "Enterprise of the Indies" proposal, declined by Portugal, was finally accepted by the Spanish sovereigns, who were in an expansive mood after the reconquest of Granada had established peninsular superiority for the first time. Columbus was offered substantial titles and commissions in the event of success.

The expedition set forth from Palos in southern Spain on Friday, August 3, 1492. Three ships sailed: two sixty-foot caravels, the *Nina* and the *Pinta*, and the eighty- to eighty-five-foot *Santa María*, the flagship. Lightly armed and loaded with trinkets and bright cloth for trading, the fleet and its ninety sailors made a final stop in the Canary Islands, another piece of luck. Had Columbus been sailing under the Portuguese colors, he certainly would have set sail from the Azores, into the teeth of the prevailing westerly winds that probably would have denied him success. As it was, Columbus caught the northeast trade winds and reached the Bahamas on October 12 after thirty-three days at sea.

After losing the *Santa María*, which was grounded off the island he had christened Hispaniola, Columbus set sail for Spain, leaving a colony of men with instructions to build a settlement and look for gold mines. Taking with him a small party of Arawak natives, Columbus made another important discovery after bearing north to clear the islands: the prevailing westerly wind that took him down to the Azores.

Columbus received a hero's welcome in Barcelona. The royal court lavished honors on him and equipped him for a second, more important voyage that included seventeen vessels, livestock, and a thousand passengers. On this crossing, after finding his settlement at Hispaniola destroyed, Columbus established a new, ill-fated colony called Isabela. Placed on an exposed and unhealthy shore, the colony never prospered and so brought criticism on Columbus himself.

In 1498, Columbus was dispatched on his third voyage. This time he found his colony, which had been moved to Santo Domingo by his brother Bartholomew, in complete turmoil. The Arawaks were virtually at war with the settlers who, in turn, were in open rebellion against Bartholomew. Columbus appeased the rebels with pardons and land grants, but his authority was permanently damaged; he was replaced as governor and sent back to Spain in irons. Despite restoration of his titles and revenues, he was never again allowed to take part in the government of the Indies.

At the age of fifty-one, Columbus set out on his final voyage, in May 1502. This trip, known as the *alto viaje*, or high voyage, was a last try for the triumph that seemed to have eluded him. Though an exploring and economic success, this new quest once again ended on a low note. Columbus sailed the coasts of Honduras, Nicaragua, Costa Rica, and Panama, collecting substantial gold, only to have his ships rot out from under him after a year at sea. Beached at Santa Gloria (now Saint Ann's Bay), Columbus composed his so-called *Lettera rarissima* (very odd letter) in which his incoherencies and enigmatic claims revealed how seriously poor health and disappointment had affected his mind.

Back entrance to Drassanes shipyard

Columbus returned to Spain with his brother and his son in November 1504. Although his fourth voyage had been an important achievement, Columbus returned to find the queen dying and the court distracted and impatient with his exaggerated demands for rights and royalties beyond what had been agreed upon. Columbus spent the last year of his life in relative obscurity, shunned by the royal court and unhappy with his share of the revenues from his Enterprise of the Indies.

In all, Columbus was a superior if rudimentary navigator; his powers of dead reckoning were said to be uncanny. Any place he had been, he could unfailingly find again. He was obsessed with gold, and years before he set sail for America, he spoke of his dream of finding a gold mine in the Indies. Knowing that his prestige in the Spanish court depended largely on his success in amassing precious materials, he was single-minded in his

152

pursuit of wealth, often cruel to Amerindians, and apt to place his trading mission ahead of exploration. Columbus has been described as a loner whose humble origins and foreign birth proved to be impediments to his leadership and administrative abilities. His natural authority at sea broke down ashore, where tact and diplomacy proved more important than navigational skills. In the end, his limitations and disappointments seemed, perhaps unfairly, to eclipse his considerable achievements and discoveries. The Columbus monument was built for Barcelona's 1888 Universal Exhibition to commemorate the explorer's return from his initial voyage to the New World, when he presented his achievement to the king and queen of Spain. Ferdinand and Isabella, the Catholic monarchs, had through their marriage united the reigns of Aragón and Catalonia with those of Castile and León. The house of Aragón's royal court was located in Barcelona in the Plaça del Rei, thus Barcelona's claim to the Columbus saga.

There are so many ironic aspects surrounding the Barcelona-Columbus connection that it's difficult to know where to start. In the first place, Columbus set out from Palos in southern Spain, not from Barcelona, as the monument may seem to imply. Furthermore, the New World was never the source of revenue for Catalonia that it was for the rest of the Iberian peninsula, and this deliberate exclusion of the crown of Aragón from America's riches has been one of the perennial sore points between Catalonia and Madrid. Whereas central and southern Spain's feudal and agricultural economy and social structure survived for centuries on the spoils of conquest and commerce in the New World, Catalonia had no choice but to develop its textile and manufacturing industries—hence Catalonia's eventual industrialization and the rise of a European-style working class along with all of Barcelona's political, intellectual, and artistic foment. In a sense the Christopher Columbus monument towers heroically over the port as the official symbol of much that never was.

As if that were not enough, there is now a serious

protest movement growing in Central and South America over the celebration of the five hundredth anniversary of the discovery of America. The charge is that what is being commemorated was, in fact, the beginning of the systematic and genocidal rape and pillage of the indigenous lands and civilizations of the New World by the conquistadores, viceroys, and legions that Spain generously provided for so many centuries. Meanwhile, in Catalonia, radical *catalanistas* boycott events related to the anniversary: choral groups refuse to perform in certain celebrations, while graffiti that protest Spain, America, Columbus, or the Catholic monarchs are likely to appear at strategic spots on significant dates. The replica of the *Santa María*, a tourist attraction on the Barcelona waterfront, was burned in 1989, apparently by La Crida, a militant Catalonian nationalist organization.

There was even controversy in 1886 when architect Gaietá Buigas erected the 150-foot iron column topped with the figure of Columbus pointing his eighteen-inch index finger directly toward Sicily—that is, southeast as opposed to west. Should he point west but inland or out to sea but in the wrong direction?

The structure itself is an elaborate work filled with allegorical sculptures representing nearly everyone involved in the discovery voyage, from the king and queen to Martín Alonso Pinzón, skipper of the *Pinta*. The column houses an elevator that climbs to the top of the monument, which affords excellent views of the port as well as the Drassanes shipyards.

Leaving the Columbus monument, the Rambla Santa Mònica, the first section of the Rambla to become known as a "promenade" after the city's second set of walls was torn down, is now the habitat for Barcelona's most varied and extraordinary street life and leads back up toward Plaça Catalunya. The Wax Museum, a sensationalist collection largely dedicated to different techniques of torture, is on the right, and the new **Centre d'Art de Santa Mònica**, a space dedicated to exhibits of contemporary art, stands on the left in what was originally the Santa Mònica Convent, built in 1636.

The corners of the Carrer de Santa Mònica and the Carrer Arc del Teatre and the sidewalk running along that side of the Rambla are traditional gathering places for Barcelona's ample and spectacular community of transvestites. They gradually accumulate as the evening progresses, and by midnight there may be anywhere from ten to two dozen buxom creatures in dazzling degrees of undress chatting animatedly in undisguisedly husky voices. The opposite side of the street, just short of and including the Pla del Teatre, is the night marketplace for the more traditional prostitutes, luckless ladies of all ages and sizes who seem especially forlorn in comparison with the exuberant counterfeiters across the street.

After dark everything from Plaça Reial to Drassanes—especially on the Raval side of the Rambla but also through Carrer dels Escudellers—turns more and more sordid and grotesque. Much of this wildness has been chronicled by, among others, Jean Genet and Henry Miller, but it will undoubtedly be gentrified as 1992 comes and goes. For now, it is a good idea not to stray far away from well-illuminated and well-frequented places.

Farther up the Rambla, near the start of Carrer dels Escudellers, the seated statue, inevitably crowned with a pigeon, is a likeness of Barcelona's most famous nineteenth-century playwright, Frederic Soler. Soler's nom de plume was "Pitarra," and he is considered the founder of the modern Catalan theater and author of the verses engraved on the 1714 war memorial in the Fossar de les Moreres (on Walk 2). The **Teatre Principal** just opposite the statue dates to 1568, when permission to build a theater was granted to the Hospital de la Santa Creu. Barcelona's first theater, and the site of the city's first opera, the Teatre Principal fell into disrepair and disuse during the nineteenth century. It was supplanted by newer and better-equipped theaters and auditoriums, such as the Liceu, the Palau de la Música, and the Romea, but has been recently restored.

Carrer Nou de la Rambla branches off to the left across from Plaça Reial. At no. 3, thirty meters off the Rambla, is the **Palau Güell**, built by Antoni Gaudí between 1885 and 1889 (despite the 1888 on the façade). The ironwork grills, the parabolic arches, the ceramic mosaics on the roof, and the sinuous horizontal and vertical lines are the building's most characteristic Gaudí devices. The interior, which until recently housed the Museu del Teatre, is particularly notable for the height of the main hall on the second floor, which reaches all the way to the glass cupola. Originally the residence of the wealthy and philanthropic Güell family responsible for commissioning many of Gaudí's most important works, the Palau Güell was turned into a *cheka*, or Communist party prison, during the Spanish Civil War. It is widely believed that one of the political prisoners held here was Andreu Nin, brother of Anaïs Nin, both believed to be children of Spanish composer Joaquim Nin. When Stalin purged Trotsky from Communist party ranks in the Soviet Union in 1937, the Spanish Republic, fighting for its life against the military uprising led by Franco and the Spanish right, found itself torn by internal strife. Nin had been Leon Trotsky's secretary in Moscow. Thus, when the Spanish Communist party, in turn, purged the P.O.U.M—Partido Obrero de Unificación Marxista (Workers' Party of Marxist Unification), which was suspected of being pro-Trotskyists (which they were not)—Andreu Nin disappeared and was never heard from again. During Mikhail Gorbachev's visit to Barcelona in the fall of 1990, one of the requests Catalan authorities passed on to the Soviet leader was for information from KGB files clarifying Nin's fate.

Back across the Rambla, the **Plaça Reial**, in spite of its present-day legions of drug dealers, thieves, drunks, and black-marketeers, is one of Barcelona's most elegant spaces. Coming into the square from the Rambla, the right-hand side belongs to the underworld, despite the strategically located mobile police trailer set up there, while the center and left end remain under friendly, if somewhat substance-enhanced, control.

Francesc Daniel i Molina, the architect who built the Plaça de Sant Josep (hidden under the Mercat de la Boquería), won the open competition held in 1848 to design the square that would occupy the space formerly inhabited by a convent. The result is one of early Barcelona's most symmetrical and orderly spaces. Uniformly arcaded, wide, and massive, the Plaça Reial's purity of line is surprising in the midst of Barcelona's twisting sprawl, especially surrounded by the Barrio Chino, although the things that go on in the square more than make up for Plaça Reial's disciplined appearance. The center of Plaça Reial is dominated by the Tres Gracies fountain and the branchlike lampposts that have small but mean-looking dragons designed by Antoni Gaudí while he was still an architecture student.

Plaça Reial is surrounded by outdoor cafés and bars, but most frequented are the ones on the left end of the square that specialize in beer, *patatas bravas*, and seafood tapas. On Sundays one of Europe's most important stamp and coin markets, first held in 1890, takes over a large part of the square. Stamps are an important theme in Barcelona; with an impressive collection of sixty-five thousand stamps on display at La Virreina on the Rambla de les Flors, as well as various clubs and societies and over one hundred listings in the yellow pages, Barcelona attracts a certain amount of tourism solely for stamp and coin collecting.

On the northwest side of Plaça Reial, the **Herbolari del Rei** is at the corner of Carrer Vidre and Carrer Heures. With its Gothic windows and the elaborately pedestaled marble bust of a wigged Linnaeus, inventor of modern systematic botany, this herb shop is one of Barcelona's most archaic and medieval hidden corners.

Leaving through the arched doorway at Passatge Madoz, Carrer Ferran leads back into the Rambla dels Caputxins, named for the convent located there until 1775. This is the prime people-perusing stretch on the Rambla, rivaled only by (and perhaps second to) the Bar Zurich at the top. In support of the Rambla dels Caputxins, however, it must be said that too many of those at the top are in an unseemly hurry to catch trains and get places, whereas the lowlife down around Rambla dels Caputxins is more playful and generally at ease. The **Café de la Opera**, **Hotel Oriente**, and **Hotel de les Quatre Nacions** are the main establishments along this well-used runway flanked by tables and chairs and terraces of studious observers. The Hotel de les Quatre Nacions dates from the beginning of the nineteenth century and has lodged celebrities such as George Sand, Marie-Henri Beyle (also known as Stendhal), and Franz Liszt. The Orient, across the way, was visited by Hans Christian Andersen in 1864.

Barcelona's official opera venue, **Gran Teatre del Liceu**, is the last building on the left before the Pla de la Boqueria opening. In Europe, only Milan's La Scala has more room than the thirty-five-hundred seat, five-tier auditorium, recognized for many years as the finest hall of its kind in the world. Originally built by architect Miquel Garriga i Roca in 1848 and restored after being gutted by flames in 1861 by architect Josep Oriol Mestres (survivor of the miraculous fall from the bridge at the Església del Pi in Walk 1), the lush interior of the Liceu is decorated with works by Barcelona's leading nineteenth-century painters. The exquisite second floor Saló de Descans, designed by Mestres, is decorated with paintings on the ceiling depicting scenes from the works of Aristophanes, Aeschylus, Shakespeare, Schiller, and Lope de Vega by Ramón Martí Alsina, Lluís Rigalt, and Antoni Caba.

The Liceu's most notorious catastrophe took place on November 7, 1893. During the second act of a performance of *William Tell* two cantaloupe-sized bombs were hurled from the upper gallery into the orchestra section. The first bomb is reported to have struck the back of a seat and exploded, killing fifteen people immediately, while the second was either a dud or—according to some reports—landed in the lap of a lady killed by the first bomb and failed to go off. In the resulting chaos, Santiago Salvador, the anarchist bomber, was able to walk out un-opposed and unpursued. He later confessed to watching at the front door as the dead and wounded were carried away. The final tally numbered twenty-two killed and fifty wounded.

After a massive roundup of suspects, Salvador was arrested in Zaragoza, tried, and executed in November 1894. While in prison Salvador admitted that he had committed the massacre as revenge for a fellow anarchist named Pallas who had been executed by firing squad just six weeks before. His last cry had been "*La venganza será terrible,*" and Salvador apparently took it literally.

The Liceu bombing was the bloodiest in a series of uprisings and reprisals in what became an ongoing war between the proletariat and the ruling classes during Bar-celona's stormy 1890s. Anarchism seemed a perfect fit for Barcelona's blend of individualism and romanticism. The idea that all of the bourgeoisie shared the guilt for the suffering and misery of the proletariat enabled a cer-tain kind of idealist to massacre with a clear conscience. The bombing of the Corpus Christi procession on June 7, 1896, was the next major anarchist strike, killing three and wounding forty-eight, many of them women and children. The state's reaction was nearly as extreme as the crime: the jails overflowed with anarchists, commu-nists, sympathizers, leftists, and liberal thinkers of all kinds. Eighty-four suspects were brought to trial; twenty-five received death sentences, with five of them executed without delay. In all, over sixty people served prison terms for the Corpus Christi bombing.

The Liceu bombing is the event that is most remem-bered, however. The choice of the Liceu as a target was a direct challenge to the city's bourgeoisie and the forces of law and order, including the Church, perceived as par-ties to the exploitation of the working classes.

The Liceu Opera House has always been a glittering

symbol of Barcelona's aristocracy, an opportunity for un-
abashed sartorial opulence. A chance to attend a gala
opening at the Liceu should not be missed. A dark suit
is appropriate if a dinner jacket is not available. The elegance of *le tout Barcelone* wearing their finest is indelible,
especially as groups of ladies in gowns and men in tux-
edos fade off into the Rambla at one or two o'clock in
the morning looking for taxis, preferring to listen to opera
rather than sleep. Meanwhile, don't forget that steaming
onion soup is available at the Gardunya Restaurant, frequented by the performers themselves, behind the Boqueria market.

The open area in the center of the Rambla between
the end of the Carrer Hospital and the beginning of Carrer
de la Boqueria on the other side, traditionally known as
Pla de la Boqueria, is a comfortable place to take a break
and have a look around, as generations of Barcelonans
have done. Despite the Rambla's present elevation, which
is the result of the construction of the subway and drainage ducts, the Pla de la Boqueria was originally a low
point where water running off from the Barcelona acropolis around Mons Taber, and from Sarrià down what is
now Carrer Hospital, joined the *ramla* riverbed, creating
a *pla*, or flat space. The area became an important gathering place outside the Boqueria or Santa Eulàlia gateway
through the walls to the city center after the second ramparts were built in the thirteenth century.

As the city developed westward, Pla de la Boqueria
became more central. Travelers from Sants and the rest
of Spain entered Barcelona through this section. Farmers
and peasants gathered here. The gallows also stood here
(the opening was also known as Pla de l'Os, or bone),
and the executed were left hanging as a warning to other
potential felons. Hangings and executions were not uncommon in and around bandit-plagued Barcelona during
the Middle Ages, as Cervantes notes in chapter 60 of *Don
Quijote* when Sancho Panza finds trees filled with human
feet, prompting Don Quijote to explain that "those feet

and legs you feel are no doubt those of some outlaws or bandits who have been hung in these trees; in these parts, when the law catches them, they hang them twenty and thirty at a time, which leads me to believe I must be near Barcelona."

Brighter than the surrounding streets and squares, this opening is decorated with a Joan Miró mosaic on the pavement, a sort of pedestrian rose window. Miró, considered one of Catalonia's artistic treasures, was born only two hundred yards away, at no. 2 Passatge del Crèdit, in 1893. Characterized by a playful use of color and form, Miró worked in Paris during the 1920s and 30s and was influenced by André Breton and the surrealist poets. Miró admired the surrealist's techniques for eluding grammatical syntax and logical structure, and aspired to free his painting from all restraints and conventions. Color and humor play important roles in Miró's creations, placing him squarely in the Catalonian tradition that is characteristic of Dalí and Gaudí. After World War II, Miró lived and worked in Palma de Mallorca and in Barcelona, permanently settling in Palma de Mallorca in 1956. Active up to the very last days of his life, this undisputed giant of Catalonian art died at his home on December 25, 1983.

Gypsies sometimes perform flamenco in the Pla de la Boqueria, and there is often a painted mime striking frozen poses, cloaked in a Roman toga. There are cafés, bookstores, newspaper stands, and waiters crossing through the traffic with full trays of coffee or drinks to serve customers seated on the terraces, as the four-way river of humanity cascades by. The Pla de la Boqueria is a Rambla midway: From Plaça Catalunya to this intersection, the world is relatively serious; from Pla de la Boqueria down, especially at night, street life plunges toward the bizarre.

The exotic, neo-Egyptian, pseudo-Japanese **Casa Bruno Cuadros** stands on the right at no. 82, with its Chinese dragon and Oriental stained-glass windows. Constructed in 1896 by Josep Vilaseca i Casanovas, Casa

Bruno Cuadros is considered an important example of pre-Moderniste eclectic architecture.

Farther up the Rambla on the left, the Moderniste shop **Antiga Casa Figueras** at no. 83 Rambla de les Flors is a colorful example of the trend in shop design that swept turn-of-the-century Barcelona. Antoni Ros i Güell designed this delicious pastry emporium in 1902, although the establishment dates back to 1820, as the corner plaque makes clear. There are some two hundred Moderniste stores around Barcelona—pharmacies, cafés,

Casa Bruno Cuadros, Pla de la Boqueria

bars, bakeries, barber and butcher shops—most of them beautifully conserved and restored inside and out, down to door handles and moldings, in the ornate and playful style that found such a willing and appreciative audience in Barcelona at the turn of the century.

Past the Boqueria market and the Rambla de les Flors, through the gauntlet of birds and beasts lining the Rambla dels Estudis, Plaça Catalunya and the center of modern Barcelona are just a couple of minutes upstream. Café Zurich, the oldest building in the Eixample, would be a fitting place to close this sweep around the Raval, Barcelona's first suburb.

Walk · 4

■■■■■■■■■■■■■■■■■■■■■

Gràcia

VILLAGE REPUBLIC

Clock tower at Plaça Rius i Taulet

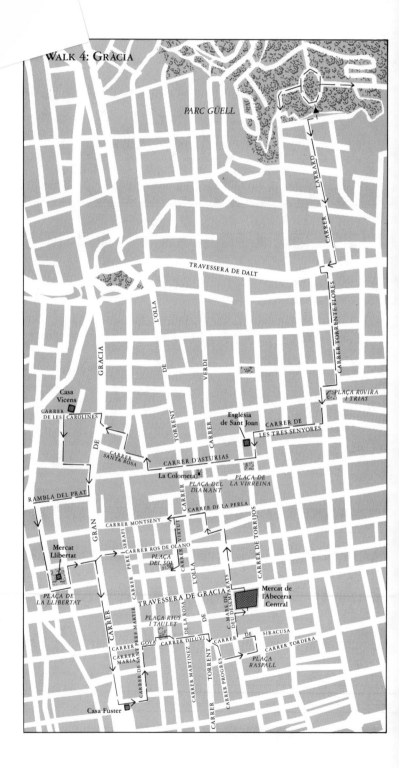

WALK 4: GRÀCIA

PARC GÜELL

CARRER LARRARD

TRAVESSERA DE DALT

CARRER DE GRACIA

L'OLLA

DE

VERDI

TORRENT

CARRER

CARRER TORRENTE FLORES

Casa
Vicens

CARRER
DE LES CAROLINES

Església
de Sant Joan

PLAÇA ROVIRA
I TRIAS

CARRER DE
LES TRES SENYORES

DE

CARRER
SANTA ROSA

CARRER D'ASTURIAS

La Colometa

PLAÇA DEL
DIAMANT

PLAÇA DE
LA VIRREINA

RAMBLA DEL PRAT

CARRER

VERDI

CARRER DE LA PERLA

GRAN

CARRER MONTSENY

CARRER

VIRTUT

L'OLLA

CARRER DE TORRIJOS

Mercat
Llibertat

CARRER PERE SERAFÍ

CARRER ROS DE OLANO

PLAÇA
DEL SOL

PLAÇA DE
LA LLIBERTAT

TRAVESSERA DE GRÀCIA

DE LA ROSA

Mercat de
l'Abeceria
Central

CARRER

DE

PERE MARTIR

PLAÇA RIUS
I TAULET

GOYA

CARRER DILUVI

TORRENT

MARE DE
DEU DEL DESEMPARATS

SIRACUSA

CARRER

CARRER
MARIA

CARRER MARTINEZ

CARRER

PROGRÉS

DE

CARRER TORDERA

CARRER DE SANT PERE MARTIR

PLAÇA
RASPALL

Casa Fuster

CARRER

Starting point: Güell Park
Metro: Plaça Lesseps
Length: Three hours. Try to start by 10:30; by 2:00 shops will be closed.

Gràcia, above all a place where people live, has been Barcelona's greatest maverick. Never content with waging perennial battle for autonomy from the city, Gràcia has repeatedly gone to war with the monarchy and the Spanish state itself, and has needed to be bombarded, assaulted, and reconquered by national troops in 1856, 1870, 1873, and 1909.

Intricately honeycombed with tiny streets and thickly flowered windows and balconies, this romantic enclave seems to bring together all of Barcelona's passion and energy in a bite-sized context—busy but intimate, fierce but friendly.

Gràcia's two markets, originally named La Llibertat and La Revolució, give an idea of the modern social history of this village-state within a city. Federalists, labor organizers, anarchists, feminists, protestants, vegetarians, Theosophists, and Esperantists have been among the liberal and progressive movements that have flourished in Gràcia since the middle of the nineteenth century. Today

Gràcia is a lively nucleus of day and night life, a youthful hub for theatergoers, jazz lovers, movie buffs, market browsers, and diners.

The name Gràcia came from the fifteenth-century monastery Santa Maria de Jesus de Gràcia founded by Alfons IV at the corner of what is now the intersection of Vía Laietana and Aragó. The 1714 War of the Spanish Succession leveled the monastery, which was alternately reconstructed and redestroyed before 1823, when the Franciscans moved it to what is now Plaça Lesseps in upper Gràcia.

During Roman times, Gràcia was a crossroads intersected by the road linking Barcelona's textile and maritime district around Carrer Montcada to the Llobregat River to the west, and the road north to Castrum Octavianum—now San Cugat—over Tibidabo and the Collserola hills. Travessera de Gràcia and Carrer Gran de Gràcia, Gràcia's two main arteries, are the contemporary remains of these ancient routes.

Gràcia extends from Güell Park on its uphill side to the Diagonal and Carrer de Corsega below, and from Vía Augusta and Princep d'Astúries on its west side to Carrer de Sardenya to the east.

Mercè Rodoreda, possibly the greatest twentieth-century Catalan-language novelist, began her moving novel, *La Plaça del Diamant*, in this popular barrio. Rodoreda's masterpiece, an account of the life of a young woman coming of age amid the chaos of the Spanish Civil War, was written after the novelist's literary and linguistic exile of nearly two decades, but it poignantly portrays the life and feel of Gràcia to this day. Of all of Barcelona's neighborhoods, Gràcia seems to speak most clearly to the unpretentious, the rank and file, including the working class, the petite bourgeoisie, students, intellectuals, and the embattled mainstream of city life. Translated by American poet David Rosenthal under the title *The Time of the Doves*, Rodoreda's novel provides unique perspective and insight into the life of Barcelona and, most especially, Gràcia.

Early in the novel, Colometa and her young husband-to-be, Quimet, meet at Güell Park. After spending some time together on a bench in one of the pathways in the park, they wander downhill through Gràcia to the Diagonal. We, too, will begin our tour at Güell Park, meandering down to the historic clock tower in Plaça Rius i Taulet and through lower Gràcia. The scenery along the way, substantially unchanged since 1930, is the Barcelona that Balzac, Dickens, or Dostoyevsky would have written about had they written about Barcelona: *la petite histoire* of the everyday people of the nineteenth century.

Güell Park can be reached most practically by taxi. Barcelona financier Eusebi Güell originally commissioned architect Antoni Gaudí to design the park as an urban development project. Güell, a Barcelona entrepreneur and art lover, was behind much of Gaudí's work. In fact, without Güell's support it is conceivable that the world might never have had the chance to contemplate Gaudí's colorful and organic dreams. Güell imagined an experimental garden community, inspired by English garden suburbs, with some sixty plots to be sold off to prospective residents. The proposal met with limited enthusiasm at the turn of the century because Barcelona gentry considered the location too remote and impractical. Only two houses were constructed between 1900 and 1914 before Barcelona city authorities accepted the park as a gift from the Güell family and made it a municipal garden. Meanwhile, Gaudí had designed some of his most surprising creations: two gatehouses, a covered marketplace under a central square, a surrealistic walkway with an arcade of leaning tree trunks pushing into the mountainside, and a serpentine bench faced with polychromatic bits of ceramic tile. The well-known bench, the detail largely executed by Josep Jujol, has been considered a precursor of abstract and surrealist painting.

The Sala de les Cent Columnes—eighty-six leaning doric columns supporting an undulating ceiling of mosaic tile—was conceived as a marketplace for the community. The bits of ceramic used to create these curved surfaces were deliberately broken up and fitted back together by the workmen Gaudí directed in the construction of the park, a procedure repeated in many of his creations. Conventional ceramic tiles were ideal for flat surfaces, of course, but could be used on curved surfaces only after being reduced to rubble, a technique known in Catalan as *trencadís*, from the verb *trencar*, to break. Two houses were actually built in the park. The upper one is now a private residence while the other, designed by Francesc Berenguer i Mestres, Gràcia's most important Moderniste architect and Gaudí's "right hand," was originally built as a model to encourage potential residents to buy plots of land. It was Gaudí's home from 1906 until shortly before his death in 1926.

The wild mushrooms atop the gatehouses—the red-and-white one is an *Amanita muscaria*, or fly ammanite—have occasionally been taken as a hint that the eccentric *modernista* was an enthusiast of the hallucinogenic mush-

Güell Park

room, although Juan Bassegoda i Nonell, director of the Catedra Gaudí, Barcelona's center for Gaudí studies, vigorously denies any relationship between the architect and the so-called divine mushroom of immortality. Debate has, somewhat playfully, lurched back and forth over this point ever since Gaudí biographer Joan Llarch suggested that Gaudí may owe some of the delirium of his esthetic vision to the so-called fly ammanite, the mushroom that typically houses squads of industrious dwarfs and the one that Alice nibbled before finding her way through the looking-glass. The other wild mushroom, the lighter-colored, mottled one on the other gatehouse, is thought to resemble the legendary *Phallus impudicus*, a remarkably priapic mushroom that sprouts and disappears in just a few hours. The mushroom motif is everywhere in Güell Park; many of the columns and supports are shaped like flowers or fungi. Gaudí, widely rumored to have been *tocat del bolet* (literally, touched by the mushroom), was known to be an ardent lover of the forest and all its magic. And while most Gaudí scholars steer clear of the subject, many experts do not altogether discount the possibility that the creator of the Sagrada Família Cathedral may have nibbled the odd mushroom, just as Baudelaire took opium or Mozart drank schnapps.

Gaudí's work and personality have always been surrounded by mystery and controversy. Born near Tarragona in the town of Reus in 1852, Antoni Gaudí i Cornet grew up the son of a coppersmith. It has been theorized that the molding and pouring of copper pots contributed to Gaudí's three-dimensional visualization of architectural shapes. After graduating from Barcelona's Escola Superior d'Arquitectura de la Llotja in 1878, Gaudí was commissioned by the ceramics mogul Manuel Vicens to build his house on Carrer de les Carolines (which you will see within the hour). Later, after meeting the wealthy industrialist Eusebi Güell, the young architect was never idle. Güell Park, the Palau Güell just off the Rambla, and the gatehouse at the Güell estate in Pedralbes all attest to this decisive relationship between patron and architect. Throughout his major works—Casa Calvet, Casa Batlló, Casa Milà (La Pedrera), and the Sagrada Família Church—Gaudí continued to develop his very personal architectural language, largely oblivious of the Moderniste movement booming around him. Gaudí stories abound: Said to have been an extravagant and epicurean dandy as a young man, he became more ascetic as he grew older and nearly starved to death fasting for Lent in 1894. A devout Catholic, religious mystic, and eccentric genius, Gaudí's affairs of the heart led to sentimental crises that finally convinced him that he, in his own words, "lacked aptitude for family life." A staunch *catalanista* on a purely emotional level, Gaudí was briefly jailed at the age of seventy-two for refusing to speak anything but Catalan to a policeman. His famous encounter with philosopher Miguel de Unamuno turned into a fiasco for the same reason: Gaudí reasoned that this learned Greek scholar should surely be able to understand Catalan, which he did not. Increasingly reclusive and otherworldly, Gaudí lived with his niece in the house in Güell Park for nearly twenty years before moving into his studio in the Sagrada Família, which was virtually the only work he did after the Casa Milà was completed in 1905. Perennially penniless, near the end of his life Gaudí was known to do without underwear and dressed in the same suit for months at a time. Mistaken for a pauper, he remained unidentified for the better part of a day after being struck by a trolley on June 7, 1926, three weeks before his seventy-fourth birthday. Gaudí, who never regained consciousness, shaped and sculpted Barcelona to a degree perhaps never attained by another architect within a single city. Buried amid the continuing saga of his great opus, the Sagrada Família Cathedral, it is as if this enigmatic genius were still alive, his vision still landscaping Barcelona many decades after his death.

Leaving Güell Park via Carrer Larrard, there are a number of inviting sidewalk cafés and restaurants on the way down. This picturesque little neighborhood is known as the **Barrio de la Salut**, named for the monastery dedicated to Nostra Senyora de la Salut. This eccentric corner at the topmost part of Gràcia was originally an enclave for weekend or vacation retreats and has many small one-family *torres* (literally, towers) or houses with diminutive gardens and a singularly quiet and rural ambiance.

After crossing under Travessera de Dalt through the pedestrian underpass to the right, Carrer d'en Torrente Flores continues down toward **Plaça Rovira i Trias**. Carrer d'en Torrente Flores is a quiet but nevertheless busy little street that begins to give an idea of the sound and sense of the town of Gràcia. In contrast to street life outside of Gràcia's intimate embrace, everyone seems to know one another along these shady, sloping streets. The pace of things eases to a brisk but not headlong clip, and in evidence are traces of humor and curiosity, not to mention a certain amount of hanging around.

The house at **no. 172 Torrente Flores** is one of the original two-floor houses typical of late-nineteenth-century and early twentieth-century Gràcia construction. Many of these small-town and country buildings, almost cottages, are being torn down and replaced by four- and five-floor apartment buildings with underground parking facilities two and three levels down. The price of real estate in Barcelona, now higher than Manhattan, is threatening the survival of these tiny, characteristic dwellings as speculation, financial pressures, and the lack of living space combine to make maintaining a house like this an unaffordable luxury.

Just downhill and to the right at **no. 30 Carrer del Cardener** is another original design that has been recently redesigned and renovated, respecting the original façade, an unusual and happy event in modern Barcelona's rush to capitalize and to survive.

The leafy garden and chemaro palm tree at no. 168 is another reminder of the Gràcia that used to be, but it may not be there much longer. The fact that palm trees flourish at all in Barcelona, especially this far up the hillside, is surprising in a city that is cold, though rarely freezing, five months of the year. There is the odd blizzard, of course, such as the famous 1954 storm when skiiers schussed from Tibidabo to the port down Carrer Balmes, using the subway as a ski lift to get back up for the next run. In January 1985 it snowed seven times in ten days.

Farther down, off to the right at **no. 108 Carrer Sant Salvador**, is another charming and diminutive original house, while still farther down Carrer d'en Torrente Flores, at **nos. 111, 113, and 115**, are three early twentieth-century apartment buildings with engravings and floral sculpture on the façades and a lushly vegetated top-floor balcony at **no. 115**. A balcony, as you have probably noted, is an indispensable feature in Barcelona architecture—partly because of its easy access to the life of the street and also as a breather from tight interior spaces.

Bar Bodega Manolo, between nos. 103 and 101, is a perfect little place, with its curving bar and dark back room where lunch is served at midday and rumors of card games drone on in the late afternoons. **Villa Esperanza**, a private home, is on the left at no. 106, another original, cozy two-floor façade. Carrer Torrente d'en Flores now opens into the Plaça Rovira i Trias. Near the center of this lively opening you will find the famous nineteenth-century architect Antoni Rovira i Trias himself in bronze, seated quietly on a bench on the far side of the square. Don Antoni, as he is affectionately and respectfully known, is usually surrounded by a few curious Barcelona natives who have never seen him before. His relaxed and unheroic disposition is unusual in a bronze monument and a little disarming. Rovira i Trias was responsible for many of Barcelona's best-known works, most notably the Mercat de Sant Antoni and Gràcia's Torre del Rellotge (clock tower), but his most famous project, drafted on the bronze plaque at his feet, was never constructed. Rovira i Trias won the municipal competition to design Barcelona's Eixample, or "widening", the gridlike new section of town built during the latter half of the nineteenth century and the setting for Walk 5. Through the intervention of Madrid and the royal family, local plans were overthrown and urban planner Ildefons

Cerdà, credited with the invention of the term *urbanismo*, was named to plan the city's new expansion. In the end it was more another Madrid-Barcelona power struggle than an architectural debate, and as usual the Barcelona solution lost and "centrism" won. The inscription around the bronze plate reads: LE TRACE D'UNE VILLE EST OEUVRE DU TEMPS PLUTOT QUE D'ARCHITECTE (A town's design is more the work of time than of an architect)—a notion some observers feel might prove embarrassing to present-day Barcelona's busy and radical urban designers and architects. A close look at Rovira's plan on the plaque itself will give you an idea of how his design differed from Cerdà's. It is a more radial, fanlike layout and lacks a Diagonal.

People often ask why the figure of Rovira i Trias isn't in the Eixample instead of in this remote corner of Gràcia. The answer is twofold: He might not have appreciated being set up (again) in Ildefons Cerdà's Eixample; and he gave Gràcia much of its municipal real estate. While the square itself is named for Rovira i Trias, the street going uphill on the left was named for another Gràcia benefactor named Rabassa. The street to the right was supposed to be called Torrente Flores after a Gràcia resident named Manuel Torrente Flores, who donated the land the street crosses. Something was lost in the translation from Castilian to Catalan however, and the street was for years erroneously named Torrent de les Flors, the Brook of the Flowers. Every other street in Gràcia called *torrent* is named for a brook or water-course.

Continuing down Carrer Rabassa to Carrer de les Tres Senyores (named for the wives of Rabassa, Massens, and Torrente Flores as a compromise when each of them attempted to have the street named for his wife), a right turn leads to a lush apartment building covered with vegetation at the corner of Carrer Robí and Carrer de l'Alzina. To the left, Carrer de l'Església runs along the lateral façade of **Església de Sant Joan** into the elegant **Plaça de la Virreina**. As you pass the wall of Sant Joan Church, you will see the

Antoni Rovira i Trias in bronze

upper part of a door embedded in the newer wall, with the heads of a man and a woman in bas-relief. This doorway was originally part of the splendid Viceroy Amat mansion constructed during the eighteenth century. The faces are said to be those of the viceroy and his child bride, the virreina, Maria Francesca Fiveller, whom we met in Walk 3.

The rector's house at the corner of Carrer Torrijos and Carrer del Or, just to the right directly facing the

church, was also designed by Francesc Berenguer, as was the Moderniste apartment building to the left on the other side of the square at **no. 44 Carrer del Or**.

Berenguer's role within the Moderniste movement was of great importance, despite the fact that he withdrew from architecture school prior to graduation and was legally unqualified to sign the plans for his buildings. Berenguer is credited with helping push Modernisme through its early derivative phase, during which "eclectic historicism" borrowed much from past architectural styles. Berenguer and Gaudí moved boldly into more creative solutions and new stylistic devices that ultimately defined some of the most original and surprising aspects of Modernisme. Berenguer was an expert at constructions sharing adjoining walls with neighboring buildings. In his Carrer del Or façade, built in 1909, he achieved one of his most admired works—a tight, steep effect crowned with pinnacles that defined the vertical stress lines over each row of the rich wrought-iron balconies. The town of Gràcia is, in a sense, Berenguer's, just as Barcelona is widely thought of as Gaudí's. Nearly all his work is concentrated here, and you will know him well by the time this walk is over.

The downtown version of the story of the Virreina is included in Walk 3 (El Raval). The uptown version, based on a handwritten account attributed to a family member, seems to describe the postnuptial festivities confirming the marriage vows, thus leaving open the possibility that the scene at the Betlem Church on the Rambla occurred as reported.

According to the Gràcia account, when the famous Virrei Amat finally returned from the New World where he had reached the pinnacle of his influence as viceroy of Peru, rumors began to circulate that he would marry the very young Maria Francesca Fiveller of the prominent Fiveller family, whose original palace was near the Sant Just Church and whose second residence was in Plaça Sant Josep Oriol next to the Església del Pi (both in Walk 1). The young bride-to-be lived and studied, as was the custom, in a convent on Carrer Jonqueres where a ceremony reportedly took place *in the viceroy's absence* because he was required at the royal court in Madrid. A celebration was held at the convent; soft drinks and sweets were served, and according to the breathless chronicler of the event, the bride wore a gown of silk and lace "so rich and exquisite that I cannot imagine where to begin to describe it."

The viceroy eventually turned up and went to his

house in Gràcia, as this same family member wrote in his diary, to rest for the ceremony confirming the marriage. On the day of the event, seven carriages with corresponding mule teams pulled out of the Fiveller palace in Plaça del Pi and drove to the house in Gràcia, where the wedding service was held in the chapel. Following the event, the owner of a well-known Rambla café catered sumptuous refreshments. The chronicler compared the house to the Palau de la Generalitat itself during the royal audience, with guests flowing up and down the stairs and elegance everywhere. The official reception was held the following day in great splendor; the towers of edibles were described as comparable to those of classical antiquity and the wedding and reception were rated as historic events in Barcelona's social history.

Three years later the viceroy was dead. The young widow would be a prominent Barcelona figure for many years, and the Palau on the Rambla as well as the house in Gràcia were both popularly called La Virreina. The Gràcia house occupied the middle of the square now occupied by the **Església de Sant Joan**. A large structure with towers on each of its four corners, the Virreina de Gràcia is reported to have been an immense and splendid display resembling a castle. During the nineteenth century the building was alternately used as a hospital, a military convalescence home, a prison, and a barracks, and was finally converted into the Església de Sant Joan between 1878 and 1884. The church was subsequently burned in 1909 during the draft rebellion that came to be known as the Setmana Tràgica, and it was restored by Francesc Berenguer in 1910.

Leaving Plaça de la Virreina by Carrer d'Astúries, **Plaça del Diamant**, where two of the most powerful scenes in Mercè Rodoreda's novel of the same name take place, is just two blocks away. Probably Gràcia's best-known square, Plaça del Diamant was named by Josep Rosell i Isbert, a mid-nineteenth-century town alderman and jeweler who succeeded in naming many Gràcia streets after precious metals: Carrer del Or (gold), Carrer de Topazi (topaz), Carrer la Perla (pearl), and Carrer Robí (ruby), among others. The square itself, traditionally the site of Gràcia fiestas and street dances, while not nearly as evocative as Rodoreda's prose, was redesigned in 1991, and the bronze sculpture of Colometa, formerly in Plaça Rius i Taulet, was finally returned to its natural habitat.

In Xavier Medina Campeny's bronze, the bare-breasted **Colometa** is surrounded (or perhaps pursued) by pigeons, while her young husband Quimet, killed in the war by steel bolts driven through his heart, remains behind her, part of her past. The sculpture—which captures the moment and the spirit of Colometa's final howl of anguish and release—fixes the young widow's naked torso as if in stocks while she struggles bravely to free herself from the plane: circumstance, the human condition.

Colometa, as a young girl, meets Quimet in the Plaça del Diamant during the annual mid-August fiesta, and years later, after surviving many hardships, returns there during a sleepless early morning fugue through the streets of Gràcia. Perhaps the novel's most famous passage occurs in the Plaça del Diamant, and Rodoreda admirers in Barcelona cannot hear the name of this magical square without a strong rush of something resembling nostalgia. In David Rosenthal's translation, the passage, which is part of the novel's conclusion, loses nothing:

> And without thinking I started walking again and the walls carried me along more than my own footsteps and I turned into the Plaça del Diamant: an empty box made of old buildings with the sky for a top. And I saw some little shadows fly across the top and all the buildings started rippling like they were in a pool and someone was slowly stirring it and the walls on the buildings stretched upwards and leaned to-

Gràcia's Colometa

ward each other and the hole at the top got smaller and started turning into a funnel and I felt something in my hand and it was Mateu's hand and a satin-tie dove landed on his shoulder and I've never seen one before but its feathers shimmered like a rainbow and I heard a storm coming up like a whirlwind inside the funnel which was almost closed now and I covered my face with my arms to protect myself from I don't know what and I let out a hellish scream. A scream I must have been carrying around inside me for many years, so thick it was hard for it to get through my throat and with that scream a little bit of nothing trickled out of my mouth, like a cockroach made of spit . . . and that bit of nothing that had lived so long trapped inside me was my youth and it flew off with a scream of I don't know what . . . letting go?

Continuing across on Carrer d'Astúries, the building at no. 65, overlooking the square, has a handsome narrow façade with heavy floral sculpture around the windows and at the center of the top floor. No. 53 has especially impressive balconies that seem almost alive, especially as the afternoon sun slants down the street illuminating the grillwork and confusing the real iron branches with its own shadows. No. 30 is another quirky façade, with twin balconies on either side of the fourth floor.

Turning right at Carrer Badia and left into Carrer Santa Rosa, past no. 14, a building with an unusual russet glow in the evening light, go right on Carrer Trilla, then left through Carrer de Santa Magdalena into the diminutive Plaça Trilla. On the right, at no. 4 coming into Plaça Trilla, is a stack of lovely Moderniste enclosed balconies, complete with stained-glass panes and curved partitions within the window frames.

Across Carrer Gran de Gràcia and uphill to Carrer de les Carolines, it is just 100 meters left to where Gaudí's first building, **Casa Vicens** (1883–85), stands at no. 24

to 26. Groups of schoolchildren busily drawing Gaudí's first project are frequently spread out on the sidewalk on both sides of the street, while cars thread carefully through the ranks of Gaudí admirers. This was one of Barcelona's first polychromatic pieces of architecture and a landmark in the new Moderniste aesthetic that would revolutionize the face of the city. It has been said that Vicens himself, a ceramist, may have encouraged the thirty-one-year-old Gaudí to use colored tile. In any case, the Moorish themes, the colors, the ironwork, and the intense ornamentation are all part of the beginning of Barcelona's explosion of Modernisme and Gaudí's major contribution to it.

Having left Güell Park only a while ago, the sharp corners and right angles are especially surprising in this early Gaudí, as is the use of unbroken ceramic tile and the absence of serpentine forms. The house is a private residence, and there are no tours of the interior, said to be even more exciting than the outside. The walls and ceiling of the main salon are decorated with exquisite murals (including a trompe l'oeil painting on the second floor), carved and polychrome wood decor, ceramics, Gaudí-designed furniture, and ornamentation, creating a monumental concentration of form and color.

Gaudí's original plans for the house, recently discovered in the Municipal Archives by Gràcia historian Jordi Cercs, are intricate and elaborately complete works of art in their own right, signed by Gaudí himself. His later drawings—for Casa Milà in the Eixample (Walk 5), for example—were much more cryptic, rudimentary, and apparently carried out freehand. From the plans and from the angles of the Casa Vicens itself, it is clear that Gaudí had not yet shaken himself free from the compass and T-square, the tools of his architectural training, as he would later.

The iron grillwork over the lower windows, crowned with Gaudí's (and Barcelona's) usual bestiary of lizards, snakes, flying crabs, bats, and dragons, offers a more indicative glimpse into later developments in the architect's imaginative case history, as do the colorful towers and turretlike chimneys on the roof. Note that the winged lizards or dragons over the right-hand ground-floor window have personalities distinct from the somewhat stranger ones on the left.

The iron fence surrounding Casa Vicens, long considered one of the most brilliant early Gaudí creations, has almost certainly been proven to be the work of his assistant Francesc Berenguer. In an article published by British architect David Mackay in *Architectural Review*, Berenguer's daughters are cited as having been present when their father became inspired with the design for the iron railings by the chemaro palm tree next door. "His daughters," stated Mackay, "actually remember him drawing it."

Berenguer's role in Gaudí's work has long been the subject of controversy. Mackay concedes from the start that Gaudí's genius is beyond debate, but other Moderniste architects, especially Berenguer, have received less attention than they deserve for a variety of reasons. Berenguer went to work young, before receiving his architecture degree, and died young, at the age of forty-eight, before he had the opportunity to assume his full stature as one of the masters of Modernisme. When in 1887, at the age of twenty-one, Berenguer married Adelina Bellvehi, Gaudí offered him work as his assistant. Berenguer gave up his studies and became Gaudí's draftsman, organizer, construction foreman, and artistic alter ego. Because he didn't have his degree, many of Berenguer's works were signed by other architects who did; thus, though Mackay lists the Carrer Gran de Gràcia apartment buildings at nos. 13, 15, 50, 61, 77, 196, and 237 as Berenguer works, the official files at the College of Architects attribute only half of these structures to Berenguer. In reality, he may have designed even more of the Gran de Gràcia residences than those Mackay has credited him with.

Berenguer and his wife produced seven children between 1889 and 1905. Berenguer had to work hard to support this brood, proving the old Spanish proverb, "Every baby's born with a loaf of bread under his arm," which addresses the relationship between necessities and solutions. The Llibertat market, the Centre Moral de Gràcia, the façade of the Gràcia Town Hall, the apartments at no. 14 Carrer Torrijos, and two dozen others, not to mention the many Gaudí projects Berenguer participated in, comprise a monumental body of work the full extent of which may never be known with certainty.

In attempting to distinguish between the Berenguer in Gaudí and the Gaudí in Berenguer (undoubtedly there was a mutual influence), Mackay described the two architects' personalities as complementary: "Gaudí emotional, idealist, and a fervent talker; Berenguer quiet, a careful organizer, and a fervent worker." Berenguer's use of three-dimensional cubism, apparent in the Gràcia Town Hall and in the Sant Joan de Gràcia restoration, Mackay shows "are clearly those of the interior elevation of the south (i.e., visually south) wall of the Sagrada Família. Gaudí himself never used this cubism."

When Berenguer died on February 8, 1914, Gaudí, deeply affected, said that he had lost his right hand. Though Gaudí himself lived another twelve years, he did no other work of importance, became a virtual recluse, and dedicated himself solely to the Sagrada Família, which, in fact, progressed little during that time.

Carrer d'Aulèstia i Pijoan, named for a noted late-nineteenth-century author and historian, leads directly away from the Casa Vicens through a typical quiet Gràcia street with some architectural details of its own. At no. 34, high on the left, is the window of a simple old Gràcia flat—the kind of place someone's widowed aunt or grandmother is probably doing quite well in—surrounded by, but protected from, the city's throbbing pace.

No. 18 is not a tomb, and I have been able to find no satisfactory explanation for this building's strange shape and color. Farther down the street, no. 15 and no.

17 are standard Gràcia apartment buildings, constructed during the first quarter of this century. On the other hand, the bright yellow building at no. 12 with the tile decoration below each balcony is one of Gràcia's more decorative uncataloged apartment buildings and includes a coat of arms at the level of the second floor, with the inevitable image of Saint George slaying the dragon. No. 10 has elaborate sculptured floral relief over the doors and windows and a heavy layer of flowers draped over the top balcony in spring. The grocery store downstairs is a typical example of the so-called *colmado*, or corner store, with an old door, antique glass, and dark interior; these are sprinkled throughout Barcelona's residential neighborhoods. To the right of no. 8 is a small glazier's shop with permanent displays of craft and an "open house" (*entrada libre*) sign for anyone who would like to look at glass sculptures and memorabilia apparently designed for fiftieth anniversaries and other sentimental occasions. No. 1 (bis) is a four-floor apartment house with interesting floral engravings, while at no. 4 a row of 300-liter wine barrels hulk in dollar-a-liter cool, fermenting fragrance.

A left turn out to Carrer Gran de Gràcia along Carrer Bretón de los Herreros threads through an often damp street filled with buildings and stores almost uniformly dull in comparison to some of the ornate structures on Aulèstia i Pijoan. With the exception of some of the smaller two-story specimens waiting to be pulled down and replaced by underground parking lots topped by banks and sterile living spaces, all of these buildings were built during the last quarter century and reflect the worst of modern Barcelona architecture: lack of funding and lack of imagination, the practical married to the dull.

The building directly across Carrer Gran de Gràcia at no. 174 is an early twentieth-century structure decorated with green floral engravings. Just downhill, the metro stop occupies the space once inhabited by an eighteenth-century farmhouse built at the site of a spring or fountain, known as La Fontana—hence the train station's name. Crossing to the Guerra Pharmacy at no. 166, a serious-looking place with a heavy wood-and-glass door, a look back at nos. 135 and 137 occupying the opposing corner offers a panoramic view of late-nineteenth-century Gràcia urbanism at its most grandiloquent. The shields indicating F/I over the doorways and around the corner at no. 2 Rambla de Prat are the initials of Francisco Iglesias, the original owner and builder of this massive structure.

At no. 160 a stained-glass tribune, or sitting space, protrudes over the sidewalk from a building decorated with Corinthian columns and women's faces sculpted into the façade.

Farther down Gran de Gràcia, past the open and fragrant bread store opposite the intersection of Rambla de Prat, on the far side of the street are three handsome buildings—nos. 129, 131, and 133. No. 129 has wonderful decks of flowers on the fourth and fifth floors. Crossing Gran de Gràcia to the corner of Rambla de Prat, a look back up to the top of no. 156 will reveal a Moderniste fifth floor with sculpted floral decoration and two windows, one a floor-to-ceiling opening with shutters and flowers on the balcony and the other smaller and higher. Intimate and cozy, this perch has the look of a miniature refuge high over Gran de Gràcia.

From no. 2, on the other side of Rambla de Prat, the mammoth, ornate, and repetitive apartment building extends down to no. 8. The dramatic sculpture on the roof, attributed to Pau Gargallo, is a series of dragons and coats of arms in powerful relief. At the foot of the main stairwell at no. 6 is a marble sculpture of Sant Jordi slaying a dragon, bronze lance and all, and floral ornamentation around the vestibule ceiling. The wooden porter's booth is another characteristic design, while the doors, door handles, and stained-glass windows inside the apartments all add up to a building of unusual splendor. From no. 10, a look back across Rambla de Prat will provide a good view of no. 9, probably the most extraordinary building on the street, with its four ornamental pinnacles crowning the façade and the floral relief supporting the curving, organic balconies. Perhaps most charming of all is the lovely young girl sculpted over the main entry; her long tresses flow up to flowers over her head and around the doorway to become garlands ending in two deep blossoms on either side of the portal.

No. 9 is also the site of a Gràcia institution: **Can Quimet**, also known as Las Guitarras, or the Guitar Bar. During the daytime Quimet's is just another not very clean window on the street, lined with photographs of customers wearing odd headgear and a poster of a large, unshaven chimpanzee. But at night this tiny, under-the-sidewalk hideaway becomes one of the city's quirkier bars, a hangout for bohemians, singers, artists, and fauna of every sort. Quimet himself hands out the hats and the guitars as customers arrive (you might get a boater or a construction worker's hard hat), and the guitars, hundreds of them, hang from the ceiling in great clumps.

The **Cinema Bosque** movie house, visible at the corner of Rambla de Prat and Avinguda Princep d'Asturies, is a historic forum that used to be the Teatre del Bosc (forest), so named for the dense garden that used to loom in the space now occupied by the movie theater's bar. Founded in 1908, the old Bosc, with its three-thousand-spectator capacity, was the scene of plays, musical comedies, operettas, vaudeville reviews, and opera as well as a venue for political rallies and campaign speeches. Pau Gargallo, the famous Catalan sculptor, author of the Valkyries equestrian scene in the Palau de la Música, decorated the original façade with haut-relief heads of Impressionist painter Isidre Nonell, artist Xavier Noguès, Pablo Picasso, and of course himself. The sculptures were saved when the building was remodeled during the 1960s and can still be seen over the movie theater's entryway: Noguès (some say it is the writer Ramón Reventós) on the left, deadpan, the moon-faced Nonell lost in laughter, Gargallo down in the mouth, and Picasso on the far right, winking.

The houses on the far side of the Rambla de Prat are a handsome series of structures from no. 15 through no. 27. No. 27, on the corner of Princep d'Asturias, is especially appealing, with its dark, textured façade of deep-green floral engravings and windows and curved balconies of exceptional balance and proportional harmony.

Rambla de Prat, of all of Gràcia's thoroughfares, is the least characteristic of this town within a city. Its width and the size of its buildings seem more appropriate to the Passeig de Gràcia's Champs Élysée–like expanse than to Gràcia's intimate charm.

Carrer de Benet Mercadé, just across from the Cinema Bosque, leads down past several interesting apartment buildings to Plaça de la Llibertat and the market built by Francesc Berenguer i Mestres. Although the present structure was built between 1888 and 1893, the **Llibertat market** was founded in 1840 and is another of Barcelona's best-known open markets. This market closes for the day at about 2:00 except on Fridays, when it remains open in the afternoon. If you're there between 11:00 and 1:00, the atmosphere hums with excitement. After a browse through the market and maybe a *tapa* of hot mushrooms cooked in garlic and olive oil at one of the seductive little bars, go out the back door of the structure into greengrocer country where the fragrance of fresh vegetables and fruit is especially strong. Looking back at the market's rear façade, Berenguer's snaillike wrought-iron creatures surround the Vila de Gràcia town shield while his iron swans swim along the rim of the roof. Up to the left, the top of the apartment building at no. 20 Plaça de la Llibertat is finished with a Moderniste floral scroll and decorated with a curious plaque showing a steam engine, a stalk of wheat, and bags and boxes of goods, presumably symbolizing the key role of the railroad and transport in uniting agriculture and the consumer. No. 22 on the corner, with its rounded corner balconies, no. 2 around to the right, with its flowery sculpted pinnacles, and nos. 3 and 5 along the right side of the market are also elabo-

Llibertat market, Gràcia

rately decorated façades with fruit, flowers, and natural themes overlooking the genuine articles being bought and sold below.

A woman passing the greengrocers asks, "Will you be here tomorrow?" The weathered saleswoman delivers the only possible response, *"Si Déu vol"* (literally, "If God wants," a little less formal than "God willing"), another reminder of life's tenuous dominion, the improvisational

and temporary make-it-up-as-you-go-along freedom built into Mediterranean life.

Heading across Carrer Cisne, across Carrer Gran de Gràcia and into Carrer Ros de Olano, you will find the **Centre Moral Instructiu de Gràcia** at no. 9 Ros de Olano, another Francesc Berenguer creation. Built in 1904, it is distinguished by its somber Mozarabic (Christians under Muslim rule) brick façade, a startling contrast to his Carrer del Or apartments or his Gran de Gràcia building at no. 77 (coming up soon). Berenguer was at one time the president of the Centre Moral de Gràcia and designed the theater inside in 1913.

Move a few steps back to **Carrer Gran de Gràcia**, the main artery up through town, known throughout the Spanish-speaking years as Mayor de Gràcia, which translates to Main Street. Carrer Gran de Gràcia's noise and fumes all but disappear once you begin to concentrate on some of its extraordinary buildings. The contrast between the quiet pace of life in Gràcia and the headlong crush of Gran de Gràcia and the Travessera de Gràcia are part of the town's traditional dynamic, dating back to the stagecoach line, later the trolleys, and then the train that connected Barcelona with Gràcia, Sant Cugat, and points beyond.

Just downhill at no. 81 is a recently cleaned Moderniste structure with wavy balconies and ample floral relief distributed around the façade. Downstairs, the **Restaurante/Marisquería Botafumeiro** is one of the best seafood places in Barcelona, a spot to keep in mind. The nautical setting—with large brass lanterns outside, waiters dressed as cabin boys, highly polished wood, and metal brightwork—is refreshing, the white wines from Galicia are cold and good, and the plates of shellfish keep materializing as if by magic.

Farther down, at no. 77, is a Francesc Berenguer i Mestre building, officially signed by another architect, Miguel Pascual. Built in 1905, the building is a compendium of Moderniste devices including *trencadís* (broken bits of tile) decorating the undersides of the balconies, ceramic trim, forged iron grillwork, sculptural framing of doors and windows, engravings, stained-glass tribunes, an interior courtyard, a curvilinear wooden doorman's booth, and painted decoration on the ceiling of the vestibule and in some of the rooms.

As you move downhill on the far sidewalk, look back at no. 74, diagonally across the intersection, a characteristically quirky late-nineteenth-century Gràcia structure with green engravings on the façade, glassed-in corner observation balconies, and the cozy **Tupinamba** bar down below.

After crossing again to the even side, farther down at no. 61 is one of Gran de Gràcia's best Moderniste houses, designed by Francesc Berenguer i Mestres (signed by Jeroni F. Granell Manresa) during the first ten years of this century. The main gallery, or tribune, a glassed-in space over the street, is especially large and ornate, with floral relief, wavy balconies, and a woman's head sculpted into the façade. The heavy molded and sculpted wooden door is another Moderniste *objet*, while the inner door handles, wall tiles, doorman's booth, glasswork, and overhead painting all contribute to the building's busy aesthetic rush.

No. 51, built during the 1890s, stands out for its first-floor glass gallery, while no. 49 (over the ancient F. Pons clothing store), built in 1905, is listed at the College of Architects as the work of architect Enric Sagnier i Villavecchia. No. 51 is authorless in the files at the College of Architects, while no. 49, though officially credited to the anti-Moderniste and conservative Sagnier, seems nothing like his work (which you will see in Walk 5); it is much too ornate and curvilinear.

Back across the street, the doors at no. 40, which have been recently refinished, will soon be one hundred years old. The initials over the door and on the glass inner entryway are for Pedro Mestres, the original owner of the building, while farther down to the right, the superimposed 1898 records the date of construction.

Looking across Gran de Gràcia, no. 35 is officially recorded as a Jeroni Granell Manresa creation built during this century's first decade. Granell is also listed as the author of no. 61, however, and there seems to be a chance that Francesc Berenguer may have designed this building as well. The intricately colored glasswork dominated by naturalist themes is by the important Moderniste glazier

Antoni Rigalt i Blanch, with whom Granell was closely associated in the glass business. Granell, Rigalt y Cia. was one of Barcelona's leading glass manufacturers at the turn of the century.

No. 23 is especially notable for its *coronacio*, or top, a scrolled floral relief reprised in the tight curves of the ornamentation over the windows and balconies below. Once again, the unknown authorship of this building brings Françesc Berenguer to mind, especially considering the façade's intense Moderniste ornamentation. The gallery on the second floor seems to have been victimized by reforms.

At its base, Carrer Gran de Gràcia opens up into a bright space filled with a series of spectacular buildings. The neo-medievalist imitation occupied by the Caixa d'Estalvis from no. 18 to no. 22, a particularly uncommunicative exercise, was built in 1906 by August Font i Carreras. Across the street, over the *Colmena* pastry emporium (the uptown branch of the original *Colmena* in Plaça del Angel in Walk 1), no. 15 is another Francesc Berenguer i Mestres creation. This building was constructed between 1906 and 1908 in full Moderniste regalia, including symmetrically placed glass galleries, wrought-iron balustrades, colored glasswork, and a richly sculpted entryway. The Moderniste apartment building at no. 7, built in 1911, was probably designed by its original owner, contractor Ramón Servent, whose initials appear over the door. The top two floors were apparently added at a later date by Servent's family, who still lives there.

Back across Gran de Gràcia, at nos. 2–4, Lluís Domènech i Montaner's **Casa Fuster**, built between 1908 and 1911, looms massively, effectively tightening Passeig de Gràcia's grandiose swath down to Carrer Gran de Gràcia's more intimate track toward Plaça Lesseps and the Collserola hills behind the city. The College of Architects' catalog describes the building as "nearly exempt" from neighboring buildings, open to our eyes on all but one side, and that one the smallest. The six-story building, chromatically more conservative than, for example, Domènech's Palau de la Música (Walk 2) and formally less extraordinary than his earlier (1905–06) Casa Lleó Morera (Walk 5), was designed in coordination with Pere Domènech i Roure, the great Moderniste's son, and certainly reflects a step away from Modernisme's most daring and radical creativity. Domènech i Montaner himself was, after all, sixty-two years old when the building was finished, while his son Pere was thirty-six and probably more than ready to impose his own taste. Remembering Flaubert's words about taste and the previous generation, it's probably a tribute to the father-son entente and professional courtesy that the building didn't turn out to be an exercise in minimalism.

In fact, the winged supports under the balconies and the massive floral support under the giant corner tower are "effects" as spectacular as any in Moderniste architecture, while the sixth-floor dormer windows and sculpted railings around the edge of the roof are warm and inviting. The absence of colored glass and the building's weightiness and power mark a different vision, however, as does the almost total absence of sculpture on the façade.

The Carrer de Gràcia cuts in behind Casa Fuster, offering a good look at the back of the building and a chance to study some of the aviary—dragons or eagles—sculpted into the marble façade. With fewer ornamental devices, the rear of the house allows the stone itself to carry the structure's expressive load, and the result is at once intimate and powerful.

The Patronat Domènech schools, founded by Adela Domènech and her husband José Llinas in 1901, stand on the corner that turns into Carrer Sant Pere Màrtir, which leads back up into Gràcia paralleling Gran de Gràcia. Even along this narrow passageway, where there is barely enough room to admire some of the sculptured trim, several of the apartment buildings are handsomely decorated with flowers, both sculpted and cultivated. The

Bar Los Hermanos is on the first corner, a quiet place to sit down for a moment, while farther up, at the corner of Carrer María, which leads back out to Gran de Gràcia, there is another ancient *colmado*, or corner grocery store, with typical one hundred-year-old light wood and glass doors opening onto both streets.

Several upstairs neighbors have been so successful with their window boxes and birds that this section of the street has an almost gardenlike quality between the din of chirping parakeets and the choked balconies. One second-floor climbing lilac plant nearly falls to the street, while the highest window, at no. 19, is a jungle of plants of at least a dozen different types. Around the corner on **Carrer Maria**, the same botanically gifted clan—whose entry is the first door on the right—have grown geraniums and wisteria in the windows as well. Carrer Maria is one of the undiscovered gems of Gràcia, with its wedgelike granite flower vessels along the street and the inlay artesan, Joan Ordóñez, working just inside the lovely wood and glass of the archaic doors of his shop at no. 6. A look down toward Gran de Gràcia reveals the back of the Mestres house (with the wooden doors) admired on the way down toward Casa Fuster.

Back on Carrer San Pere Màrtir, up at the corner of Carrer Goya, the restaurant **La Querencia** is a fine place to break for lunch, a cool spot with a superb slab of mahogany for a bar and polychrome Moderniste lamps hanging from wooden ceiling beams. La Querencia specializes in thirty-three different codfish dishes, along with a complete selection of other foods. There is also a bread store directly across the street on Carrer Goya, always a sensorial bonanza and a good stop to make.

Coming into **Plaça Rius i Taulet**, Francesc Berenguer i Mestres's town hall façade is at the lower end of the square. The 125-foot *Rellotge*, or clock tower, and its bell, built in 1862 in a combined project directed by architect Antoni Rovira i Trias, came to be known as the Campana (bell) de Gràcia after rallying the revolutionaries of 1870. The bell or bells (there were two: one of almost three and a half tons for the hours and another bell half that size for the quarters) pealed incessantly until the army shot it out with an artillery barrage launched from the intersection of what is now Provença and Paseo de Gràcia. Ever since then the bell has been the symbol of Gràcia and its struggle against the army, the monarchy, centralized power, industrial exploitation, and the ruling classes.

Gràcia's history as an incubator of workers' movements and rebellions started in 1855 when a group of weavers refused to go to work in factories on mechanized looms, preferring to stay at home and continue as independent operators. Little did ownership then suspect what problems collectivization would soon bring.

José Barceló, a leader of one of the Gràcia workers' organizations, had been convicted of armed robbery and put to death on the *garrote vil* shortly before, so Gràcia's antiauthoritarian sentiment was already aroused. The events of 1855 were solved without bloodshed in Gràcia. Josep Anselm Clavé, the choral director who created Barcelona's famous workers' choruses, was especially successful in Gràcia, where more than one seditious meeting "was turned philharmonic." A demonstration with placards reading BREAD AND WORK was as far as Gràcia went in 1855, but the groundwork was laid: The working class was organizing.

It was a different story in 1856. In the midst of generalized workers' uprisings in various Barcelona districts, a detachment of soldiers was trapped in the Casa de la Marquesa at the top of Passeig de Gràcia. After surrendering, a colonel and six officers were lynched by revolutionaries from Gràcia. In reprisal, eighteen local volunteer militiamen were captured by the army, taken to the top of the Passeig de Gràcia, and executed by firing squad. Gràcia historians have recorded the bitter irony of the carpenter who was charged with building the wooden altar where the condemned took their final sacraments before execution, not suspecting that his own son would be one of them.

Another *desastre de la guerra* was the story of the

executed hunchback. As told by Gràcia historian José María de Sucre, a Spanish army officer was assassinated by a man described by witnesses as a hunchback. When a suspect fitting the description was captured, a summary court-martial found him guilty of murder and sedition, and sentenced him to die by firing squad. The presiding officer carried out the sentence without delay, only to discover—when another, guiltier, hunchback was rounded up—that they had executed the wrong man.

The uprising of 1870, known as the Sublevació de les Quintes (Draft Revolt), was a protest against military conscription as well as a result of cumulative disaffection with centrist rule and the domination of the working classes by the traditional ruling oligarchy. Gràcia, which had long fought for municipal independence from Barcelona, was not convinced that its sons should be required to fight and die for the Spanish Crown in distant wars.

The bombardment of Gràcia by the army during the first days of April 1870 preceded the surrounding of and final assault upon the rebel forces. The troops, under the direction of General Eugenio de Gaminde, who was later offered (and declined) the title of Duque de Gràcia by the monarchy, stormed Gràcia via Carrer Gran de Gràcia, entering the town through Carrer Buenavista and the intersection of Plaça de la Llibertat and Carrer de Perill. Meanwhile, another body of troops circled around what is now Carrer Tuset to Sant Gervasi and entered Gràcia across Rambla de Prat. A third group approached Gràcia along the Travessera. This three-pronged advance eventually pushed across Gràcia and trapped the rebels, led by a charismatic cobbler named Francisco Derch, at the Torrent del Pecat (now Carrer d'en Torrente Flores) on the far side of Plaça Rovira i Trias.

On April 10, Palm Sunday, the troops entered Gràcia and began to arrest citizens who had taken part in the uprising. According to the late Gràcia historian Duart Bonafont, some two hundred women were involved in the rebellion in various roles—principally burning the municipal files to destroy evidence of draftable conscripts—but none were arrested. Four months later the rebels were released en masse. Even Francisco Derch was permitted to return to his shop on Carrer Teatro, where he lived peacefully for the rest of his life, concerned only with his customers and with the Red Cross, of which he was the Gràcia president.

José María de Sucre, in his chapter recounting the events of April 1870 in *Album Histórico y Gráfico de Gràcia*, reports the difficulty of the flanking maneuver because of the terrain at that time. The route taken was exposed and dangerous, winding through the deep draws and *rieras*, or dry riverbeds, then creasing the area. Luckily, recounted Sucre, the *caps calents* (literally, hotheads) were not strategically placed, or a slaughter of government troops might have occurred, with, in all probability, dire consequences for the rebellious town of Gràcia.

Sucre's grandfather, according to a family story, had taken cover with his wife and seven children on the floor of his flat. Sheets were draped from the balcony as a signal of neutrality, and mattresses were stacked in the windows for protection from flying rifle rounds, errant or otherwise. Watching the advance of the troops, the elder Sucre decided that something had to be done to avoid a catastrophe. Donning his ornate railroad official's uniform, he went out to meet the attacking army, which he managed to pacify before a shot was fired. As Sucre reported the story, the invading army captain placed himself under the dazzling railroad official's command, and part of Gràcia, at least, was taken without bloodshed.

In 1873 during the First Republic, another rebellion broke out when, on January 5, 1874, General Manuel Pavía led a coup d'état that overthrew the Spanish government. Gràcia immediately went on general strike in support of the Republic, and barricades once again occupied strategic points around the town. Joan Martí i Torres, known as "el Xic de les Barraquetes" (the Kid of the Barricades), a much-chronicled and mythologized revolutionary who was eventually dealt with by the authorities, led local volunteers in bloody confrontations with police and regular army units. Son of a prosperous Martorell innkeeper, Martí was known to have inherited substantial wealth at an early age, a key factor in his legend as a defender of the cause of the rank and file. Described as a loyal federalist when a young man (antimonarchist supporter of the Republic), Martí volunteered for the army but deserted when his unit was mobilized. Hunted down by the army, Martí and his group of rebels were defeated. Condemned to death, he fled to France but returned after receiving a government pardon. Soon afterward he was involved in the events of 1874, was defeated again, and once more fled the country. This time, however, the amnesty that lured him back to his wife and family was a trap. When he was taken prisoner in Martorell, a mob of friends materialized and sent the Guardia Civil running for reinforcements, allowing Martí to escape. Sick and exhausted, el Xic de les Barraquetes hid in a shepherd's hut, where he was finally discovered by a new contingent of soldiers who—according to one illustrated account—"finished him off" with rifle butts and bayonets. Joan Martí i Torres was buried in Martorell as a hero of the Republican cause, another name in Gràcia's long roll call of fallen rebels.

The so-called Setmana Tràgica of July 1909, known in working-class circles as the Revolució de Juliol, was a spontaneous and citywide revolt again sparked by the conscription of reservists to fight a colonial war for the Spanish Crown in Morocco. As in 1870, the mothers and wives of the soldiers to be packed off to North Africa were among the most violent catalysts of this uprising. The leadership of women in collective conflicts throughout the Iberian peninsula has not been unusual. The pattern has been chronicled as far back as Lope de Vega's famous play, *Fuenteovejuna*, in which a village in Galicia rises up against the local state authority, thrusting the men into a bloody conflict that ends tragically. Doctoral theses have been written addressing the apparently unusual leadership of women in a society generally held to be one of the last bastions of uncontrite machismo. Many of these studies conclude that, despite certain appearance and customs, much of the real power and influence in private life below the Pyrenees is generally, if somewhat discreetly, wielded by women.

In the end, federal forces prevailed. The Guardia Civil reported, "The rebels were almost all staunch Republicans and had great pride. They shouted 'Visca la República' as they were executed, and one officer admitted before he died that 'what I most regret is to be killed by Republican bullets, I who have been a Republican all my life.' "

During the Setmana Tràgica, seventy-six barricades were thrown up in the streets of Gràcia. Paving stones, rocks, trolley tracks, sewer covers, and bedsteads blocked key intersections, and once again shots were fired against Spanish troops. The fact that some two hundred reservists from Gràcia were called up to fight in the Spanish war in Morocco seemed too heavy a burden for the modest population of *gràciencs*. Despite the outbreak of church and convent burning, the revolt was initially against a war no one in Gràcia understood or supported. Anticlerical extremists burned sixty-four religious structures throughout Barcelona; eighty-two citizens died and 126 were wounded. The Guardia Civil lost two killed and thirty-nine wounded, and army casualties were reported as three killed and twenty-seven wounded. Following the uprising, which lasted from Sunday, July 25, to the following Sunday, August 1, four persons were executed by firing squad, including one who was found guilty of dancing with the mummified remains of a nun.

The ideological repression that followed the Setmana Tràgica included the suspension of 139 publications throughout Barcelona and the closing of fifteen cultural centers and lay schools. Françesc Ferrer i Guardia, a teacher and founder of the progressive Escuela Moderna, was judged guilty of providing the ideological provocation and support for the uprising. His active participation was never proved, but he was executed by firing squad in what has been described as the Catalan Dreyfus case.

Sitting here on a bench or at a sidewalk café in Plaça Rius i Taulet, which has also been known as Plaça de l'Orient, de la Constitució, de la Campana, del Rellotge, and de la Torratxa, you are at the rallying point for almost all of Gràcia's revolutionary uprisings. The bell tower and clock, never known to be very exact, were the inspiration for some caustic local doggerel that circulated around Barcelona in the 1860s:

Alla en la Vila de Gràcia	Out in the town of Gràcia
Pasan la vida muy bien	They live in a happy way
Pues las gentes que alli moran	Folks who roam around out there
Nunca saben la hora que es.	Never know the time of day.

After the events of 1870 the clock and the tower were no longer a laughing matter. A liberal and progressive newspaper, *La Campana de Gràcia*, was founded, later suppressed, and then republished as *L'Esquella de la Torratxa*. The bell tower's success as a symbol of liberty grew as a result of its mute testimony to the bombardment that put it out of action. The clock remained stopped and the bell silenced for years, until a local carpenter convinced the town hall to let him repair it. After filing down and welding a crack, the bell was again a bell, but the clock was still broken. For a number of years someone went up to the tower and hammered the bell twelve times every noon—in those days an important public service essential to life in Gràcia.

In 1929 when a proposition was approved to melt the larger bell and use the bronze to pour two smaller ones, the protest was once again total and instantaneous. The bell was soon replaced, and finally in 1947 restored completely.

The clock tower stands today as a symbol of Gràcia's long collective struggle for what Francisco Derch, the leader of Gràcia's militia forces during the 1870 *Sublevació de les Quintes*, looked upon as the common cause. Derch, in his memoir of the events of that April, when attempting to describe the reason his men were willing to die resisting the Spanish state's intrusion into their lives, wrote that his loyal troops were willing to sacrifice "for the Republican idea, as defenders of the cause of the people, which is the cause of humanity."

Leaving Plaça Rius i Taulet, a walk through the lower part of Gràcia offers a chance to see an even less bourgeois part of town. On the corner of the square and Carrer Diluvi, the 123-year-old pharmacy, **Farmàcia Gras**, occupies a low, two-story original Gràcia town house that was built in the middle of the nineteenth century. The colorful advertisement for CALLICIDA (callus or corn remover) has been there for seventy-two years, not counting, the pharmacist will point out, when it had to be redone in 1939 to replace the old Catalan version with a Spanish one when Franco's Movimiento Nacional was in power and busily unifying the Iberian peninsula's bothersome divergent cultures. The notion that corns and calluses in Catalan were regarded as potentially subversive may seem ludicrous in today's democratic and open regime, but as late as 1975 it was against the law to fill out a birth certificate with a Catalan name such as Pau, Neus, or Jordi (Pablo, Nieves, and Jorge in Spanish). Thus, Jordi's legal name was Jorge. Catalans of the 1940s and 1950s had been treated to signs in official places commanding "No ladres! Habla el idioma del Imperio Español" (Don't bark. Speak the language of the Spanish Empire) or given instructions to "Habla en Cristiano" (Speak Christian) from impatient Spanish patriots and nationalists.

Follow Carrer Diluvi to Torrent de l'Olla, make a right

down to Carrer Siracusa and a left one block to the corner of Carrer Progrés. One of Gràcia's secret bars, **El Raïm**, known to serve the best mussels in Barcelona, stands darkly behind large floor-to-ceiling shutters and rickety doors of glass and wood. Moving down through Carrer Progrés, there are a series of modest houses, decorated with bright splashes of scarlet-and-orange-flowered balconies. The far corner of Carrer Tordera and Carrer Progrés is the site of another classic old Barcelona bar and café known as **Can Tofol** (short for Cristofol). This cavernous space is ringed with wine barrels and stacks of beverage cases, a kind of combination warehouse and café. The nearly ninety-year-old woman who tends the bar in the morning is hard of hearing, so it is essential to point at the coffee machine if coffee is what you want or to the wine barrels or Coca-Cola advertisement, or whatever.

A left down Carrer Tordera will lead across Carrer Fraternitat to Plaça Raspall, which according to some Gràcia historians was an attempt to name the square for the French revolutionary Jean Raspail. Others believe it was for broom and brush (*raspall*) makers who used to work in that part of town. Plaça Raspall, a mostly unimproved and naturally tumbledown concentration of houses, is the nucleus for Gràcia's Gypsy community. Said to number around 250, Gypsies have been part of Gràcia life since its founding. On Sundays the square is a meeting place for families of Gypsies, and the new Unió Gitana de Gràcia (Gracia Gypsy Union) is located at no. 20 Carrer Tordera. The **Bar Resolís** on the corner of Carrer Tordera and Carrer Tagamanent, on Plaça Raspall, is another regular gathering place for Gràcia's Gypsy community, a stately and hospitable group more closely resembling landed nobility than wandering bohemians. Gràcia's Gypsies are almost all Catalan-speaking and are involved in a variety of pursuits, from scrap metal and junk collection to used-car commerce and banking.

Walk up through Plaça Raspall, make a left on Carrer

Gràcia doorways

Siracusa, and go one block up Carrer Mare de Deu dels Desamparats to the market formerly called Mercat de la Revolució, now known as the **Abecería Central**. This is another garden spot with outside booths for selling wooden tableware, old magazines, lingerie, and costume jewelry, and it is a fresh place to browse through. "You can tell a lot about a city by its markets," explained Colman Andrews, author of the book on Catalan cuisine, "whether the people are exuberant or repressed, what private life might be like. It's a little like being in a kitchen; people seem to relax around food."

Walk up Mare de Deu dels Desamparats and past the factory building—a reminder of Gràcia's important industrial history—and the handsome corner building at no. 24, which has engravings on its façade and unusual rounded balconies, to the Plaça de la Revolució de Setembre de 1868. Named for the events that brought Queen Isabel II to power, this square was also the site of the market named Revolució (and later Isabel II) until it was moved down a block to its present location.

Moving straight uphill from the square on Carrer

Verdi, a left turn at the heavily ornamented building at the corner of Carrer Vallfogona will lead down to Carrer Guilleries. A right turn here will take you up to Carrer la Perla, where you will be able to catch a glimpse of Plaça del Diamant, a long block uphill. A left leads across the intersection of Carrer Montseny and Carrer Torrent de l'Olla, where you should look up for a view of the singular tower on top of the building at no. 49, which is nearly impossible to see unless you find the right opening. On the opposite corner is a Moderniste sculpture—a girl and flowers—outside an outlet for cement and construction supplies.

The **Teatre Lliure**, at no. 47 Carrer Montseny, is one of Barcelona's most important experimental theaters and musical auditoriums. The theater has a quiet restaurant upstairs that is open for lunch or dinner after performances. Moving downhill, Carrer Virtut opens into **Plaça del Sol**, one of Gràcia's liveliest squares, especially at night.

Near the center of the square the famous Arbre de la Llibertat once stood, a fir tree planted to commemorate the execution of a trio of young revolutionaries caught in flagrante delicto with a small cannon or artillery piece during the rebellion of 1870. Surprised in their meeting place on the street running from Plaça del Sol to the Travessera—now named Carrer Canó (cannon) in memory of the event—they were taken to the middle of the Plaça del Sol and summarily executed by firing squad.

Outdoor cafés and tiny restaurants with a certain easy intimacy ring the Plaça del Sol. At night the street lamps in all of these Gràcia spaces, with their antique nineteenth-century gaslight frames, produce something like candlelight: yellow and subdued. Bar browsing throughout Gràcia is a favorite pastime of the young and not-necessarily-so-young. Carrer Verdi is almost solid saloons from the Travessera de Dalt down to the Plaça de la Revolució; interesting new bars and cafés open almost daily. What is it that makes these places so appealing?

There are different theories, to be sure, but the consensus seems to be that there is something stimulating about Gràcia itself: a sense of all the things the streets are named for: liberty, fraternity, progress, revolution, danger (mainly in the sense of excitement), and, yes, even Venus. Gràcia is an aphrodisiac; people feel comfortable and alive there.

Walk · 5

▨▨▨▨▨▨▨▨▨▨▨▨▨▨▨▨▨▨▨▨

L'Eixample

MODERNISTE BARCELONA

Sant Jordi on Casa Amatller

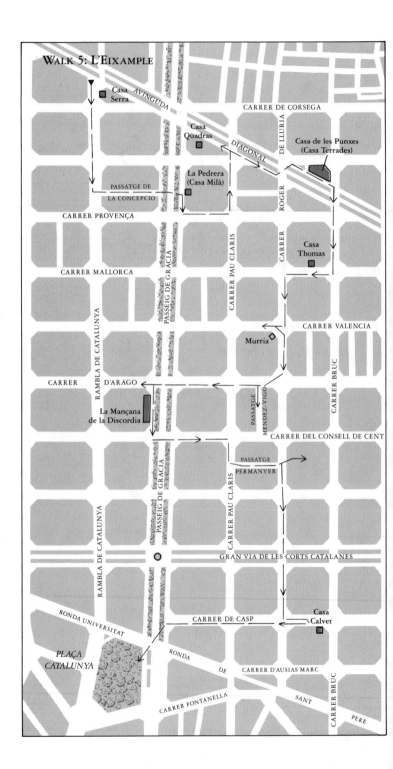

WALK 5: L'EIXAMPLE

Casa Serra
AVINGUDA
CARRER DE CORSEGA

Casa Quadras
DIAGONAL
DE LLURIA
Casa de les Punxes (Casa Terrades)

La Pedrera (Casa Milà)
PASSATGE DE LA CONCEPCIO
ROGER

CARRER PROVENÇA

CARRER PAU CLARIS
CARRER
Casa Thomas

CARRER MALLORCA

PASSEIG DE GRACIA

RAMBLA DE CATALUNYA
CARRER VALENCIA

Murria
CARRER BRUC

CARRER D'ARAGO

La Mançana de la Discordia
PASSATGE MENDEZ-VIGO
CARRER DEL CONSELL DE CENT

PASSATGE PERMANYER
CARRER PAU CLARIS

PASSEIG DE GRACIA
RAMBLA DE CATALUNYA

GRAN VIA DE LES CORTS CATALANES

RONDA UNIVERSITAT
CARRER DE CASP
Casa Calvet

PLAÇA CATALUNYA
RONDA
DE
CARRER D'AUSIAS MARC

CARRER BRUC

CARRER FONTANELLA
SANT
PERE

Starting point: Rambla de Catalunya at Avinguda Diagonal

Metro: Diagonal or Provença

Length: About three hours

Ebullient and swashbuckling, Barcelona's Eixample, or "widening," is filled with the city's most surprising Moderniste buildings, a concentration of creativity and economic power unique in modern urban design. Splashed with color and form, the Eixample reflects the ambition and the taste, the grandeur and the grandiloquence of the turn-of-the-century Barcelona bourgeoisie.

Once an uninhabited open space crisscrossed by dry river beds, Roman roads, and the occasional gulch or swale, the Eixample is now a wide grid of city blocks containing some of the city's most characteristic architecture. "Widening" precisely describes the mid-nineteenth-century plan to tear down Barcelona's third set of walls in order to open out into the largely unused space between the ramparts and the outlying towns of Gràcia, Sant Gervasi, Sants, and Sarrià. The Eixample's symmetry contrasts sharply with the anarchical patterns traced by old Barcelona, as well as by Sants, Gràcia, and Sarrià. The labyrinthine repetition of the blocks and *xamfrans*—the openings or squares created by beveling off the corners of each block—is nearly as confusing to Barcelona natives who have crossed the Eixample for generations as it is to newcomers. Whereas, for example, Manhattan's streets and avenues are numbered, Barcelona's are not, and many longtime residents have their share of trouble remembering whether, say, Consell de Cent or Diputació comes after Valencia.

The so-called Battle of the Cerdà Plan, designed by Ildefons Cerdà in 1859, involved a broad cross-section of players from Barcelona and Madrid, including landowners, architects, politicians, army officers, and even the Spanish royal family. Initially it was the military that worried about the city walls and the compromise of Barcelona's traditional system of defense. With the Napoleonic invasion still a fresh memory, the Ministry of Defense argued that Barcelona's significance as a strategic stronghold would be jeopardized without the deployment of thousands of additional troops, for which they had no budget. Implicit was the fear that the city, which occupation troops had so conveniently shelled from the fortresses of Montjuïc and the Ciutadella, might get out of range. Life within the walls, in any case, had become overcrowded, unhealthy, and impossible (the only squares were paved-over church graveyards), and Barcelona unanimously recognized the urgent need to burst out of its walls and spread into the hinterland.

Much more than a struggle among city planners, the Cerdà dispute, which continues even today, was about who ran Barcelona, municipal or central government authority, Barcelona or Madrid. Queen Isabel II first assumed control of the Madrid-Barcelona debate over whether or not to tear down the walls by *ordering* them removed, thus retaining at least the appearance of authority. Then, while city officials organized an open competition to determine who would design the Eixample, Madrid first imposed a candidate and then, via royal decree, his appointment, over the objections of Barcelona authorities. Antoni Rovira i Trias, the local candidate and winner of the competition, was bypassed in favor of Cerdà, who has never been forgiven despite his stature as a progressive and innovative genius of city planning. Opposition to the Cerdà Plan has held fast for over a century; in fact, many of the Eixample's shortcomings are the result not of Cerdà's plan but of Barcelona's visceral urge to subvert it. Thus, Cerdà's green spaces never appeared; the projected residential nature of the neighborhood was adulterated with businesses and commercial establishments; buildings were altered and heightened; and the interior squares, originally planned as gardens and parks, were often filled with structures of all kinds.

The Eixample, however, represents something quintessentially Barcelona: Modernisme. In the rest of the world it was just another passing artistic movement, but Modernisme caught Barcelona's "widening" at a moment of nationalistic and cultural renaissance and literally exploded in the streets of the new city. Known as "Modern Style" in English-speaking countries, "Art Nouveau" in France and Belgium, "Sezessionstil" in Austria, "Jugendstil" in Germany, "Liberty" or "Floreale" in Italy, and "Modernismo" in the rest of Spain, this international cultural revolution, an attempt to break with the past in favor of new forms and ideas, flourished nowhere as it did in Catalonia.

Characterized by a preference for the curved (natural) line over the straight (man-made) line, asymmetrical shapes, elaborate and often pigmented decorative detail, Modernisme made frequent use of natural and vegetable forms as well as that of the female figure. Part of the international reaction to early nineteenth-century optimism about the roles of science and technology in solving humanity's social, economic, moral, and spiritual problems, Modernisme reflected a trend away from the rational toward emotion, instinct, and intuition. Disillusion over technology's failure to solve humanity's material and spiritual problems triggered a movement away from order and discipline toward spontaneity and passion. Irrationalism triumphed over logic and reason, nature over artificiality, the aesthetic over the practical, and the simple life over the quest for material wealth.

The human reaction to all this became evident when the bitterly disappointed working classes espoused revolutionary ideologies such as anarchism, which led to terrorist catastrophes on the order of Santiago Salvador's 1893 bombing of Barcelona's Liceu Opera House (Walk 3). Architecture emerged from early nineteenth-century historicism (an attempt to invoke Catalonia's glorious medieval epoch in neo-Gothic, neo-Romanesque, and neoclassical revivals) and eclecticism (the use of a mixture of styles) into this new movement in search of novelty, passion, authenticity, and national identity. (The American 1960s might provide an interesting parallel: the "greening" of Catalonia; loss of faith in the values of technology, consumerism, and the military/industrial juggernaut.)

The quantity and the varieties of the architectural expression of Modernisme in the Eixample are nearly infinite. The façades, the stores and pharmacies, the *porterias*, or entryways, the interior patios, the passageways, the sculptures, woodwork, and furniture on many of the *principales*, or main (second) floors, are all worthy of—and have been published and photographed as—monographic studies.

There is an inherent schizophrenia about the Eixample. What at first seems patternless, an exercise in confusing symmetry to replace the old city's confusing anarchy, is in fact vertebrate. The Carrer de Balmes—railroad tracks until they were put underground during the 1920s—is considered the dividing line between the *Dreta* (right) and the *Esquerra* (left) sides of the Eixample, a division of absolutely fundamental social significance, similar to Manhattan's East Side and West Side. Just as life inside Cerdà's blocks is divided into *davant* (front) and *darrera* (back)—the interiors of the flats are either in the front over the street or in the back over the interior patio—the grid itself is either bourgeois *Dreta* or working class *Esquerra*. The distinction is not absolute, of course, and is becoming less so. Nevertheless, there remains a certain pride in being of the Dreta or of the Esquerra, not as virulent but nearly as profound as the basic Barcelona rivalry, the spiritual abyss dividing supporters of the Futbol Club Barcelona and the Real Club Deportivo Español, the city's two professional soccer clubs.

In modern Barcelona the Eixample is no longer the hinterland but the center. The Collserola hills behind the city are the only walls left, and soon the urban sprawl will leave the Collserola behind, too; tunnels have been constructed and developments of bedroom communities are springing up in Terrassa, Sabadell, and beyond. Barcelona's Eixample—art, architecture, design, commerce, offices, homes—has become and will remain the nerve center and the living museum of Moderniste Barcelona.

The only serious problem for a walking tour of the Eixample is its very wideness, the sheer expanse of the area to be covered. One solution is to leave some of the more remote—and major—attractions for special half-day visits in themselves and concentrate on an area that can reasonably be walked in a few hours. Thus, Antoni Gaudí's Sagrada Família, the Hospital de Sant Pau i de la Santa Creu, the *Encants* (Barcelona's picturesque but increasingly inflationary flea market) at Plaça de les Glòries Catalanes, and the Mercat de Sant Antoni (a Sunday market for books and coins across town at the edge of the Raval), though strongly recommended, will not be included in this treatment of the Eixample.

The Sagrada Família, Gaudí's unfinished masterpiece, is especially important, virtually a chapter or a book of its own. In 1891 Gaudí was given full authority over the project, which was begun in 1882 by Françesc P. Villar as a neo-Gothic structure, and he continued to work on it until the end of his life.

Debate over whether or not the temple should be finished, and if so, how, has gone on for more than half a century. At the time of Gaudí's death only one tower had been completed; the other three were still covered with scaffolding. The anticlerical violence of the Spanish Civil War spared only the Sagrada Família, known as "the church of the people" as a result of its radical design, and the Cathedral of Barcelona. The structure's designs and scale models were almost completely lost or destroyed, however, and architects have had to extrapolate based on the general notions left by Gaudí or insinuated by the work in progress. Jordi Bonet, the architect in charge of the project, is the son of one of Gaudí's assistants and remembers playing among the rocks and rubble of the construction site as a child. Jordi Cusso, another architect, has been working on the façades since 1967, building models based on clues gained by piecing together fragments of the original plans.

Barcelona artist Josep Maria Subirachs, an avowed atheist credited with having declared that "God is one of man's greatest creations," has somewhat ironically been given complete freedom to create sculptural work for the structure's *Pasión* façade. Criticism has been bitterly and liberally applied from all quarters, but Subirachs holds firm, stating that his work has "nothing to do" with Gaudí's. Meanwhile, Japanese sculptor Etsuro Sotoo is restoring and completing the *Nacimiento* façade in a style rigorously faithful to Gaudí's original work.

Funding, which has stopped construction often during the years following the Spanish Civil War, is no longer a problem, and the roof is expected to be on the nave by 1995. The projected central tower, 200 feet taller than the other three, is under study, but as yet no one knows if Gaudí's plans for this giant spire will prove viable, even with the aid of modern technology and materials of space-age lightness and strength. In any case, don't bet against *cava* corks popping to celebrate the Sagrada Família's completion on or about June 7, 2026, one hundred years to the day after Gaudí's death.

* * *

Starting downhill from the Diagonal, Rambla de Catalunya is a cool and leafy promenade leading down to Plaça Catalunya where it joins the top of the original Rambla. Originally a watercourse known as *la riera d'en Malla*, which collected the runoff from Sant Gervasi and Gràcia and flowed directly into the lower Rambla, the dry riverbed was covered for the Universal Exposition of 1888. The *riera* was considered the original Eixample meridian separating the Eixample's left and right lobes. Later, after Rambla de Catalunya was paved and turned into a graceful promenade, Carrer Balmes became the natural barrier between the Eixample's two personalities.

Rambla de Catalunya's central walkway is now lined by shops, hot chocolate emporiums, sidewalk cafés, movie theaters, and late-nineteenth- and early twentieth-century buildings of varying architectural importance.

The first building on the left side of the Rambla de Catalunya is **Casa Serra**, built between 1903 and 1907 by Josep Puig i Cadafalch, one of the great architects of Barcelona's Eixample. Nearly torn down during the 1970s, Casa Serra was saved after an uprising of architects and journalists succeeded in paralyzing plans to sell the land and demolish the building in favor of a more profitable structure. Since that time the provincial government—Diputació de Barcelona—has taken over Casa Serra and erected the modern gray office building behind it.

Originally commissioned in 1900, Casa Serra seemed doomed from the start. Economic difficulties slowed construction, the Serra family never did occupy the building, and the congregation of Santa Teresa de Jesús eventually bought it to use as a school. In 1945 two floors were added to the Diagonal side. Architect Josep Pericas directed this project with the assistance of Josep Puig i Cadafalch, who was not permitted to practice his profession after the Spanish Civil War because of his prewar political prominence as a Catalonian nationalist.

"Indiano," Rambla de Catalunya

The building occupies an irregular block, cut on one side by the canted path of the Diagonal, bordered by three streets, and favored with four façades as a result of its two *xamfrans*, the characteristic cornerless blocks of the Eixample created to maximize light and space while cutting down walking distances. The plateresque sculptural ornamentation (that is, floral relief, scrolls, heraldic escutcheons, and so forth) and the cylindrical tower connecting the two main sections of the house are among its most spectacular features. The building falls within the spirit of Modernisme's early medievalist revival movement, as opposed to the movement's more imaginative second stage associated with the first years of this century.

Moving down Rambla de Catalunya, the façade occupying the *xamfran* at no. 124 is a handsome beige-and-maroon grid, especially when illuminated by the afternoon sun. The building at no. 125 is also a typical Eixample structure with bas-relief ornamentation, colorful engravings, and sculpted heads of a man and a woman over the door on the second-floor balcony. The building at no. 112 has a Moderniste second-floor stained-glass window with floral ornamentation, while at no. 110 the strikingly Eurasian features of the face over the entryway may reflect, in the opin-

218

ion of certain historians, the peculiar style and look of the "indianos," nineteenth-century adventurers who returned rich from the New World and built grandiose houses to display their successes abroad.

The Passatge de la Concepció cuts left through the block opposite no. 113 Rambla de Catalunya. Lined by small and graceful houses and rich in vegetation, these passages are among the Eixample's secrets. There are forty-six of them spread throughout the blocks of the grid, each with a distinctive and intimate charm. At no. 5 Passatge de la Concepció there is a unique town house that has been restored and converted into a modern restaurant, the **Tragaluz** (skylight). Tragaluz is an ingeniously designed space with a sloping glass roof, traveling blinds to regulate the amount of sunlight during the day, and moon and starlight at night. The plates were designed by Javier Mariscal, the artist who created the puckish and controversial Olympic mascot, Cobi (a comic cross between a typical Catalonian sheepdog and a cartoon cat). There are also chairs, bar stools, and even bathrooms created by Barcelona's leading designers, all manifestations of the contemporary, late-twentieth-century surge of confidence that has broken out with Spain's return to democracy. Nearly a century after the nineteenth-century *Renaixença* erupted in the Eixample's unbashful Modernisme, art and design are again flourishing. Just as Barcelona's Universal Exposition of 1888 proved to be a psychological lift that caused feverish creativity, construction, and reurbanization, the present coincidence of the restoration of democracy, the recognition of Catalonia's autonomous institutions, and the excitement and confidence generated by the promise of the 1992 Olympic Games have all combined into a boom unparalleled in Barcelona history.

Emerging from the Passatge de la Concepció, directly across the Passeig de Gràcia at no. 96, just uphill from Gaudí's Casa Milà, is **Vinçon**, one of the city's finest stores, specializing in design and interior decoration. The marble plaque on the façade contains verses by the great

Moderniste poet Rubén Darío dedicated to Santiago Russinol, Barcelona's famous nineteenth-century poet and artist who lived here.

Gloria al buen Catalan	Glory to the good Catalan
que hace a la luz su misa	who makes light his Mass
jardinero de ideas	gardener of ideas
jardinero del sol;	gardener of the sun;
al pincel y a la pluma	to the paintbrush and pen
a la barba y a la risa	to the beard and the laughter
con que nos hace	with which he brightens
la vida alegre Rusiñol.	our lives, Russinol.

One of Catalonia's first impressionists and greatest painters, Ramón Casas, Russinol's inseparable colleague and friend, also had a studio in this building, and it is probable that his famous 1892 oil painting, *Interior al aire libre*, a portrait of his sister and her husband having tea under an awning, was painted in the interior patio.

Ramón Casas, sometimes described as the Toulouse-Lautrec of Catalonian painting, was perhaps the central figure among the Moderniste artists who gathered at Els Quatre Gats café on Carrer Montsió (in Walk 2). Widely considered the most talented artist of the early Modernistes, Casas was heir to a fortune amassed by his father in the West Indies as well as to his mother's textile industry. By fifteen Casas had given up his studies in favor of painting and attended a famous Parisian center for young artists. Casas quickly mastered the formal techniques of the Impressionists, returned to Barcelona, and became the painter of choice for the city's bourgeoisie. When his painting *Garrote Vil* was exhibited at the Sala Parés (Walk 1), lines formed to see it. *Plein Air* (1891), *La Madeleine* (1892), *Interior al aire libre* (1892), *Garrote Vil* (1894), and *La Carga* (1899), along with his posters, represent the artist's finest works.

The *principal* (second floor) is the site of one of the most spectacular displays of Moderniste woodworking in Barcelona. The fireplace is ablaze with form and texture, as are the ceilings and their gilt trim, the window casings, and the moldings. The interior courtyard is one of the two or three best in the Eixample; it is shaded by a jungle of plane trees and surrounded by colorful tiles. The courtyard has been called *el jardí dels guerrers* (the garden of the warriors), named for Gaudí's helmeted chimneys that loom over the open space from the neighboring building, **La Pedrera**, while offering an unusual view of the architectural masterpiece next door.

Vinçon is an exciting store to visit under any pretext: people watching, architecture browsing, even shopping.

Gaudí's Casa Milà, normally known as La Pedrera, undulates around the corner of Passeig de Gràcia and Carrer Provença. You won't miss it. The term *pedrera*, meaning quarry, was coined by skeptics during the controversy that raged during and after the building's construction in 1905. The Milà family, who commissioned Gaudí to design a combination home and apartment building after admiring his work on the nearby Casa Batlló, was reportedly shocked when the finished work was unveiled. Senyora Milà, in particular, is said to have disliked the twisting stone expanse, stating that it looked like a place for "snakes and wild animals" to live in. The plans Gaudí showed the Milàs as he began construction, reproductions of which can be found in Juan Bassegoda i Nonell's book *La Pedrera de Gaudí* (Caixa d'Estaluis de Catalunya, 1987) gave only a hint of the structure's final appearance. During construction the building was hidden by huge tarpaulins; the Milà family's astonishment when the cavelike façade was finally revealed is interesting to imagine.

The best view of La Pedrera is from the middle of Paseo de Gràcia; this may look dangerous, and make no mistake, it is, but the lights do concede occasional breaks in traffic. A few seconds may be enough to get the feel of this monolithic abstract sculpture from one of the few points close enough to be part of it and far enough away to see it all. La Pedrera manages to seem much bigger than it is; the horizontal lines and the sand-colored limestone make the structure seem enormous. The doorways, interiors, moldings, door handles, and the roof with its hooded sculptures are all Gaudí designs. The entryway and the roof are the only parts of La Pedrera open to the public at the moment. A tour of the roof of Casa Milà is presently offered Tuesdays through Saturdays at ten, eleven, twelve, and one o'clock, and should not be missed. The distant towers of the Sagrada Família Church, as well as the views of Tibidabo, Montjuïc, and the Eixample below are spectacular. Gaudí's chimneys, ominous and hooded figures finished with broken bits of ceramic (*trencadís*), are thought to be knights or soldiers by some art historians, while others see the veiled countenances of Arabian women. The Greek crosses subtly camouflaged in these figures reflect Gaudí's constant preoccupation with religion. The smaller chimneys with twisted stems are original Gaudí, while the straight ones were built later by another architect. Looking over the eastern façade, a small cavelike terrace can be seen—the hideaway of one of the last tenants of the rooftop apartments added to the building over the years.

Sinuous and wavy, as if borrowed from some windswept strand in the Ebro delta, La Pedrera—as indeed all of Gaudí's work—seems a perfect answer to the Eixample's checkerboard rationalism, with wild fungi sprouting in the middle of the urban maze.

A few steps down Carrer Provença and up Carrer Pau Claris to the Diagonal no. 373 (just around the corner to the left) is **Casa Quadras**, another building by Josep Puig i Cadafalch. Built in 1904 for Baron Quadras, this richly decorated structure combines neo-Gothic and plateresque (leafy and intricate) elements in another early Moderniste historicist evocation of Catalonia's rich past. Now the home of Barcelona's Music Museum (open from nine to two except Mondays), the sculptural detail features intricate Eusebi Arnau sculptures over the windows

La Pedrera (Casa Milà)

overlooking the Diagonal, including another exquisitely rendered portrayal of Sant Jordi slaying the dragon.

Across the intersection is Casa Terrades, more commonly known as **Casa de les Punxes** (spikes), another Puig i Cadafalch creation. This remarkable structure of stone and brick, with its six-pointed conical towers, was built just before La Pedrera by Gaudí's young colleague in yet another example of early Moderniste medievalist revival, in this case inspired by Nordic Gothic architecture. Occupying a separate wedge-shaped block, Casa de les Punxes is one of the few structures in the Eixample to stand alone and apart, visible from 360 degrees. The Terrades family allowed Puig i Cadafalch to score what Barcelona novelist Manuel Vázquez Montalbán described as a "macabre double" by commissioning him to design their family mausoleum as well, a project done somewhat less exuberantly—as if, Vázquez Montalbán noted, they were taking no chances on the possibility that the Divine Father, like the Pope who disapproved of Modernisme, might have more classical tastes.

Coming down Carrer Bruch to Carrer Mallorca, a right turn will take you to Lluís Domènech i Montaner's **Casa Thomas**, at no. 291–293 Carrer Mallorca, built for Josep

Thomas in 1895. Originally constructed over the Thomas graphic arts industry, at that time one of Europe's leading printers and engravers, the building's upper stories were designed and constructed in 1912 by Domènech i Montaner's son-in-law, Francesc Guardia i Vidal (under the supervision of his famous father-in-law) as living space for the Thomas heirs. Guardia carefully moved the original two towers to the new roof and decorated the new central portion of the façade in the Moderniste style used in the original structure nearly twenty years earlier. During his lifetime Josep Thomas had vigorously refused to allow any construction that might interfere with the natural lighting he considered fundamental to his industry. The Thomas printing business closed in 1973, and the building was taken over in 1979 by *Bd*, Barcelona Design, one of Barcelona's most innovative and dynamic enterprises in the design of lamps, chairs, and all manner of indoor furniture. The lower floor was rebuilt for *Bd* by the Studio PER, respecting Domènech i Montaner's original design.

Crossing Carrer Mallorca to the sidewalk opposite Casa Thomas, you will get a better look at the house itself. To the west, back toward Carrer Roger de Llúria, are two typical Eixample entryways, at no. 284 and no. 282, deep and dark spaces, wood-beamed, and richly ornamented, with the standard wood-and-glass cubicle for the doorman next to the elevator. The elevators of Barcelona's older buildings, many of them considered important pieces of Moderniste art, have been the subject of photographic essays and books. Slow, creaky, and usually deliciously decorated with mirrors and woodwork, these noble hoists have never taken too long for the admirers of the Eixample's at once stately and exciting turn-of-the-century elegance.

At the intersection of Carrer Roger de Llúria and Carrer Mallorca, the building on the far corner, on the uphill side at no. 283 Carrer Mallorca, is **Palau Casades**, now the Lawyers College, an example of eclectic Moderniste architecture with its Pompeyan patio. At no. 235 Carrer

Mallorca, **Palau Montaner**, begun by architect Josep Do-mènech i Estapà in 1889, was completed by Lluís Do-mènech i Montaner and Antoni Gallissà between 1891 and 1893. The interior staircase and the colorful ceramic friezes at the top of the façade are the most memorable features of this graceful structure, now the seat of the Delegació del Govern, representatives of the Madrid gov-ernment. Palau Montaner may be visited on Saturday mornings from eleven o'clock to one o'clock.

Moving down Carrer Roger de Llúria, an important concentration of Modernisme is gathered around the inter-section with **Carrer Valencia**. At the upper left corner, at **no. 339 Carrer Valencia**, is a corner tower of glassed-in porches with stained-glass panes. The building is an-other Gallissà creation with Moderniste ornamentation and details.

The **Murria** store across the intersection at the lower right-hand corner is one of the most colorful of Barcelona's Moderniste shops with bright, painted glass showcases. The store, originally known as La Puríssima after the nearby Església de la Concepció, has a popular store window ad-vertising Anis del Mono. The bright representation of a monkey with a bottle of anise under his arm, walking hand in hand with a colorful lady with plumes, dates from 1904. The paintings were done *al fuego*—applied under heat—from the back side of the glass and are taken from the famous poster by the Barcelona painter Ramón Casas.

Across the street at no. 80 Carrer Roger de Llúria is a fossillike corner tower, the balconies of **Casa Villa-nueva** built in 1906 by Juli M. Fossas i Martínez. The combination of ornamentation, organic forms, and curved lines are redolent of both Domènech i Montaner's Casa Lleó Morera (especially in the spiked cupola) and Gaudí's Casa Batlló (coming soon), both built shortly before Fos-sas designed Casa Villanueva.

A short detour to no. 302 Carrer de Valencia will take you to **Casa Elizalde**, the local civic center, which has one of the Eixample's best interior patios, now used for concerts and art exhibits. Built in 1888 by architect Emili Sala i Cortes, Casa Elizalde is a good example of the kind of town houses, or *palacetes*, Barcelona's powerful bourgeoisie built for themselves during the last quarter of the nineteenth century, influenced by the style and spirit of France's Second Empire. The building barely survived in 1974 when its owner illegally began to tear it down; an injunction halted the demolition, and Casa Elizalde was added to the Architectural Patrimony's list of protected sites. The stairwell's ornate stained-glass tower, rising from the rear of the exhibition hall, and the interior patio located straight in through the main entryway are the building's most interesting features.

Continuing on down Carrer Roger de Llúria, at no. 74 is **Farmacia Robert**, now owned by M. Ferrer Argelaguet. Built in 1906, this Moderniste drugstore is nearly enough to make you feel better all by itself: Designer doors inspired by Gaudí, beams and floral wall relief, stained glass, and hand-carved wooden ornamentation create a sense of magic that is popular in many Barcelona shops, but especially—perhaps in deference to pharmacology's supernatural properties—in pharmacies.

At no. 72 is **Casa Pere Salisachs**, built between 1904 and 1906 by architect Salvador Viñals i Sabaté. This colorful building houses a permanent display, open to the public, of Orfebres Artesanos (goldsmiths). Designers of jewelry, these artesans have restored the façade entryway, and the main (second) floor in soft pastels, while restoring the sculpture already present. The plaque on the street reads: " 'Give me the form and I will become the message,' said gold to the goldsmith, and the craftsman patiently filled his hands with love and made *joia*" (which in Catalan means both jewel and joy).

Carrer Aragó hurtles across Barcelona in a high-speed six-lane crush at the next corner. Crossing to the far sidewalk, walk to the right for forty yards to Passatge Mendez-Vigo. A wide, wrought-iron archway leads down between the Italian School, the Italian Center, and the Italian Cultural Center, all grouped in this overgrown alley surrounded by some of the city's widest and busiest thoroughfares. There is usually a security guard at the gate who claims never to have stopped anyone from entering, so do not be intimidated. You're welcome to go in. One house that is especially spectacular is nearly invisible behind some of Barcelona's wildest inner-city vegetation; it is for sale at $27 million.

Because they have recently decided to close the lower end of Passatge Mendez-Vigo, the way out is back to Carrer Aragó. A block and a half to the left over to Passeig de Gràcia will place you across the street from the upper corner of one of Barcelona's most extraordinary concentrations of architecture. This chaotic enumeration of houses has been popularly tagged **la Mançana de la Discordia**, a pun on the words block and apple (both *mançana* in Catalan), thus the Apple (Block) of Discord. Barcelona's three greatest Moderniste architects—Antoni Gaudí, Josep Puig i Cadafalch, and Lluís Domènech i Montaner—are represented in this design sampler, along with the more traditional Enric Sagnier i Villavecchia. Although Gaudí's Casa Batlló usually gets most of the attention, all four of the buildings are intricate and intriguing statements by four distinct personalities.

This upper corner of Carrer Aragó and Passeig de Gràcia is probably the best spot for a wide-angle look at the Mançana de la Discordia, depending on the time of year. But before making a closer inspection from the far sidewalk, a quick detour down to **Casa Montaner i Simon** at no. 255 Carrer Aragó will offer a view of the Moderniste structure originally built for the Montaner i Simon publishers in 1880 and now housing the Fundació Tàpies. Domènech i Montaner's building, cited as the first manifestation of Moderniste architecture, is crowned with an unruly and controversial tangle of steel called "Núvol i cadira" (Cloud and Chair) by contemporary artist Antoni Tàpies. Barcelona journalist James Townsend Pi-Sunyer even suggested that the Bulgarian-born artist

Christo wrap it in one of his macro installations, thus twice blessing the city—"once with a work of art and again by covering up that Tàpies monstrosity."

Back around the corner in front of Gaudí's Casa Batlló, an exploration of the Mançana de la Discordia and the architectural debate around it tells much about the people and politics of Moderniste Barcelona.

This clash of styles came about not completely by chance. The Lleó i Morera, Amatller, and Batlló families, and later the Milàs up the road, not to mention the other powerful families of Barcelona's upper middle class, were apparently locked in one of history's more spectacular neighborhood competitions, all goaded on by a nationalistic need to celebrate the economic power and cultural solvency of fin de siècle Catalonia.

The **Casa Lleó Morera** by Lluís Domènech i Montaner, decorated in a distinct floral Moderniste style redolent of his Palau de la Música, is at the corner of Carrer del Consell de Cent and Passeig de Gràcia. The lower floor was redesigned ("mutilated" is the term normally applied to this event by Barcelona chroniclers) in 1943, in a style described by critics as "funeral parlor," by the clothing store, Loewe. The Town Hall's tourist office, Patronat de Turisme, presently occupies the main floor above. The next house uphill, at no. 37 Passeig de Gràcia, is Enric Sagnier i Villavecchia's **Casa Mulleras**, a Louis XVI revival structure outstanding (in this company) for its stiff but unassuming classical formality. Puig i Cadafalch's Netherlands-style, neo-Gothic **Casa Amatller** is next up the block, all right angles and flat expanses of engravings, while the brightly colored and undulating **Casa Batlló** spectacularly closes the cycle in Gaudí's personal and unmistakable idiom.

The four architects—Domènech i Montaner, Sagnier i Villavecchia, Puig i Cadafalch, and Gaudí—were men of their times, influenced by the Moderniste movement and by the surge of Catalan nationalist fervor. Yet each carried very different personal, political, and aesthetic baggage:

Domènech i Montaner, in his 1877 article *"En busca d'una arquitectura nacional,"* considered by many to be the Moderniste manifesto, established himself as one of the intellectual leaders of his generation. Domènech i Montaner's politics appear to have been rational, coherent, consistent, tolerant, and moderate. Neither obsessed with religion nor fanatically *catalanista*, Domènech hoped for a Catalonia of "illustrated" tolerance, open and eclectic.

Sagnier i Villavecchia was archconservative and had little or nothing to do with Catalan nationalism and mainly distaste for the ideas and aesthetics of Modernisme. Sagnier, rooted in the French baroque and English neoclassical traditions, was the architect of Barcelona's upper crust, traditionally non-Catalan-speaking monarchists (known as *botiflers*, Catalans who sided with the Bourbons in the War of the Spanish Succession) who resisted revolutionary change in all areas.

Puig i Cadafalch, eighteen years younger than Domènech i Montaner and fifteen years younger than Gaudí, was a politician, historian, and archeologist as well as an architect. Dedicated to the recovery of Catalonia's proud past, his designs never completely departed from the historical revivalism of the first epoch of Catalonia's Moderniste movement. Mayor of Barcelona, senator to the Spanish Cortes or parliament, head of Barcelona's provincial government, Puig i Cadafalch's brilliant career as a statesman culminated in the presidency, in 1917 at the age of fifty, of the Mancomunitat de Catalunya, Catalonia's first home rule initiative since 1714.

Gaudí, the most spontaneous and radical of the four, was both a fervent *catalanista* on a purely personal level (he had nothing to do with organized politics) and a devoutly religious mystic who lived in a world of his own devising, oblivious of aesthetic schools and movements.

Thus, the Mançana de la Discordia represents more than three or four clashing architectural styles. Starting from Domènech i Montaner's Casa Lleó Morera, we see an enlightened and open Catalan Modernisme, with all the movement's aesthetic conceits and devices. Next comes Sagnier i Villavecchia's shrug, ignoring the Moderniste madness with a lofty statement of European (French and English) baroque and neoclassical rationalism. In Casa Amatller, Puig i Cadafalch's eclectic historicism searches for Catalonia's identity in its past, while Gaudí's Casa Batlló is an entirely original creation, a playful return to natural lines and unchecked fantasy.

After a careful study of the Mançana de la Discordia, **Casa Batlló** still stands as the most surprising and appealing structure on the block, and the crowds snapping pictures on the sidewalk know it. Even before identifying the rooftop dragon's scaly back, the cross of Saint George impaling his tail, the skull-like masks of the dragon's victims stacked below as balcony balustrades, or the femurs and tibias framing the lower windows, the colorful façade and undulating surfaces of the building are intriguing. Gaudí reportedly "painted" the façade personally from the center of the Passeig de Gràcia, directing workmen on scaffolding equipped with baskets of different-colored bits of ceramic tile.

Casa Amatller, at no. 41, was the first of the four houses to be refurbished. Planned in 1898, the reforms were finished in 1900 when architect Josep Puig i Cadafalch was just thirty-three years old. The leading sculptors, stonemasons, ironsmiths, ceramists, and woodworkers collaborated on the richly ornamented structure in an attempt to give it the air of a typical Gothic town house lived in by a single family. The façade's sharp angles, inspired by Flemish or Netherlands house design, contrast sharply with adjacent buildings, while the elements of Romanesque, Gothic, sixteenth-century, and baroque ornamentation continue in Puig i Cadafalch's use of different architectural styles from the past. The Eusebi Arnau sculptures on the lower part of the façade include Sant Jordi slaying the dragon over the center column between the doorways, a woman grappling with a dragon (perhaps the maiden Sant Jordi saved) to the right, and on the left, a man with a missing hand beating a drum for a dancing bear on a leash. Over the doorway is a figure entitled "La Princesa," perhaps Antoni Amatller's only daughter, Teresa. Above appear figures of a scheming Celestina, the crone matchmaker of Fernando de Rojas's late-fifteenth-century drama, and a photographer taking a picture of her (Antoni Amatller was a great photography enthusiast). The playful groups of animals distributed across the façade include one group pouring chocolate, the source of the Amatller fortune, a writer-donkey dressed as Cervantes, and again a photographer.

Casa Mulleras, next door at no. 37, was reformed by Enric Sagnier i Villavecchia in 1910–11. The last of the houses of the Mançana de la Discordia to be redecorated, Casa Mulleras is an exercise in the Louis XVI style, characterized by order, harmony, and understatement. Clearly a different vision is at work. Sagnier used some art nouveau floral ornamentation in an attempt to give his work a certain contemporary flair, but his thinking as well as his aesthetic vision obviously had little to do with the Moderniste excitement that had captivated Barcelona's bourgeoisie. Sagnier was not the only critic of Modernisme. George Orwell, for one, described Gaudí's Sagrada Família Cathedral as "the ugliest building in the world" and expressed regret that the anarchists had failed to blow it up when they had the chance. Even the radical Salvador Dalí is reported to have stated that Modernisme was all "supremely creative bad taste." During the first seventy-five years of this century, leading Barcelona critics and pundits proposed a wide range of revisions, including demolition, of treasures now as universally cherished as the Palau de la Música itself. Josep Pla, one of the most respected chroniclers of Catalonia's natural and artistic treasures, who once wrote that the Sagrada Família reminded him of "a bunch of immense chicken guts," called for a reform of the Palau (see Walk 2), along with many other post-Modernistes.

Sagnier, for those who remain queasy about Modernisme, kept his head when all about him were swept away by momentary fashion. Credited with one of the most important innovations in Barcelona urban planning, Sagnier conceived the fore-and-aft distribution of the Eixample houses, placing the main living spaces over the street and over the interior patio with a connecting corridor between.

Domènech i Montaner's **Casa Lleó Morera** was originally built in 1864 and then redecorated between 1902 and 1906 for Francesca Morera i Ortiz and, after her death, for Dr. Albert Lleó i Morera. Lavishly decorated with exterior and interior sculptures, stained glass, and mosaics, the house is all but a private version of the ornate Palau de la Música Catalana by the same architect and many of the same sculptors, glaziers, and mosaicists.

The story of the sculptures by Eusebi Arnau on the main floor and their meaning in the history of the Lleó Morera family were recently revealed by historian Manuel García-Martin in his book on the family and the house, *La Casa de Lleó Morera*, published in 1988. Gloria Lleó i Miralbell, granddaughter of Albert Lleó i Morera, was born in the building at no. 35 Passeig de Gràcia but moved shortly afterward when the building was sold.

I had always heard about the house [she wrote to García-Martin] . . . about the mosaics of the country picnic scene and the sculptures over the street with the women holding the modern inventions: the phonograph, the light bulb, the telephone, and the camera . . . and my father even told me that among Eusebi Arnau's sculptures inside on the main floor was one of himself as a newborn baby . . . but I never understood why or how. I had almost resigned myself to never actually seeing the inside of the house when the Patronat de Turisme took it over. It was a strange feeling, the first time I went in, like walking into a dream, surrounded by places so often described and imagined, a sense of recognizing a place I had never been. It was like discovering a world in the past, actually many worlds, that I had known nothing about and that now have become a part of my present.

The Eusebi Arnau sculptures, sumptuous marble haut-relief tucked over the archways on the main-floor vestibule, depict scenes from the popular lullabye *"La dida de l'infant del Rei"* ("The King's Baby's Nanny"), an ancient ballad recounting the story of the miracle of the king's baby lost in a fire.

Dr. Albert Lleó i Morera married Olinta Puiguriguer in 1898, and their first child, Francesca, was born in 1899. Albert, their second, died soon after birth in 1902, and in 1904 another son, whom they also named Albert, was born and lived until 1967. Glòria Lleó i Miralbell is the second Albert's third daughter.

In the ballad the king goes off to hunt; the nurse is left alone with the baby, who won't sleep *"ni en breçol, ni en cadira"* (in neither cradle nor chair), in the song and as sculpted by Arnau. The *dida* is shown nursing the baby. Later she builds a fire, falls asleep, and awakes to find the baby *cendra viva*, burned to a crisp. The nurse prays to the Virgin Mary, promising to make the Infant Jesus crowns of gold and silver if she brings the king's baby back to life. When a page finds her grief-stricken, the *dida* says she has lost the king's golden apple; the page gives her a bag of gold (in the sculpture over the archway to the left) to buy another. On the road to town the *dida* encounters the Virgin Mary and repeats her promise and plea for help, at which the Virgin tells her to return to the palace, where she will find the baby playing in his crib. The *dida* finds the baby alive and well, is overjoyed, and swears eternal devotion to the Virgin.

García-Martín, in his study of Arnau's sculptures, confirms that the sculpture of the king's baby is in fact an exact likeness of the second Albert, and that the *dida* as sculpted—a bust of great sweetness and nobility—is the nurse that Albert II had. The sculptures portray the miracle of the lost child brought back to life, the story of the two Alberts.

Continuing across Passeig de Gràcia on Carrer del Consell de Cent and turning right on the far side of Carrer

Pau Claris, **Passatge Permanyer** cuts through the middle of the next block, a leafy stroll through a row of one-story houses with tiny gardens and a distinct English flavor inspired in John Nash's neoclassical Regent's Park terraces with their formally designed town houses. Cerdà's plan for the entire Eixample envisaged spaces of this kind, a more residential, less commercial atmosphere. But this vision was systematically rejected by the majority of the property owners, who built whatever they thought they needed in the Eixample's blocks. Once the zone inhabited by Barcelona's aristocracy, who have since moved to the upper reaches of the city—Pedralbes, La Bonanova, and Sarrià—Passatge Permanyer has always possessed a poetic appeal. It has been the home of artists such as the pianist Carlos Vidiella and the poet, musician, and illustrator Apel.les Mestres, one of Barcelona's most fascinating turn-of-the-century personalities.

Apel.les Mestres was the author of some forty thousand drawings, caricatures, and illustrations before failing eyesight halted him in 1912. An agile and popular poet, he published his first book of verse, *Avant,* in 1875 at the age of twenty-one and went on to publish a dozen more volumes of poetry as well as fiction, biography, and an autobiography. At the age of sixty-eight, Mestres turned to music and wrote madrigals, ballads, and love songs before his death in 1936. Mestres, son of Josep Oriol Mestres, the architect who not only redecorated the Liceu Opera House but survived the fall from the footbridge at the Església del Pi, was a perfect match for Passatge Permanyer's oasislike hideout. A photograph of a room in his house from Cristina and Eduardo Mendoza's excellent book *Barcelona Modernista* (ed. Planeta, 1989) shows piles of books, paintings, drawings, sculptures, mandolins, French horns, and an endless tangle of knickknacks, odds and ends, and general debris. Mestres was the con-

Passatge Permanyer

235

summate Moderniste, a precursor of the all-around creative supermen of Barcelona's late-nineteenth-century cultural boom.

Emerging on Carrer Roger de Llúria, almost directly across the street there is a tunnel at no. 56 that leads into one of the few open interior patios in the Eixample, the so-called **Pati de les Aigues**, named for the Torre de les Aigues (water tower), originally built over a spring. A children's swimming pool and some trees fill this hidden space, which affords an interesting look at the back of some typical Eixample apartments and the (generally illegal) private building that has gone on for years on back balconies and rooftops.

Another block downhill is the Gran Vía de les Corts Catalanes. The statue and fountain in the middle of the intersection is Venancio Valmitjana's Diana, Roman goddess of the hunt, moon goddess protector of the forest and of wildlife. The hotel at the far corner is the **Barcelona Ritz**, a landmark in its own right, richly adorned with sculpture on the façade at the intersection. The downstairs bar is a cool, dark place for a drink.

Another block down, Carrer de Casp crosses Carrer Roger de Llúria near Gaudí's **Casa Calvet**, halfway down the block to the left at no. 48. Built between 1898 and 1900, Casa Calvet marked an important step in the style that would distinguish Gaudí's singular architectural vision. The houses Gaudí built after the Casa Calvet (Casa Batlló and Casa Milà) were another move away from conventional design and closer to his organic conception of form in space. While the practical elements of the Casa Calvet—the way the rooms are distributed and the mechanics of the structure itself—are perhaps the most conventional of all Gaudí's buildings, the façade, the vestibule, the elevator and stairwell, the windows, ornamentation, and furniture (much of which is now in the Gaudí museum in Güell Park) all lead directly to the architect's best and most characteristic later work.

In a recent article, Juan Bassegoda i Nonell, Barcelona's leading Gaudí expert, described how Gaudí became Gaudí. Quoting Gaudí's famous "originality is a return to origins," Bassegoda explains his use of parabolic (naturally looping) arches as a functional consideration rather than as a matter of stylistic intent. Gaudí had observed that, throughout the history of architecture, architects had been limited to the use of forms they could draw with the compass and the T-square. All buildings came from these instruments, which could only draw circles, triangles, squares, and rectangles. In three dimensions these shapes become prisms, pyramids, cylinders, and spheres with which pillars, planes, columns, and cupolas can be constructed. Gaudí, an architectural innocent, noted that in nature these shapes are unknown. Gaudí admired the structural efficiency of trees, for example, and of mammals, noting that "neither are trees prismatic, nor are bones cylindrical, nor are leaves triangular." Observing natural forms, Gaudí saw that bones, branches, muscles and tendons are all composed of fibers. Thus, surfaces curve but are supported from within by fibers, a type of geometry known as "ruled geometry," with which hyperboloids, conoids, helicoids, or parabolic hyperboloids can be constructed. These are all complicated names for simple and familiar shapes: The femur is almost hyperboloid; the way shoots grow off a branch is helicoidal; the web between your fingers is a hyperbolic paraboloid. All of these shapes are peerlessly functional but never used by architects, who were confined to prisms, spheres, and rectangles. Gaudí, whom Bassegoda describes as "innocent and honest," revolutionized architecture, but his revolution was retrograde, a return to shapes much older than the ones invented by architects.

Casa Calvet, unassuming as it may seem, catapulted Gaudí definitively into his most surprising and original civil projects: Casa Batlló and Casa Milà and, finally, into his mystical and dreamlike Sagrada Família Cathedral. Whereas Casa Vicens, his first house, used looping arches and many of the devices present throughout his career

(color, broken tile, wrought-iron sculpture), it wasn't until after 1900 that his forms acquired the organic quality he achieved through the use of natural forms and ruled geometry.

Gaudí's work always maintained a certain natural innocence and playfulness that many of his critics found difficult to accept. Gaudí's ultimate accolade, as reported by Bassegoda, came from the mother of a childhood friend who, upon seeing Barcelona and her old friend's architecture for the first time, commented that the famous Moderniste was "just doing the same things he always did as a kid."

Moving back toward the Passeig de Gràcia along Carrer Casp, **Casa de Sant Jordi**, with reliefs of Sant Jordi by the early twentieth-century Catalan sculptor (born in 1899) Joan Rebull, stands at the corner of Carrer Pau Claris. Built by architect Francesc Folguera in 1929, the façade, Germanic in style, reflects a cooling of Modernisme's most radical moment. The house at no. 22, Casa Camprubí by architect Adolfo Ruiz i Casamitjana, is another example of post-Moderniste decor. The **Tivoli** movie theater is a famous landmark for Barcelona couples, one of the city's first and best-attended movie houses. The **Bracafé** (Brasil café) next door is and has been one of the city's key points for a cup of espresso and something more: a cosmopolitan, big-city intimacy. Enclosed by glass in winter, Bracafé sets up tables on the sidewalk during the warmer months—a good place to meet, people watch, read the newspaper, or have breakfast. In short, it's a great place to almost get something done.

After crossing to the far side of the Passeig de Gràcia, across what was once, in rainy weather, a rushing river where strong young men carried ladies across *coll i be* (piggyback, actually, in Catalan, "lamby neck") in return for a *petó* (a kiss), a step across the Ronda San Pedro will

Doorbell at Gaudí's Casa Calvet

bring you to **Plaça Catalunya** from the uphill side. This wide circle of empty space, possibly Barcelona's worst-kept secret, the center for train and subway communications to nearly everywhere, has a surprisingly interesting history as well as a bright future. Originally an empty lot outside the city walls between Barcelona and the neighboring town of Gràcia uphill in the distance, the area became more important when Barcelona residents began to build summer houses and weekend retreats in what is now the upper part of the city: Sarrià, Sant Gervasi, Pedralbes, and La Bonanova. When the walls were demolished in 1860, this broad plain became once again a battleground between city planning by the city itself and federal planning by the *Estat*: Madrid.

The Cerdà Plan backed by Madrid called for the extension of the Rambla to a great square that would occupy a space between the Gran Via de les Corts Catalanes and Carrer del Consell de Cent in what is now the Passeig de Gràcia. The municipal plan directed by Antoni Rovira i Trias called for a large space—800 by 400 meters—in the area occupied by the present square. As a result of the city's resistance to the Cerdà Plan, in 1868, Miquel Garriga i Roca devised a system for linking the old city to the new Eixample, including a square not unlike the present Plaça Catalunya. As discussion, suits, countersuits, and controversy raged, private citizens began building in the empty lot. Huge palaces were constructed by, among others, the Gibert and Estruch families until the mayor stepped in and ordered the demolition of all buildings occupying what is now Plaça Catalunya. In 1927, Francesc Nebot designed and constructed the modern Plaça Catalunya, which is presently being redesigned by chief city planner Oriol Bohigas.

With an area of 50,000 square meters, Plaça Catalunya's measurements are comparable to those of the Place de l'Étoile in Paris or Saint Peter's Square in Rome, while Moscow's Red Square is slightly larger with a total area of almost 60,000 square meters. Plaça Catalunya is bordered by seven banks, most notably Banco Español de Crédito on the northwestern side, located on the site where the old Hotel Colón used to stand. The Colón was the headquarters for the P.S.U.C., Catalonia's socialist party, during the Spanish Civil War, festooned with enormous portraits of Marx, Lenin, and Stalin hanging over the façade. George Orwell's account in *Homage to Catalonia* of warring factions within the Spanish Republic skirmishing around Plaça Catalunya places anarchists atop the telephone building at the far (eastern) edge of the square where Telefónica still stands. Orwell's wife and Orwell himself, until he became a hunted man tainted by his service with the supposedly Trotskyist militia and took to the streets, lived in the Hotel Continental, which was then on the eastern corner of the Rambla, now the Banco Central and presently at no. 138 Rambla de Canaletes.

The Corte Inglés department store in its quilted aluminum garishness looms massively to the northeast. The roofs and towers of the buildings farther up the Passeig de Gràcia, best seen from the center of Plaça Catalunya, are **Casa Pascual i Pons** at nos. 2–4 Passeig de Gràcia and **Cases Rocamora** just uphill at nos. 6–14. Enric Sagnier i Villavecchia built the first of these two monoliths in 1890–91, a symmetrical neo-Gothic structure with conical towers and overhanging wooden eaves now housing, among other tenants, the Catalana Occidente insurance company, as emblazoned on the corner tower. The Cases Rocamora on the next block were built between 1914 and 1917 in a similar medieval revivalist style. The lower side of Plaça Catalunya overlooks the Banco Central and the top of the Rambla.

The sculptures distributed around the square include Josep Clarà's marble "Goddess," which stands between the lighted fountains in the center of the upper side, and Pau Gargallo's "Shepherd Playing a Flute," which occupies the corner nearest the telephone building. The extended Rambla de Catalunya joins the main Rambla at the Rambla de Canaletes in front of the popular and by now familiar Café Zurich which, though threatened, is a good bet to survive.

Plaça Catalunya—a space often hurried past, hulking, as it does, astride Barcelona's subway and railroad nerve center, often too bright, too hot, too big—has been the setting for three of the major events of Barcelona's history in this century. Franco's troops took possession of the city in 1939 in a military parade that ended with the removal of the Plaça Catalunya signs. Barcelona's central nucleus temporarily became Plaza del Ejército (Army Square), which was the start of forty years of what has been described as "internal exile."

On September 11, 1977, Plaça Catalunya was one of the focal points for the massive *Diada*, the first celebration of Catalonia's National Day since Franco's 1939 occupation of the city. An estimated quarter of a million people filled the streets in what may have been the largest popular demonstration ever held in Spain.

Nearly a half century after the end of the Spanish Civil War, on October 17, 1987, at quarter of two in the afternoon, International Olympic Committee president— and, not coincidentally, a Catalan—Antonio Samaranch announced that Barcelona had been chosen as the site of the 1992 Olympic Games. The city collapsed: schools closed; traffic stopped; total strangers leaped from automobiles and embraced; the din of car horns, fireworks, and howls of joy was impenetrable. Friends and families tried to get through to one another by phone; the telephone system went down; all of the office buildings (including Telefónica) had emptied out into Barcelona's central square to join the melee. Plaça Catalunya soon filled with laughing, weeping, dancing *Barcelonins* in one of those moments people remember for the rest of their lives: where they were, what they were doing, initial thoughts, words, and actions. Much more than a chance to line pockets or even to promote the city, the choice of Barcelona confirmed Catalonia's age-old universalist aspirations—that is, the need for international recognition of the Catalan language and culture.

Barcelona's Olympic Movement, originally a contender for the 1924 games, nearly won in its 1936 candidacy. Only uncertainties about the political stability of the Spanish Republic undermined the city's selection as the seat of the Olympics eventually held in Berlin. The "popular Olympics," an antifascist protest gesture, was about to begin when history intervened.

Fifty-six years after Barcelona's 1936 Popular Olympics were canceled on opening day by the military rebellion that started the Spanish Civil War, Catalonia's Olympic dream will come true. Popular playwright and poet Josep Maria de Sagarra, whose lyrics to the 1936 Olympic anthem came to seem a tragic omen of the events about to unfold in Spain and around the world, would have been proud to hear them echo through the cavernous spaces of Montjuïc's Olympic stadium in 1992.

No es per odi,	It's not from hatred,
no es per guerra	it's not for war
que venim a lluitar	that we gather to compete
a cada terra.	in every land.
Sota el cel blau	Under the blue sky
l'únic mot que ens escau	the only word that describes us
es un crit d'alegria:	is a single joyous cry
la pau.	of peace.

Restaurants, Hotels, Shops, and Museums

RESTAURANTS

Making a short list of restaurants in a city with no fewer than 3,423 dining establishments is no picnic, but the following choices will cause few disappointments.

More Expensive

Azulete, Via Augusta, 281. Tel: 203-5943. Superb dining in a restored chalet in Tres Torres (near Sarrià). The dining room is a greenhouselike backyard garden filled with trees. The international cuisine is superbly orchestrated by new chef Jean-Luc Figueres, previously of Eldorado Petit.

Eldorado Petit, Carrer de Dolors Monserdà, 51. Tel: 204-5153. A garden spot above the Bonanova in upper Barcelona. Colman Andrews ranks it among the top two or three restaurants in town. Reservations are indispensable.

Can Isidre, Carrer de les Flors, 12. Tel: 441-1139. Not far from the theaters and dance halls of the Paral.lel, this small restaurant is carefully and passionately managed down to the last detail by chef Isidre Gironès. (Raval. Walk 3)

Casa Leopoldo, Carrer de Sant Rafael, 24. Tel: 241-3014. Not far from Carrer Hospital, this oasis of gentility in mid-Raval is a favorite for artists and *illuminati* in search of a good dinner in semi-slum chic. (Raval. Walk 3)

Passadis del Pep, Pla del Palau, 2. Tel: 310-1021. A well-known but out-of-the-way spot near Santa Maria del Mar, this small and always crowded bistro starts serving wonderful selections of wine and *entreteniments*—canapés, hors d'oeuvres, delicacies—as you come through the door. Reservations essential. (Sant Pere i La Ribera. Walk 2)

Botafumeiro, Carrer Gran de Gràcia, 81. Tel: 218-4230. Oysters, shellfish, ribeiro wine—Galician seafood in the middle of Gràcia. (Gràcia. Walk 4)

Set Portes, Passeig Isabel II, 14. Tel: 319-3033. Tucked under the neoclassical *Porxos*, arcades, built in 1836 by Josep Xifré, Set Portes (Seven Doors) is unique. Alive and open, always boiling and boisterous, piano, old world ambience, Set Portes serves from 1:00 P.M. to 1:00 A.M. Excellent dining at any hour. Reservations are difficult; if you make them, they may not hold them past 2:00 or 9:00, depending on the number of people waiting. (Sant Pere i La Ribera. Walk 2)

Agut d'Avignon, Carrer Trinidad, 3. Tel: 302-6034. This is the better of the two Aguts, a lively, rustic setting with a quiet, discerning clientele. Tiny Carrer Trinidad is the first right off Carrer Avinyó, to the left off Carrer Ferran between Plaça Sant Jaume and the Rambla. Excellent traditional Catalan cuisine. (Near Barri Gòtic. Walk 1)

Tram-Tram, Major de Sarrià, 121. Tel: 204-8518.

Named for the end of the old trolley tracks, Isidro Soler's fresh and original cuisine and his wife Reyes' pastries and poise are making Tram-Tram one of Sarrià's newest surprises. Ask for the back room on the garden.

Less Expensive

Agut, Carrer Gignàs, 16. Tel: 315-1709. This is a comfortable little bistro usually filled with young people. The menu has a wide variety of Catalan selections, served up cheerily and expertly by a family staff that has been running Agut for three generations. (Equidistant from Walks 1 and 2).

Bilbao, Carrer de Perill, 33. Tel: 258-9624. At the corner of Venus and Perill (which means danger), the Bilbao seems indeed to be perilously cozy and delicious. The upstairs, downstairs distribution seems to create intimate spaces; the local cuisine is excellent. (Gràcia. Walk 4).

Egipte, Carrer Jerusalem, 12. Tel: 317-7480. Tiny balcony tables for two, semiprivate rooms upstairs, corners in the window over the street. There's a certain Henry Fieldingesque ambience about this brawling place. The fact that Egipte is always full is its best recommendation. Just behind the Boqueria market. (Raval. Walk 3)

La Gardunya, Carrer Morera, 17–19. Tel: 302-4323. In the back of the Boqueria market, this is the place to visit late on opera nights or at midday on market days. (Raval. Walk 3)

La Morera, Plaça Sant Agustí, 1. Tel: 318-7555. Another good place to break up the Raval walk, this conveniently located bistro is comfortable, unpretentious, and complete. It offers good value and an ample selection of Catalan specialties. (Raval. Walk 3)

Raïm, Carrer Pescateria, 6. Tel: 319-2998. Please don't tell the owners how you found out about this restaurant. It doesn't look like much, but Raïm serves genuine Catalan cuisine in a simple, rustic setting. (La Ribera. Walk 2)

Can Lluís, Carrer de la Cera, 49. Tel: 241-1187. This busy and popular restaurant serves well-prepared Catalan specialties of all kinds. The clientele is predominantly young and discerning, the atmosphere sophisticated and alive. (Raval. Walk 3)

HOTELS

To accommodate all tastes and budgets, a number of alternatives deserve mention here, but there are really only two places to stay: the **Hotel Colón** or the **Hotel Jardí**. Both are near the center of the Ciutat Vella, the old city, and both have a certain traditional and simple charm. The Colón is more comfortable, while the Jardí is—though impeccably scrubbed and decent—a hostel.

The **Hotel Princesa Sofía** is the solution for travelers who prefer comfort and modern surroundings over local charm and convenient access to Barcelona itself, while the **Hotel Ritz**, exquisite and impeccable, is the obvious choice if you really don't care what it costs. Another good option is the centrally located **Hotel Condes de Barcelona**, a five-star hotel deliberately rated at four stars to provide top services at somewhat more palatable rates.

Hotel Colón (Avinguda Catedral 7, 08002 Barcelona. Tel: 301-1404) is in the middle of everything and has an old world ease and decor that nicely matches Barcelona's best characteristics.

Hotel Condes de Barcelona (Paseo de Gràcia, 75–77. 08008 Barcelona. Tel: 215-7931) is located in a Moderniste building near the middle of the Eixample. Full comfort and full service, this new place has the advantage of being stationed midway between Gràcia (Walk 4) and the Barri Gòtic (Walk 1).

Hotel Gran Vía (Gran Vía, 642. 08007 Barcelona. Tel: 318-1900) is another good choice. Moderniste stairways and early twentieth-century trappings give this centrally located place a familiar and friendly feel.

Hotel España (Sant Pau, 9–11, 08001 Barcelona. Tel: 318-1758) was designed by Moderniste Lluís Domènech i Montaner, author of the Palau de la Música and much of the architecture you will see in the Eixample. The rooms are, perhaps inevitably, disappointing compared to the splendor of the hotel's public spaces, but the Eusebi Arnau sculptures around the fireplace and the mermaid mural in the breakfast room can go a long way toward cheering you up about your sleeping quarters.

Hotel Continental (Rambla de Canaletes, 138. 08002 Barcelona. Tel: 301-2570) was where George Orwell and his wife stayed during the spring of 1937 after Orwell had been shot through the throat and, nearly completely recovered, was undergoing therapy for his damaged vocal cords while trying to survive the purge of the suspected-Trotskyist militia with whom he had fought. What is now the Continental was then an annex around the corner from the original hotel. The Continental is high enough over the Rambla to be relatively quiet, not too expensive, comfortably furnished, and is *the* place to read *Homage to Catalonia* (again).

Hotel Princesa Sofía (Plaça Pius XII, 4. 08028 Barcelona. Tel: 330-7111) is far out the Diagonal, handy for the airport, and supremely luxurious and comfortable.

Hotel Ritz (Gran Via de les Corts Catalanes 668, 08010 Barcelona. Tel: 318-5200) is the best hotel in town and reasonably well located for seeing the city.

Hotel Jardí (Plaça Sant Josep Oriol, 1. 08001 Barcelona. Tel: 301-5900) is conveniently located halfway between the Rambla and the cathedral, a clean and economical base of operations over one of the city's most charming squares.

Paseo de Gràcia (Passeig de Gràcia, 102. 08007 Barcelona. Tel: 215-5828) is another budget selection with comfortably furnished rooms overlooking the Eixample and some with rooftop terraces facing northwest to Tibadabo and the hills behind the city.

SHOPS

Barcelona, rapidly reaffirming itself as one of Europe's design capitals, is an exciting place to shop for clothes and original household articles. Passeig de Gràcia, Rambla Catalunya, and the Diagonal as far up as Plaça Francesc Macià are the main shopping areas. The best shops for antiques and books are around the Carrer de la Palla and Carrer Banys Nous. Leather goods, wicker products, ceramics, and Lladro items are all standard purchases in Barcelona, but the only bargain left is saffron, which can be bought here for a fraction of what it costs abroad. Olive oil, another good buy, is heavy and somewhat precarious to transport but probably a good idea anyway.

Leather

While leather is no longer cheap in Barcelona, the quality and design of the best products available are undeniably fine. The best locale of a **Loewe**'s department store is under the Lleó Morera house at no. 35 Passeig de Gràcia, but the uptown shops at no. 570 Diagonal and no. 8 Johann Sebastián Bach, are also good and may be less crowded. Shoes, bags, and leather goods of all kinds are found around Porta del Angel and along Carrer Pelai, as well as throughout the main shopping areas.

Design

Since designer Javier Mariscal's invention of the Olympic mascot Cobi, designed to resemble, if not all of zoology, at least a confusing combination of several species, Barcelona designers have come into a new surge of confidence and creativity. Catalan design is obviously the heir of a playful wink passed down from, among others, Gaudí to Dalí to Miró to Tàpies. **Gimeno** (at Passeig de Gràcia, 102), **Vinçon** (Passeig de Gràcia, 96), **Bd** (Barcelona Design, at Carrer Mallorca, 291–293), or **Dos i Una** (Carrer de Rosselló, 275) are all filled with new ideas for lamps, chairs, glasses, and an endless list of delightful knickknacks and paraphernalia.

Fashion

Bulevar Rosa (at Passeig de Gràcia, 55, and Diagonal, 474) offers a cluster of different shopping opportunities. **Adolfo Dominguez** (Passeig de Gràcia, 89) is one of Spain's top designers. Toni Miró's two **Groc** establishments (at Carrer Muntaner, 385, and Rambla Catalunya, 100) have the latest looks for men, women, and children. Carrer Tuset is a hot area for shops, especially **Conti** for conservative men's wear at Tuset, 30. Conti, which produces the Barcelona soccer team's traveling threads, also has stores at Diagonal, 512; Pau Casals, 7; and Rambla Catalunya, 78.

Department Stores

Barcelona's big stores include the two **Corte Inglés** giants, one at Plaça Catalunya, 14, and the other out on the Diagonal at no. 617. **Galerías Preciadas** has two stores, one at Porta del Angel, 14, and the other at Diagonal, 471-473, near Plaça Francesc Macià. Both of these stores are convenient because they remain open through the lunch hour.

Antiques

The area around the junction of Carrer Palla and Carrer Banys Nous is the antique center. Ancient books, old maps, furniture, and *objets* of all kinds can be found in these eclectic emporiums of the past. The Thursday antique market known as the **Mercat Gòtic** (Walk 1) is also a good time and place to get lucky.

Rope soles

La Manual Alpargata at Carrer Avinyó, 7, is a unique store, probably the largest collection of rope-soled footwear assembled anywhere.

Ceramics

While the big department stores offer good selections of the most rustic earthenware pots, plates, and bowls at normal prices (and in exchange for credit cards), **La Cerámica** at Carrer Avinyó, 27, just past its intersection with Carrer Escudellers, has a wide selection of mammoth coffee cups and handsome ceramic tableware from La Bisbal on the Costa Brava. *Molsa*, at no. 1 Plaça Sant Josep Oriol, and *La Roda*, at no. 18 Carrer del Call, are also good spots for ceramics.

Saffron

Saffron is available in the big stores, but for buying in bulk and at a better price try the wholesalers **Jobal** at Carrer Princesa, 38 ($1,500 for a kilo) or **La Barcelonesa** at Carrer de Comerç, 27.

MUSEUMS

Barcelona has many excellent museums, probably more than you can see in a lifetime, much less in a single visit. Nevertheless, Picasso's childhood doodling and early works must not be missed, nor should you fail to see the Miró Foundation, or—perhaps most of all—the Museu d'Art de Catalunya on Montjuïc, one of the world's finest Romanesque collections.

The city maps presently being handed out free by the tourist information stations at the airport, the Sants train station, at the Palau de la Virreina, Rambla, 99, and at the City Hall at Plaça Sant Jaume list on the back all thirty-eight of Barcelona's museums as well as the most recent and up-to-date hours, addresses, and phone numbers. Below are the especially recommended ones:

Museu d'Art de Catalunya: Palau Nacional. Parc de Montjuïc (at the end of Carrer Lleida). The world's largest collection of Romanesque art (eleventh to the thirteenth centuries). These murals, polychrome wood carvings, and paintings on wood were found in the more than one thousand Romanesque chapels built all over Catalonia when Christianity took to the hills seeking safety and religious freedom in the face of the Moorish invasion beginning in the eighth century. These works were carefully packed on mules and donkeys during the early part of this century, and the originals were replaced by exact copies. The museum is virtually a lesson in the geography of Catalonia as well as a superb collection of particularly moving art since each piece is presented with maps showing the location of the chapel where it was originally found.

Museu d'Arte Modern: Plaça d'Armes. Parc de la Ciutadella. Primarily nineteenth-century Catalan artists and sculptors, this excellent collection may soon be moved to another location, but wherever it goes, follow it. Isidro Nonell, Ramón Casas, Marià Fortuny, Santiago Russinol, Josep Mariá Sert, Pau Gargallo, Miquel Blay, Josep Clara, and the others will make it abundantly clear that, far from anomalies, Catalonia's universally famous artists—Gaudí, Picasso, Dalí, Miró—emerged very naturally from this rich context. The building housing the museum was originally the arsenal for the Ciutadella fortress, thus explaining its massively thick walls.

Galeria de Catalanes Ilustres: Carrer del Bisbe Cassador, 3. Palau Requesens. This museum is part of Walk 1 and is a good chance to see the inside of one of the Ciutat Vella's extraordinary buildings. Displaying portraits of illustrious Catalans from the tenth to the twentieth centuries, this Gothic structure houses the Academia de les Bonas Lletres.

Museu Frederic Marés: Plaça Sant Iu. This private collection of sculptor Frederick Marés includes pre-Romanesque pieces as well as works from the twentieth century and a collection of household and everyday artifacts from the fifteenth to the early twentieth centuries.

Museu del Futbol Club Barcelona: Estadio del FC Barcelona. Carrer Arístides Maillol. Seeing a game in this stadium with a capacity of 130,000 is an unforgettable spectacle, but if that's not possible, soccer enthusiasts will have an opportunity to see some of the greatest goals ever scored on the five-screen video in the club museum.

Casa-Museu Gaudí: Carrer Olot. Güell Park. This Francesc Berenguer–designed house was Gaudí's residence until just before his death when he lived in the Sagrada Família Church. Filled with busts, portraits, and furniture designed by the great Moderniste architect, the house-museum brings visitors closer to Gaudí in a smaller, more intimate setting than the monolithic structures he built.

Museu d'Història de la Ciutat: Plaça del Rei. Although part of Walk 1, this museum, like many that appear on the walks, might be better saved for a separate visit. The Roman ruins and early Iberian discoveries help to make the city's two-thousand-year history three-dimensional.

Fundacío Joan Miró: Plaça Neptú. Parc de Montjuïc. Josep Lluís Sert's building is the perfect showcase for what may be the most complete collection of Joan Miró's art, including paintings, drawings, sculptures, tapestries, as well his complete graphic work. There are also frequent exhibitions of contemporary work as well as lectures, films, and puppet shows for children on Sunday mornings.

Museu Monastir de Pedralbes: Baixada del Monestir, 9. Just beyond Sarrià in Pedralbes, this three-decked Gothic cloister tells much about life in a monastery, which is removed from the clamor and rush of daily life in the city. The ancient glass in the windows, the monks' cells, the view of the garden below all strongly suggest that maybe it really would be possible to figure something out about our lives and times if left alone for long enough in such surroundings. The church and square next to it are also lovely.

Museu Picasso: Carrer Montcada, 15-19. The thirteenth-century palaces housing the Picasso collection are nearly as spectacular as the work within. Although the works present in the museum include few of his masterpieces, the drawings, early works, and studies show much about Picasso's raw talent and how it was developed that a look at a cubist or a surrealist work may not provide. The postcards, prints, and catalogues for sale in the bookshop are among the best opportunities the museum offers.

Museu de la Sagrada Família: Carrer Mallorca, 401. Plans, projects, and scale models answer many of the questions you will have about Gaudí's unfinished masterwork.

Museu Verdaguer: Vil.la Joana. Vallvidrera. A pilgrimage to the house of Mossèn Jacint Verdaguer, the literary priest known as the father of modern Catalan, offers several opportunities. The view of Barcelona from Vallvidrera is breathtaking, especially on a clear day when you can see far out into the Mediterranean. Verdaguer, author of the immortal poem *Canigó*, among other famous works, was, with playwright Ángel Guimerà, responsible for the rejuvenation of Catalan language and literature during the latter half of the nineteenth century. Verdaguer died—defrocked, impoverished, and disgraced—at the age of fifty-seven in June 1902, after having become one of the most popular figures of his time.

Further Reading

The earliest Catalan literature available in English is Joanot Martorell's *Tirant lo Blanch* (1490), translated by David Rosenthal. Described by no less a literary figure than Miguel de Cervantes as "the greatest book ever written," *Tirant lo Blanch* is, like *Quijote*, a Renaissance knight novel, with more psychological depth than the novels of intrigue and adventure published up to that time. If you have managed to read *Tirant lo Blanch* before arriving, you will automatically qualify as a serious *Catalanista*, although the work may prove to be of limited help in gaining an understanding of present-day Barcelona.

George Orwell's *Homage to Catalonia* is a portrait of the "people's" Barcelona at the outset of the Spanish Civil War in 1936. Orwell's account of the ironies and confusions (many of them his own) of politics and military operations in revolutionary Barcelona provides a penetrating and sardonic view of Republican Catalonia.

Mercè Rodoreda's *Plaça del Diamant* (an excerpt from David Rosenthal's translation, entitled *The Time of the Doves*, begins on page 180 of this book) is an intimate look into the life of Gràcia, the Barcelona village-turned-neighborhood toured in Walk 4. Although critics occasionally mistake the protagonist as a symbol of womanhood rather than of humanity, the novel stands as a moving chronicle of the human condition as well as a living slice of Gràcia street life.

Eduardo and Cristina Mendoza's *Barcelona Modernista* may be available in translation by the time this book is in print. If so, don't hesitate to use it to amplify and illustrate the treatment of the Eixample that appears in Walk 5. The text and the book's spectacular graphic work are both superb.

Other recommended works in English include Jan Read's *The Catalans*, a history of Catalonia; Richard Ford's nineteenth-century *Handbook for Spain 1845*, of which eighty pages in volume 2 deal with Catalonia; and *Forbidden Territory* by Juan Goytisolo, an account of Barcelona during the Franco regime. *Getting to Know Catalonia*, a coffee-table-sized book with excellent plates and text by Josep-Maria Puigjaner, published by the Generalitat de Catalunya in 1990, is yet another excellent and contemporary introduction to Barcelona and its context. For food and wine as well as a sense of where you are, don't miss Colman Andrews's *Catalan Cuisine*.

Following is a bibliography including the works mentioned above as well as additional resources.

Ajuntament de Barcelona. *Guía de arquitectura de Barcelona*. Barcelona: Col.legi d'Arquitectes de Catalunya, 1990.

Amades, Joan. *Històries i llegendes de Barcelona*. Barcelona: Edicions 62, 1984.

Andrews, Colman. *Catalan Cuisine*. New York: Atheneum, 1988.

Bassegoda Nonell, Juan. *La bibliografia de Gaudí*. Barcelona: Salvat, 1987.

——*La pedrera de Gaudí*. Barcelona: Caixa d'Estalvis de Catalunya, 1987.

———*El gran Gaudí.* Sabadell: Ausa, 1989.

———*La arquitectura de Gaudí.* Barcelona: La Vanguardia, 1990.

———*Gaudí, arquitecto del futuro.* Barcelona: Salvat, 1984.

Benet, Josep and Martí, Casimir. *Barcelona a mitjan segle XIX.* Barcelona: Curial, 1976.

Carandell, José María. *Nueva guía secreta de Barcelona.* Barcelona: Martinez Roca, 1982.

Carreras i Candí, Francesch. "La ciutat de Barcelona" in *Geografía general de Catalunya*, Vol. 5. Barcelona: A. Martin, 1913–1918.

Cirici i Pellicer, Alexandre. *El arte Moderniste Catalan.* Barcelona: Ayma, 1951.

———*Barcelona pam a pam.* Barcelona: Teide, 1971. (Updated, 1985.)

Domènech i Montaner, Lluís. "En busca de una arquitectura nacional." *La Renaixença*, año VIII, tomo I, num. 4 (28 Febrero, 1898), 149–60.

Duran i Sanpere, Agustí. *Barcelona i la seva història.* Barcelona: Curial, 1972.

———*El barrio gótico.* Barcelona: Ayma, 1956.

Fabre, Jaume and Huertas, Jesus Maria. *Tots els barris de Barcelona.* Barcelona: Edicions 61, 1976.

Ford, Richard. *Handbook for Spain.* London: Centaur Press, 1845.

García-Martin, Manuel. *Els oficis Catalans.* Barcelona: Catalana de Gas, 1977.

———*Portals modernistes.* Barcelona: Catalana de Gas, 1979.

———*Vidrieres de un gran jardin de vidrios.* Barcelona: Catalana de Gas, 1981.

———*El palau de la música Catalan.* Barcelona: Catalana de Gas, 1987.

———*La casa de Lléo Morera.* Barcelona: Catalana de Gas, 1988.

Gilot, Françoise and Lake, Carlton. *Life with Picasso.* New York: Avon, 1981.

Mackay, David. "Berenguer." *Cuadernos de arquitectura.*

(Col.legi d'Arquitectes de Catalunya) 58 (4th Trimester, 1964), 45–47.

McCully, Marilyn and Isidre Molas, et al. *Homage to Barcelona*. London: The Arts Council of Great Britain, 1985.

Mena, Jose María de. *Curiosidades y leyendas de Barcelona*. Barcelona: Plaza & Janes, 1990.

Mendoza, Cristina and Eduardo Mendoza. *Barcelona Moderniste*. Barcelona: Planeta, 1989.

——*La ciudad de los prodigios*. Barcelona: Planeta, 1986.

Orwell, George. *Homage to Catalonia*. London: Penguin Books, 1988.

Palau i Fabre, Josep. *Picasso vivent: 1881–1907*. Barcelona: Poligrafa, 1976.

Permanyer, Lluís. *Història de l'Eixample*. Barcelona: Plaza & Janes, 1991.

——*Establiments i negocis que han fet història*. Barcelona: La Campana, 1990.

Puigjaner, Josep-Maria. *Getting to Know Catalonia*. Barcelona: Generalitat de Catalunya, 1990.

Read, Jan. *The Catalans*. New York: Faber & Faber, 1979.

Reglá, Juan. *Història de Catalunya*. Madrid: Alianza, 1974.

Riquer, Martín de. *Cervantes en Barcelona*. Barcelona: Sirmio, 1989.

Rodoreda, Mercè. *La Plaça del Diamant* (translated as *The Time of the Doves* by David Rosenthal). New York: Taplinger, 1980.

San Agustín, Arturo. *Ramblistas*. Barcelona: Penalba, 1980.

Sucre, Jose María de. *Memorias*. Barcelona: Ediciones Barna, 1963. Arolas, 1950.

Roure, Conrat. *Recuerdos de mi larga vida*. Barcelona: Diluvio, 1925.

Various authors. *Album histórico y gráfico de Gràcia*. Barcelona: Arolas, 1950.

Vázquez Montalbán, Manuel. *Barcelonas*. Barcelona: Empuries, 1990.

Vila, Pau and Lluís Casassas. *Barcelona i la seva rodalia al llarg dels temps*. Barcelona: Aedos, 1974.

Index

Index

Index

Index

Index

THE HENRY HOLT WALKS SERIES

For people who want to *learn* when they travel, not just see.

Look for these other exciting volumes in Henry Holt's best-selling Walks series:

PARISWALKS, Revised Edition, by Alison and Sonia Landes
Five intimate walking tours through the most historic quarters of the City of Light.
288 pages, photos, maps $12.95 Paper

LONDONWALKS, Revised Edition, by Anton Powell
Five historic walks through old London, one brand new for this edition.
272 pages, photos, maps $12.95 Paper

VENICEWALKS by Chas Carner and Alessandro Giannatasio
Four enchanting tours through one of the most perfect walking environments the world has to offer.
240 pages, photos, maps $12.95 Paper

ROMEWALKS by Anya M. Shetterly
Four walking tours through the most historically and culturally rich neighborhoods of Rome.
256 pages, photos, maps $12.95 Paper

FLORENCEWALKS by Anne Holler
Four intimate walks through this exquisite medieval city, exploring its world-famous art and architecture.
208 pages, photos, maps $12.95 Paper

VIENNAWALKS by J. Sydney Jones
Four walking tours that reveal the home of Beethoven, Freud, and the Habsburg monarchy.
304 pages, photos, maps $12.95 Paper

NEW YORKWALKS by The 92nd Street Y, edited by Batia Plotch
One of the city's most visible cultural and literary institutions guides you through six historic neighborhoods in New York.
288 pages, photos, maps $12.95 Paper

BARCELONAWALKS by George Semler
Five essays touring one of the Mediterranean's cultural and artistic centers—habitat for names such as Gaudí, Miró, Picasso, Casals, and Dalí.
272 pages, photos, maps $12.95 Paper

JERUSALEMWALKS, Revised Edition, by Nitza Rosovsky
Six intimate walks that allow the mystery and magic of this complicated city to unfold.
350 pages, photos, maps $14.95 Paper

BEIJINGWALKS by Don J. Cohn and Zhang Jingqing
Six fascinating walking tours through a city that is as old as Chinese civilization itself.
280 pages, photos, drawings, maps $15.95 Paper

RUSSIAWALKS by David and Valeria Matlock
Seven walks through Moscow and Leningrad, with a special emphasis on architecture and political history.
304 pages, photos, maps $12.95 Paper

Available at your local bookseller or from Special Sales Department, Henry Holt and Company, 115 West 18th Street, New York, New York 10011, (212) 886-9200. Please add $2.00 for postage and handling, plus $.50 for each additional item ordered. (New York residents, please add applicable state and local sales tax.) Please allow 4–6 weeks for delivery. Prices and availability are subject to change.